LICENCE TO LOOT

LICENCE TO LOOT

How the plunder of Eskom and other parastatals almost sank South Africa

STEPHAN HOFSTATTER

PENGUIN BOOKS

Published by Penguin Books
an imprint of Penguin Random House South Africa (Pty) Ltd
Reg. No. 1953/000441/07
The Estuaries No. 4, Oxbow Crescent, Century Avenue, Century City, 7441
PO Box 1144, Cape Town, 8000, South Africa
www.penguinrandomhouse.co.za

Penguin
Random House
South Africa

First published 2018
1 3 5 7 9 10 8 6 4 2

PUBLISHER: Marlene Fryer
MANAGING EDITOR: Robert Plummer
EDITOR: Alice Inggs
PROOFREADER: Dane Wallace
COVER AND TEXT DESIGNER: Ryan Africa
INDEXER: Sanet le Roux

Set in 10.5 pt on 14 pt Minion

Printed by **novus print**, a Novus Holdings company

MIX
Paper from
responsible sources
FSC
www.fsc.org   FSC® C022948

Penguin Random House is committed to a sustainable future for
our business, our readers and our planet. This book is made
from Forest Stewardship Council ® certified paper.

ISBN 978 1 77609 312 0 (print)
ISBN 978 1 77609 313 7 (ePub)

To all the whistleblowers who had the courage to tell me their stories

Contents

Preface

While on assignment for the *Guardian* newspaper in 2016, a photographer friend of mine, James Oatway, took a picture of a young man – I guess he must have been in his early twenties – collecting firewood at a dump in the veld near his home. Behind him, barely two kilometres away, a forest of cranes and the half-built boiler towers of Kusile, one of the world's largest coal-fired power stations, rise into the Highveld sky.

For me, this image encapsulates everything that's wrong with South Africa's power utility, Eskom.

At a time when the world is moving away from mega projects that use polluting fossil fuels to generate electricity, Eskom built not one but two giant plants whose combined output would satisfy almost a quarter of the country's power needs. Before long these projects became bogged down in mismanagement and corruption. The ANC made a handsome return in success fees and dividends through its investment arm Chancellor House's dodgy partnership with Japanese boilermaker Hitachi, and some Eskom officials and their families became millionaires overnight. As a result, the cost of building the new power stations doubled to more than R300 billion. Taxpayers have been saddled with skyrocketing electricity prices and a crippling debt burden that threatens the economic wellbeing of the entire country, while rural communities continue to scavenge for winter fuel.

Things went from bad to worse for villagers living near the construction sites. Already eking out a precarious existence on sparse grasslands, many were relocated to places where watercourses had dried up or were contaminated. Thickets once used for firewood were cleared to make way for open-cast coal mines. The villagers found themselves subjected to the constant din of coal trucks thundering past their homes, choking on the toxic plumes of mine dust that made their children ill.

Eskom's stated mission is to build a power base that fosters shared economic growth and development in order to ensure an even spread of prosperity. If anything, it has achieved the opposite. Instead of investing in cleaner, localised small-scale energy sources, Eskom has stubbornly clung to an outdated mode of centralised power generation that favours gigantic, expensive projects that destroy the environment. This monolithic model, coupled with rampant mismanagement, has allowed or encouraged looting on a grand scale, ultimately constraining economic growth and putting the entire country in hock. Today South Africa is the most unequal country in the world. For this, Eskom must shoulder a fair portion of the blame.

Eskom's implosion also serves as a salutary lesson for those demanding the nationalisation of land, mines and banks – that total state control of the country's productive resources, especially when clean governance remains a low priority, is a recipe for plunder and economic ruin.

This was not an easy story to tell. The looters and their parastatal deployees put a lot of effort into creating an elaborate smokescreen to cover their tracks. This was mostly done by shrouding scientific or financial complexities in impenetrable technical jargon, and trotting out red herrings to deflect attention from their wrongdoing. When these ploys failed, they resorted to outright lies. Sifting fact from fiction and spin became a constant hazard of the job.

An army of helpers guided me through this maze. Many still fear retribution and will have to remain anonymous. You know who you are and the debt of gratitude I owe you. Others, such as Grace Silaule, Mosilo Mothepu, Bianca Goodson, Suzanne Daniels and Khulani Qoma, feature in the pages of this book.

The work of Chris Yelland, Mzukisi Qobo, Anton Eberhard and his MBA student Marisane Thobejane was especially valuable in helping me unravel the intricacies of this complex subject.

A special thanks goes to my colleagues at the *Financial Mail*, *Business Day* and the *Sunday Times*. I'm deeply grateful to Sikonathi Mantshantsha, Mzilikazi wa Afrika, Kyle Cowan, Rob Rose, Genevieve Quintal, Carol Paton and Sabelo Skiti for collaborating on stories with me or comparing notes and engaging in robust debate. Your contributions have immensely enriched my work. The same goes for Jessica Bezuidenhout at the *Daily Maverick* and Geoffrey York at *The Globe and Mail*.

A big thanks too to Shirley de Villiers for her invaluable insights and encouragement, and to my editors at Penguin Random House South Africa, Robert Plummer and Alice Inggs, for their unwavering faith, patience and painstaking attention to detail.

Without all of you this book would not have been possible.

STEPHAN HOFSTATTER
JOHANNESBURG
JULY 2018

Abbreviations

ANC: African National Congress
BEE: black economic empowerment
COSATU: Congress of South African Trade Unions
CSA: coal supply agreement
DA: Democratic Alliance
DRC: Democratic Republic of Congo
EFF: Economic Freedom Fighters
GCIS: Government Communication and Information
    System
JSE: Johannesburg Stock Exchange
MEC: member of the executive council
MK: Umkhonto we Sizwe
MP: member of Parliament
NPA: National Prosecuting Authority
PIC: Public Investment Corporation
PRASA: Passenger Rail Agency of South Africa
SAA: South African Airways
SABC: South African Broadcasting Corporation
SACP: South African Communist Party
SOE: state-owned enterprise
UAE: United Arab Emirates

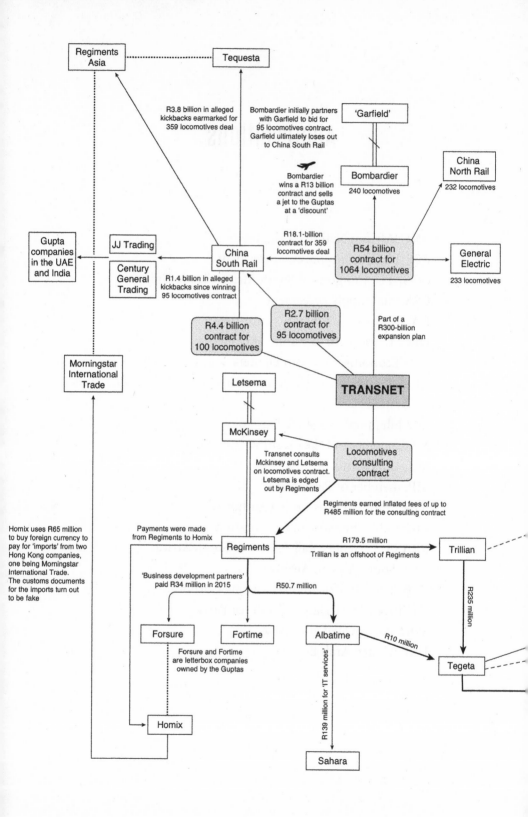

The deals and money flows in the Transnet/Eskom saga

The connections between the various entities represented in this diagram and the flows of money are indisputable in some cases and circumstantial in others. This diagram does not imply wrongdoing on the part of every listed entity, its directors or shareholders. It is intended to aid readers in their understanding of the various links explained in the book and cannot be viewed in isolation. For a proper understanding of the different roles played by the listed entities and individuals, readers are advised to read the book in its entirety.

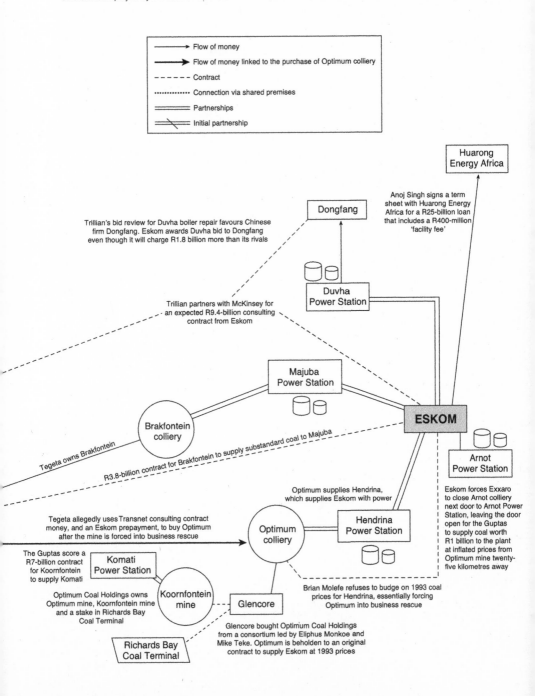

Legend:
- Flow of money
- Flow of money linked to the purchase of Optimum colliery
- Contract
- Connection via shared premises
- Partnerships
- Initial partnership

Huarong Energy Africa

Dongfang

Duvha Power Station

Trillian's bid review for Duvha boiler repair favours Chinese firm Dongfang. Eskom awards Duvha bid to Dongfang even though it will charge R1.8 billion more than its rivals

Anoj Singh signs a term sheet with Huarong Energy Africa for a R25-billion loan that includes a R400-million 'facility fee'

Trillian partners with McKinsey for an expected R9.4-billion consulting contract from Eskom

Majuba Power Station

Brakfontein colliery

Tegeta owns Brakfontein

R3.8-billion contract for Brakfontein to supply substandard coal to Majuba

ESKOM

Arnot Power Station

Optimum supplies Hendrina, which supplies Eskom with power

Tegeta allegedly uses Transnet consulting contract money, and an Eskom prepayment, to buy Optimum after the mine is forced into business rescue

Optimum colliery

Hendrina Power Station

Eskom forces Exxaro to close Arnot colliery next door to Arnot Power Station, leaving the door open for the Guptas to supply coal worth R1 billion to the plant at inflated prices from Optimum mine twenty-five kilometres away

The Guptas score a R7-billion contract for Koornfontein to supply Komati

Komati Power Station

Koornfontein mine

Glencore

Brian Molefe refuses to budge on 1993 coal prices for Hendrina, essentially forcing Optimum into business rescue

Optimum Coal Holdings owns Optimum mine, Koornfontein mine and a stake in Richards Bay Coal Terminal

Richards Bay Coal Terminal

Glencore bought Optimum Coal Holdings from a consortium led by Eliphus Monkoe and Mike Teke. Optimum is beholden to an original contract to supply Eskom at 1993 prices

1

Zuma's Dubai Bolthole

It's a Friday evening in April 2016. I'm standing in my hotel room in Dubai looking out at the world's tallest building, the Burj Khalifa, when my phone rings. It's one of my best contacts. Let's call him Calvin. He's one of those guys every journalist wants as a source: well connected in the world of high finance and close to some very senior ANC politicians. He also claims to be a longtime acquaintance of leading members of one or two of the world's more interesting intelligence services.

I've never been able to figure out how Calvin managed to become so connected. He once ran a company with links to the ANC's informal intelligence structures and was involved in mining deals throughout Africa, but that doesn't really account for the depth and range of his contact network. Calvin is often on the money but he rarely provides me with a paper trail or any way of corroborating his tip-offs, which is why I seldom publish anything he tells me, no matter how juicy the story, until I can find a way of verifying it independently.

'Steve,' he says. 'Brian Molefe just gave the Guptas R2 billion to buy Optimum.'

I take a deep breath. The Guptas are a controversial immigrant family which has cultivated close ties with South Africa's political elite. Brian Molefe is the chief executive of Eskom. The national power utility operates thirty power stations that generate 45 000 megawatts of electricity, mostly from burning coal, making it the largest in Africa by far. It earns R177 billion a year from selling power to South Africa and its neighbours, which is almost three times the revenue generated by the country's second-largest parastatal, the ports and rail authority Transnet. Eskom is a company that more than any other in the public or private sector holds the fate of the South African economy in its hands. Without a regular power supply, mines, smelters, commercial farms and the retail, manufacturing and hospitality industries would grind to a halt. It's been estimated that the economy lost up to R1 billion a day during the height of rolling blackouts in 2014. When Eskom sneezes, the entire country catches cold. It is therefore vital for the economy that the utility is run properly.

Eskom spends R140 billion a year on operating expenses alone – almost four times more than Transnet does. This excludes the R337 billion being spent over several years to build the mega power stations Medupi and Kusile and the Ingula pumped-storage scheme, R23 billion a year in interest on ballooning loans, and billions more on maintenance and refurbishment. Buying coal accounts for R50 billion of Eskom's annual operating costs, the parastatal's single biggest expense. At one point, it was also spending R1 billion a month on diesel to fuel its emergency generators. Eskom spends R33 billion a year on salaries for its 48 000-strong workforce – up from 35 000-strong a decade ago, even though the utility sells less electricity today. The rest is spent on forking out massive – and often inflated – fees to consultants and contractors. Eskom was ripe for looting.

One of the biggest stories in 2016 exposed how Brian Molefe and mineral resources minister Mosebenzi Zwane helped the Gupta family buy Optimum coal mine from Glencore shortly after President Jacob Zuma's son Duduzane Zuma became a shareholder in Gupta mining company Tegeta. Molefe was a key player in the saga, having forced Optimum into business rescue by refusing to renegotiate uneconomical coal prices. This left Optimum open to takeover by the Guptas, who would have no trouble in getting a better deal from Eskom once they'd laid their hands on the mine. But the deadline for the Guptas to come up with the purchase price of R2.15 billion was 14 April 2016. Just days before the deadline, they were still scrambling to find the money. Then, at the last minute, an announcement was made that they'd come up with the cash.

The big mystery was where the money came from. And now here was Calvin, on the phone to me twenty-four hours later, claiming it was Molefe. It was a great scoop, but it sounded too good to be true.

'You're saying Brian Molefe, the CEO of Eskom, gave the Guptas the money to buy Optimum?' I ask Calvin.

'Yup. Eskom gave them the money up front for future coal deliveries. Brian authorised the deal. A forward purchase agreement. Why don't you ask him?'

'Who told you this?'

'It's true, Steve. Just write it! This is gospel. I'm telling you now, it's 100 per cent. Just ask Brian. He'll have to tell you.'

I decide to check in with a banking source who used to work in the coal industry and still has connections at Eskom.

'Yes, it's true,' he says.

'How would you know for sure?'

'I've spoken to two people directly involved.'

'Can I talk to them?'

'Look,' he says, sounding exasperated, 'that was always the plan. The Guptas wanted to break into the big league in the coal supply game. To do that, they needed to own a mine like Optimum. And they wanted Eskom to help them pay for it.'

'By making the prepayment?'

'Yes. Eskom paid the Guptas up front for coal supplied by Optimum to help them pay for the mine. That's how it was done.'

Another question that nagged at me was why the Guptas would want to buy Optimum in the first place. The mine was haemorrhaging R100 million odd a month after being locked into a long-term contract with Eskom to supply the adjacent Hendrina power station at the price of R150 a ton. By 2015, it was costing Optimum R300 a ton to mine the coal. The colliery desperately needed to negotiate a more favourable rate, or it would go out of business. Molefe refused to budge. Instead, he imposed a R2.2-billion fine on Glencore for previous deliveries of substandard coal.

I ask my banking source what the Guptas would want with a lemon. 'They're looking for better opportunities down the line,' he explains. 'Optimum supplies Hendrina. But I was told they will also supply Arnot power station for a higher price.'

Arnot is twenty-five kilometres away from Optimum. This arrangement would have an added advantage: while transport costs to Hendrina power station were minimal because the coal was shunted directly to the plant on a conveyor belt, the Guptas could slap on inflated trucking costs to Arnot on top of higher-priced coal. 'That's how they will make their money back,' he says.

At the time, I thought the story sounded far-fetched. It was too brazen. Surely, given all the adverse publicity surrounding the Guptas and their business dealings with Jacob Zuma's family, Eskom wouldn't dare help them buy a coal mine. The notion that the power utility's chief executive could have personally authorised a shady deal benefiting the president's son seemed absurd. South Africa has been through some pretty bad corruption scandals, but there's usually some attempt to preserve a fig leaf of respectability. 'We're not Russia or the DRC,' I remember thinking.

In hindsight – after a deluge of leaked emails originating from the server of a Gupta company laid bare just how deeply Zuma, his cabinet and a host of parastatal bosses were in the family's pocket – my qualms seem somehow quaint. That moment would come to feel like another country.

On Saturday 16 April I decide to give Molefe a ring, just to see what he says. If this whole thing's been fabricated by sources who tend to see a Gupta plot under every rock and behind every tree, then Molefe can easily clear things up. That's if he picks up the phone.

To my surprise, he answers almost immediately. He sounds gruff and put out when I ask about the Gupta prepayment.

'I'm at a funeral. You can send your questions to the Eskom spokesperson.'

I apologise for disturbing him. 'But this involves you personally. Can you tell me if you authorised that forward payment or not?'

He accepts my apology but doesn't answer my question.

'Are you denying that you authorised the prepayment to the Guptas?' I persist. 'Can you at least tell me that?'

'I've already told you to ask my spokesperson. I'm at a funeral.'

That's the end of our conversation. He's not commenting on the Gupta prepayment, but he isn't denying it happened either.

I dash off an email to Eskom's media desk to ask whether the utility made a prepayment to help the Guptas buy Optimum, whether Molefe authorised it and if the Guptas will be supplying Arnot power station as well as Hendrina from Optimum colliery.

To kill time, I go for a stroll around the old Al Fahidi district off Dubai Creek, an enclave of tranquillity in this frenzied monument to excess. I wander through narrow alleys and ornamentally cobbled squares surrounded by restored villas built with coral stone walls and wind towers that funnel sea breezes into the rooms. After ambling around the old fort, I buy a few Omani limes at a nearby souk to take back to South Africa, before settling down to lunch.

It takes two hours for Eskom to return my call. The utility's spokesperson, Khulu Phasiwe, flatly denies the prepayment even exists. 'We are currently not aware of any valid or enforceable contract as described by you,' he declares piously.

This was a very curious thing to say. In fact, it amounted to an outright lie. It later emerged that the Guptas had only managed to scrape together R1.5 billion of the R2.15 billion they needed, but on Wednesday 13 April, just three days before I'd spoken to Molefe, Eskom had paid them R660 million for future coal deliveries from Optimum mine even though they hadn't even bought it yet. Molefe would later be able to claim plausible deniability: he hadn't actually signed off on the prepayment himself; that task was left to one of his deputies, Eskom's head of generation, Matshela Koko. Nevertheless, given the body of evidence that subsequently emerged regarding Molefe's tight relationship with the Gupta family, it's highly unlikely that he didn't approve, or at least know about, the payment. The next day, 14 April, Glencore received its outstanding R600 million. The prepayment had come just in the nick of time. Without it, the Guptas could not have bought the mine.

Two years later, with the mine forced into business rescue and workers' salaries going unpaid, it was clear that the Optimum deal had allowed the Guptas to extract billions of rands from Eskom and probably divert large sums to front companies in Dubai. They had been given a licence to loot.

* * *

A pivotal moment in this story took place four months earlier. On 9 December 2015, a day that's been dubbed '9/12', Zuma fired respected finance minister Nhlanhla Nene and replaced him with small-town mayor Des van Rooyen. Within days, R170 billion was wiped off the value of shares traded on the Johannesburg Stock Exchange and the rand plunged to record lows. By Monday 14 December, Zuma had caved in to intense pressure from bank executives to reverse the decision. He replaced Van Rooyen (who subsequently landed the nickname 'Weekend Special') with highly regarded former finance minister Pravin Gordhan, who had been moved sideways eighteen months earlier after becoming an outspoken critic of parastatal looting. The change came too late: the country's financial credibility lay in tatters.

A week later, the Economic Freedom Fighters' deputy president, Floyd Shivambu, published an incendiary blog titled 'SA is under colonial administration', which set the tone for the surge of anger against the Guptas and their elaborate looting scheme.

'The reason Nhlanhla Nene was removed was to open space for the looters, the Gupta led criminal syndicate, to loot state resources for private enrichment,' Shivambu railed. He went on to describe the family as 'a criminal syndicate masquerading as genuine business people, headquartered in Saxonwold' who had 'colonized South Africa for some time now, with Zuma being the Chief Colonial Administrator'.

The Guptas had infiltrated the ruling party to install 'puppets' in every tier of government, and they had influence over the premiers of the Free State and North West provinces, cabinet ministers, and the heads and boards of state entities.

Zuma's appointment of Van Rooyen as finance minister was a Gupta-orchestrated plot to 'capture' Treasury, wrote Shivambu. As evidence, he pointed to Van Rooyen's visit to the Treasury offices just a day after he took over, where he introduced his newly appointed Gupta-linked advisors to senior management. Now that the Gupta plot to capture Treasury had been foiled, Shivambu warned, 'they will resort to other means of looting'.[1]

There was some consolation in that the Guptas had failed to get their hands on the keys to the national vault. The country had survived '9/12', but the family's audacity in attempting the heist in the first place enraged South Africans.

These feelings reached fever pitch in March 2016, when reports sur-faced that the Guptas had offered deputy finance minister Mcebisi Jonas the job of finance minister shortly before Nene was fired. Jonas later told Public Protector Thuli Madonsela that he'd been offered a R600 000 cash bribe and was promised another R600 million if he agreed to take the job to do the Guptas' bidding.[2] Shivambu weighed in again, issuing a statement saying the Guptas had already 'started packing their bags and are in the process of moving their assets to Dubai'. He added that the family had already sent R2 billion of their loot abroad. When the EFF's sensational claims were met with indignant howls of denial and cries of defamation from the Guptas, the party challenged them to sue. They never did.[3]

The EFF now turned on Zuma. On 28 March 2016, the president paid a three-day 'working visit' to the United Arab Emirates, starting in Dubai, to 'promote South Africa as a top global tourism destination for visitors from the Gulf region'.[4]

The presidential jet had barely touched down in South Africa when EFF leader Julius Malema dropped a bombshell at a press conference: 'This was not an official visit, it was a personal one,' Malema declared. 'Zuma took money to UAE. That is where they are dumping money. The Guptas have taken R6 billion to Dubai.'[5]

Zuma threatened to sue Malema for spreading 'preposterous and mali-cious' rumours.[6] Atul Gupta dismissed the allegations as 'nothing more than a politically-motivated campaign against us'.

'It is correct that we know president Zuma in a personal capacity,' he told the *Times of India*. 'However, we have never benefited commercially from this relationship. In fact, less than 1% of our group's revenue comes from government business.'[7]

This was a blatant lie. In its annual results statement, released six months later, Oakbay declared that 9 per cent of its total revenue came from government business.[8] Atul Gupta also sidestepped two salient facts. First, the Guptas' mining ventures were entirely reliant on licences and approvals granted by the government departments they had infiltrated. Second, evidence unearthed later suggests that the Guptas acted as brokers for multinationals bidding for large state contracts, earning kickbacks worth billions in return. This was made possible by engineering key appointments to Zuma's cabinet and the boards and executive committees of state entities. In fact, the Gupta business empire was almost entirely dependent for its survival on government largesse, bestowed thanks to the family's close ties with the president.

On 10 April, ten days after Malema's memorable press conference, the EFF leader upped the ante: 'We received unconfirmed reports that Zuma wants to leave the country and seek asylum in Dubai because he doesn't feel safe in his country!' he tweeted.

On the same day, *City Press* ran a story claiming that the Guptas had fled the lynch mob in South Africa 'with a mountain of luggage loaded onto the business jet ZS-OAK'. The aircraft, the Rolls-Royce of private jets made by Canadian train and plane manufacturer Bombardier and financed by the Canadian government's export bank, was destined for Dubai. Gupta family spokesperson Nazeem Howa told *City Press* that the Gupta children 'have been taunted at school and university' and the Gupta brothers had withdrawn from public life. By then, all four major banks that serviced the Gupta companies had closed their accounts or were about to. Duduzane Zuma had also announced that he planned to resign from the boards of all Gupta companies and would be 'exiting' his investments. It looked as though the exodus had begun.[9]

The most disturbing aspect of the whirlwind of events in those few weeks in March and April 2016 was the suggestion that the president and his family were about to follow in the footsteps of so many leaders who'd plundered their countries and fled abroad with the loot to escape jail or being lynched by their angry and impoverished subjects. It suddenly didn't seem that far-fetched that Zuma might follow suit. In *Talk of the Devil*, Italian journalist and author Riccardo Orizio tells of spending several years traversing the globe to track down fallen dictators in exile. Most had looted their countries, massacred their subjects and fled with a sizeable chunk of their nations' wealth. Some, like Uganda's Idi Amin, were living in relative comfort many years later. Orizio interviewed Amin in a large white villa in Jeddah shortly before the former president died in a state-of-the-art Saudi hospital in 2003. Others, like Jean-Bédel Bokassa, had returned home from exile. Orizio found him living out his last days in poverty in his crumbling villa in the Central African Republic capital of Bangui.[10] I once met one of Bokassa's successors, François Bozizé, in a drab hotel on the outskirts of Paris. Months earlier, Bozizé had been toppled in a French-sponsored coup that had cost the lives of fourteen South African soldiers and hundreds of civilians. He was shabbily dressed and looked like a broken man, a far cry from the military strongman whose government, like Zuma's, had dished out lucrative state contracts to his family.

I wondered how Zuma would meet his end. Would he land up like Amin, pampered and protected by his Emirati hosts thanks to the money his family and the Guptas had siphoned from state contracts and diverted to Dubai? Or would he, like Bozizé, end up penniless and friendless once he was no longer useful to either the Guptas or the Emiratis, haunting the shabby lobbies of Dubai's seedier hotels, a shadow of the man who once had it all. Most likely he'd follow in Bokassa's footsteps, returning home to face the music rather than rotting in a foreign city – even if it meant being jailed for corruption before spending his dying days in a run-down Nkandla.

It turned out that *City Press* had jumped the gun. The Guptas would only flee South Africa almost two years later, in 2018, when arrest warrants were issued for them. The idea that they were making preparations as early as March 2016 to disinvest from South Africa and move abroad, though, wasn't that implausible.

Even so, by March 2016 my colleagues at the *Sunday Times* and I had heard from several independent sources that the Guptas were moving large sums of money to Dubai and buying up properties there, echoing the EFF leaders' claims. The properties included a villa bought by Rajesh 'Tony' Gupta for $25 million in cash in the plush expatriate suburb of Emirates Hills, a collection of ostentatious homes built around an artificial lake and golf course, and dubbed the 'Beverly Hills of Dubai'. We heard that Tony had already moved there, but when I called his mobile number, one of his employees who told me his name was Nazeem answered the phone. 'I don't know why he bought a house in Dubai. Just because he's bought a house doesn't mean he lives there,' he said and hung up.

I obtained home-affairs and flight records that showed the Gupta brothers and Duduzane Zuma regularly flew to India and Dubai, as well

9

as between the two countries. Our sources said that Zuma's son spent most of his time in Dubai to attend to his business interests in the region. 'He is consolidating his assets there and is in the process of moving there,' said one.

The most explosive piece of information we received was that the Guptas had actually bought the house in Emirates Hills as a retirement home for President Zuma. Malema's claim that Zuma was about to seek asylum in Dubai suddenly sounded credible. My *Sunday Times* colleague Mzilikazi wa Afrika and I decided it was time to head to Dubai and track down the president's bolthole; who knew, we might arrive to see a fugitive Zuma and his Gupta benefactors roll up at the gates of their villa carrying suitcases bulging with cash. With these thoughts running through my mind, I settled down on Flight SAA 7162 to Dubai, landing at 8 a.m. on Tuesday morning, 12 April 2016.

* * *

Dubai is an unreal city, a densely populated coastal strip of low-rise apartment buildings, residential villas, factories, warehouses, markets, international hotels, giant glitzy malls, and futuristic towering skyscrapers clad in blue-tinted glass. Upmarket suburbs and gleaming hotel complexes have been built on artificial islands just off the coast. On the outskirts of the city, gated villages are clustered around artificial lakes and golf greens, eventually giving way to the desert, a wasteland of sandy scrub stretching far into the distance.

After we check into our hotel in the financial district on Sheikh Zayed Road, a twelve-lane highway that cuts a swathe through the city and runs parallel to a raised metro, I call my contact. He used to occupy a senior position in the Emirati government and remains close to people who still do. He wants to meet right away at a Starbucks around the corner. Despite the blistering heat, he looks fresh and unruffled as he walks in wearing a flowing white *kandura*. He orders a cappuccino. After sitting down and exchanging a few pleasantries, he studies his hands before looking up warily. He explains that he only agreed to meet us because Calvin vouched for me. 'A friend of his is a friend of mine,' he says, then holds up his hand. 'Please, I live here. I do business here. You can't ever use my name or tell anyone that you spoke to me.'

First, he gives us some tips on how to survive Dubai. 'The police and the government officials you meet will always be very friendly and courteous,' he says, but warns that this is just for show. A PR gimmick illustrates his point. In 2013, the Dubai government supplied the police with supercars to patrol tourist districts. Officers driving Porsches, Bugattis and Bentleys encourage visitors to pose for selfies with them. The fanciest cars are reserved for female officers. 'We're not looking to just show off with the car, we're looking to show tourists how friendly the police is here in Dubai,' a police official told CNN.[11]

But beneath the glitzy veneer that welcomes first-time visitors is the brutal machinery of a police state that uses mass surveillance and arbitrary detention to crack down on dissent, and an army of lowly paid migrant workers crammed into overcrowded housing complexes built on the scrubland on the edge of the city, enjoying few rights and little recourse to the law when subjected to abuse from employers.

'Don't be fooled,' our guide tells us, suddenly glancing around nervously. 'The secret police are everywhere. Dubai is open for business to everyone, but if you step out of line, especially if you threaten the business interests of the sheikh and his family, there will be consequences.' These consequences range from deportation to beatings, torture and disappearance. 'Especially as a journalist, you must be very careful,' he continues. 'The Dubai government does not like bad publicity. It's bad for business. If you plan to write anything you must make sure you leave the country before you publish your story.'

We ask him about the Guptas – their businesses, their properties, and the money they brought here. 'The Guptas are causing problems for the government,' he sighs. 'Your president too. We want to enjoy good relations with your government. There is a lot to offer with a strong relationship – in trade, in tourism. But the Dubai government doesn't like bad publicity.'

He promises to make some enquiries for us, and then gets up to leave. Walking down Sheikh Zayed Road in his flowing robes, he looks just like any other Emirati – unobtrusive, giving away nothing about his wealth or status. He could be a telecoms tycoon taking a morning stroll before climbing into a gold-plated Bentley, a cobbler returning to his shop down a side street, or a mysterious former functionary who still has access to state secrets...

The bleak picture he paints is brought home to me a few days later during a conversation with a Czech journalist whose colleague narrowly escaped torture, or worse, at the hands of the secret police. She'd been detained after writing something unflattering about the government and was only released after convincing her interrogators that she had a personal relationship with the sheikh.

'You will see them outside the Burj Khalifa,' the journalist says, referring to the ubiquitous secret police. 'There are a lot of Russians there: arms dealers, oil barons, oligarchs. They like to spend their money here. The Dubai government makes sure there is no trouble.'

Gradually, using information supplied by our sources in the ANC, people close to the Zuma family, and our mysterious guide and his business associates in Dubai, including a senior attorney and an official at Sharjah Islamic Bank, we are able to piece together elements of the story. We can confirm that the Guptas have bought the $25-million villa in Emirates Hills, but we can't corroborate the claim that it is intended for Zuma. Our efforts to verify information we'd received that the Emirati government had frozen $240 million of the Guptas' assets in a bonded warehouse in one of the UAE's free economic zones also draw a blank.

However, we are able to establish that Duduzane Zuma and Salim Aziz Essa, a Johannesburg businessman at the heart of the Gupta looting machine, bought luxury apartments in the Burj Khalifa. 'We cannot confirm registration,' says one of my sources of Duduzane Zuma's purchase. 'He would have done it through a shelf company, but he's the beneficial owner. He's there at least ten days a month, but hasn't been seen there in the last month.'

The Burj soars almost a kilometre above Dubai and is billed as 'the world's most prestigious address, home to a select few'. The place reeks of new money. Prices range from $800 000 for a small studio to as much as $8 million for serviced apartments designed by Giorgio Armani. The complex boasts indoor and outdoor pools, state-of-the-art gyms, jacuzzis, and sky bars and restaurants where patrons can take in spectacular views of the city and the Persian Gulf.

An estate agent agrees to take us on a tour of Emirates Hills. The estate is surrounded by high walls and fences, and access is strictly controlled. Inside, an atmosphere of moneyed tranquillity prevails, with residents jogging or cycling around artificial lakes, strolling down the broad avenues or driving past in Rolls-Royces and Bentleys. Surveillance cameras track our every move.

Architectural plans must be approved by the developer, the state-backed Emaar Group, which also constructed the Burj Khalifa. Styles range from Arabic, Moroccan and neoclassical to 'modern contemporary', the estate agent informs us. At night, residents put up coloured lights that twinkle in the dark. Wild parties take place out of eyeshot. 'People have discos in their basements for private parties. Kylie Minogue was brought in secretly to sing at someone's birthday party.'

Anyone with a pile of money can buy a villa here with no questions asked. 'People come here in their private jets to buy properties with cash,' the estate agent says. 'When the Saudis come here, they don't come with credit cards. They bring hard cash. We're on the border with Iran, which is one of the biggest money-laundering countries in the world.'

Finding proof of property ownership is notoriously difficult in Dubai and one of the reasons the country is so popular with arms dealers, narco traffickers and oligarchs with money to launder. If you wanted to buy property here and remain anonymous, you'd first register a company in one of the UAE's (tax) free economic zones and appoint local nominee shareholders, which would ensure your identity remains hidden. The names of directors and shareholders of companies and the beneficiaries of trusts registered in the free zones aren't publicly available, and deeds and records can't be accessed without permission from the owner.

'I can get a company set up for you in five days, then you can purchase a property,' the estate agent explains over drinks at the Address Montgomerie, a luxury hotel at the estate's golf club. 'Within fourteen days you can transfer the title. If you have to declare it back home, that's up to you. If you don't declare it, you don't declare it. There's no chance of a Panama Papers situation here.'

This comes in handy for tax avoidance. 'If you have to pay tax back in South Africa you just open a Jebel Ali offshore company. It will cost you about 3 000 dirham. The company owns the asset, and you have share-holders. [The registrar] will not disclose their identity to any government.' Buyers take cash or bank transfers. 'If you've got money in the bank you can do a money transfer. If the money is in cash, which means it's not legit, we have to find other means. But it's not a problem.'

If Zuma were to take up residence in Emirates Hills, he would be in illustrious company. The former president of Pakistan, Asif Ali Zardari, has a house here. Zardari was jailed for eight years for arms deal corrup-tion and money laundering and moved to Dubai after his release in 2004. Another resident is Thaksin Shinawatra, the former prime minister of Thailand. Shinawatra was deposed in a coup in 2006 and convicted in absentia after being accused of corruption, tax evasion and abuse of power.

Some of the more established expatriate residents have a sardonic view of the constant stream of new arrivals. 'You need twenty to thirty million dollars to buy a property here,' says one, sitting on a park bench in the estate, feeding scraps to a swarm of cats. 'Maybe you brought along some dirty money you want to wash?'

Although we couldn't prove at the time that the Guptas had bought Zuma a house in Dubai, a year later a piece of evidence from the so-called 'Gupta leaks' landed in our laps that suggested this was their intention all along. It came in the form of an email sent by Ashu Chawla, the chief executive of Gupta-owned company Sahara Computers, to Duduzane Zuma on 16 January 2016. Two draft letters were attached to Chawla's email. One was addressed to the crown prince of Abu Dhabi, Sheikh Mohammed bin Zayed Al Nahyan, and the other to Sheikh Mohammed bin Rashid Al Maktoum, the prime minister of the UAE and ruler of Dubai. Both letters were drafted in the name of 'Jacob G Zuma, President of South Africa'.

The fawning letter to Sheikh Mohammed bin Zayed compliments the Abu Dhabi crown prince for his successes 'in the areas of education, economic development and environmental protection'. These, it says, are 'worthy of emulation for us in the African Continent and specially in South Africa, where we continue to pursue transformation for our Citizenry, through various government initiatives'. The letter goes on to fondly recall Zuma's meeting with the sheikh 'and the gracious hospitality and warmth extended to me during my visit', and it concludes: 'It is with this sentiment that I am happy to inform you that my family has decided to make the UAE a second home. It will be a great honour for me and my family to gain your patronage during our proposed residency in the UAE.'

The second letter drafted in Zuma's name, this time to the ruler of Dubai, Sheikh Mohammed Al Maktoum, is even more obsequious. It congratulates him for 'completing 10 years of dynamic rule and visionary leadership that has transformed the landscape of Dubai, making it one of the most advanced and efficient governments in the world'. The sheikh's 'visionary approach to governance' is a personal inspiration. The letter concludes by informing the sheikh of Zuma's intention 'to make the UAE, and specifically Dubai, a second home', requesting his 'patronage during our proposed residency in the UAE'.

In a revised draft of this letter, Sheikh Mohammed Al Maktoum is informed that Zuma has 'already acquired a residence located at Emirates Hills, Dubai (Villa L35, Lailak Street No1)'. It asks the Emirati leader to 'kindly grant an audience to my son, Mr Duduzane Zuma, to meet with you and formally introduce the family to you'.

Villa L35 on Lailak Street is a palatial mansion. Photos posted on the website of estate agent Knight Frank show that it has ten bedrooms, thirteen bathrooms, a double grand staircase and nine reception rooms boasting white marble, mosaic and gold interiors, and parking for eleven cars.

Documents contained in the Gupta leaks also confirm that the villa was bought by Tony Gupta. However, in July 2015, a draft agreement was drawn up between the seller, Lebanese businessman Adib Hassan Ataya; Tony Gupta; and an opaque entity registered in Jebel Ali Free Zone called Mahila Investments. The new draft agreement voided the sale agreement between Tony Gupta and the Lebanese businessman, transferring ownership of the property to the 'new buyer', Mahila Investments. The beneficial ownership of Mahila Investments is not disclosed, which means it's possible that the Mahila Investments shares were intended to be held by the Zuma family or their nominated proxies.

The idea that the Zuma family may have planned to relocate to Dubai with the help of the Guptas is reinforced by the fact that Duduzane Zuma obtained a Dubai residency permit in October 2015. Leaked emails show that he bought his apartment in the Burj Khalifa two months later, for R18 million, through Wens Holdings, a company co-owned by the Guptas.

When our story about 'Zuma's Dubai palace' was published in the *Sunday Times*, the president branded it 'a fabrication'. He insisted that he didn't own any real estate outside South Africa and had never asked anyone to buy property for him abroad. 'The President has also not received or seen the reported emails and has no knowledge of them,' his spokesperson, Bongani Ngqulunga, said in a statement.[12]

This sidestepped an important issue: If Zuma were completely unaware of the existence of letters drafted in his name that declared his intention to relocate to Dubai and live in the Emirates Hills mansion he'd bought, Chawla would surely be guilty of misrepresenting the intentions and actions of the president, with the full knowledge of the president's son Duduzane, to whom he'd forwarded the letters. This in itself should have been of grave concern to Zuma, demanding immediate action against both Chawla and Duduzane, yet as far as is known, none was taken.

Democratic Alliance leader Mmusi Maimane challenged the president to sue the *Sunday Times* if he believed the story to be false. 'The claims made in the story are not trivial and go to the very nub of state capture by the notorious Gupta family,' Maimane said. 'The allegations are serious, and cannot simply be dismissed via a press release. Therefore if the story is in fact false – as the Presidency claims – the DA challenges the President to take legal action against the newspaper for publishing false and defamatory information about him and his good friends, the Gupta brothers.'[13]

To date, no legal action has been brought against the newspaper.

* * *

Flying back to South Africa from Dubai, I replay the conversation I had with Calvin about Brian Molefe's prepayment to the Guptas in my mind.

It gets me thinking. Calvin is seldom wrong, but Eskom flatly denied the transaction took place. I couldn't publish the story without any further corroboration. I only discovered later that this wasn't the first or the last time the power utility had blatantly lied to the media about its dealings with the Guptas. At the time, the story struck me as implausible: if the Guptas had really succeeded in persuading the head of Africa's biggest and most powerful utility to come up with the R2 billion they needed to buy a coal mine, then they must have some serious sway. The only way to pull off a stunt like that is if you have the president in your pocket.

2

President for Hire

Shortly before 8 a.m. on Friday 10 October 2008, a jet took off from Lanseria Airport. On board were Zwelinzima Vavi, Blade Nzimande and the newly elected president of the ANC, Jacob Zuma. Their destination was Equatorial Guinea. The oil-rich West African country is ruled by Teodoro Obiang Nguema Mbasogo, one of the continent's most corrupt dictators. Obiang had invited Zuma to attend his country's Independence Day celebrations, which took place two days later.

The three men were a coalition of the disgruntled, rather than ideological bedfellows, united in one thing only: their opposition to President Thabo Mbeki. Vavi, the charismatic trade unionist, and Nzimande, the acerbic head of the South African Communist Party, had both decided to throw their weight behind Zuma to oust Mbeki at the ANC's elective conference in December 2007. Vavi and Nzimande felt Mbeki had sold out the working class by adopting neoliberal economic policies that had failed the poor. They also regarded Zuma as a victim of Mbeki's abuse of state institutions – the police, prosecuting authority and intelligence services – to settle political scores and neutralise rivals.[1] Ironically, Zuma would use the same tactics to even more devastating effect when he took over the country.

With just months to go before the April 2009 general elections that would propel Zuma to the highest office in the land, Vavi and Nzimande wanted some time alone with the man whom they'd helped put in power. The trip to Equatorial Guinea was an ideal opportunity to whisper a few suggestions in the ANC president's ear before he chose his cabinet. What they hadn't bargained on was a chance encounter with one of the Gupta brothers and bearing witness to a seminal moment in the future 'state capture' saga.

* * *

By the time Vavi and Nzimande flew to Equatorial Guinea with Zuma, a large body of evidence already existed suggesting the newly elected ANC president was corrupt. For a start, there was the conviction in June 2005 of Zuma's former financial advisor, Schabir Shaik. During his trial, Shaik had admitted to making hundreds of small payments to Zuma totalling almost R1 million. He claimed that they were loans or gifts to his former comrade in the anti-apartheid struggle. Prosecutors argued that Shaik was bribing Zuma to further his business interests, including with French arms and electronics maker Thomson-CSF (later renamed Thales), which had won a R2.6-billion contract from the South African navy in 1997 to fit four new German frigates with combat suites.

Next came the dramatic raids by the Scorpions.[2] In August 2005, the elite crime-fighting unit swooped on Zuma's home in the leafy Johannesburg suburb of Forest Town (situated a stone's throw from the now notorious Gupta compound in Saxonwold), as well as on his Nkandla homestead in rural KwaZulu-Natal, the offices of his lawyer Michael Hulley, and Shaik's home in Durban. The raids yielded 93 000 documents, apparently providing investigators with valuable evidence in their corruption investigation.

Following the raids, former KPMG investigator Johan van der Walt compiled a detailed forensic report into Zuma's financial affairs that underpinned his indictment for corruption in 2007. The report identifies 783 payments totalling R4 million that Shaik made to Zuma. He spent over R500 000 on school fees for fourteen of Zuma's children and dependants, including Duduzane and Duduzile Zuma; he took care of Zuma's car repayments and repairs, household expenses and travel and medical costs; and he regularly handed Zuma wads of cash.[3]

Shaik's business model was simple and not uncommon. He was close to politicians with the power to decide who got awarded lucrative state contracts. A company that wanted a contract had to cut him in on the deal. Shaik would then broker bribes for the politicians or use the proceeds of his partnership to bankroll their lavish lifestyles. In Zuma's case, Shaik did both.

The Guptas would later deploy a variant of the same scheme. The family cut Zuma's son Duduzane in on government deals and, the evidence suggests, used their influence with the president to ensure multinationals were awarded large contracts in return for lucrative partnerships and kickbacks.

Van der Walt's report, which is likely to constitute a key piece of evidence in the case against Zuma that was reinstated in March 2018, also sets out the nexus between Zuma, Shaik and Thales. It details how Zuma leaned on Thales executives to cut Shaik in on the deal while his financial advisor was bankrolling him to live beyond his means. The money Shaik earned from an arms deal brokered by Zuma with Thales was finding its way straight back into Zuma's pockets.[4]

It gets worse. Within six months of Zuma's appointment as deputy president in June 1999, the auditor-general, the Heath Special Investigating Unit[5] and Parliament all began investigating corruption allegations related to the arms deal. Companies that had bribed their way into contracts now needed political protection from prosecution.

An item of evidence that was instrumental in Shaik's conviction was a handwritten note that Alain Thetard, the local director of Thales, had written after meeting Zuma in Durban in March 2000. Thetard's note said that Zuma had agreed to be paid a bribe of R500 000 a year in return for protecting Thales in the arms deal investigation and for 'support for future projects'. Investigators found that Thales later paid R250 000 towards renovations at Zuma's Nkandla homestead, funnelled through one of Shaik's companies.[6]

Van der Walt's evidence, together with what came out during Shaik's successful prosecution for fraud and corruption, should have been enough to sink Zuma, but by 2007 he had mustered a 'tsunami' of support, as Vavi put it. Zuma employed what his lawyer Kemp J. Kemp described as a 'Stalingrad defence', fighting from 'burning house to burning house', contesting every technicality. At court appearances, his supporters, egged on by Vavi and Julius Malema, vowed to 'take up arms and kill for Zuma'.[7]

Vavi, Nzimande and Malema (who headed the ANC Youth League at the time) had convinced themselves that the deputy president was the innocent victim of Mbeki's political machinations, not someone who deserved to go to jail because he was corrupt.

Zuma's lawyers finally persuaded the National Prosecuting Authority's acting head, Mokotedi Mpshe, that there was enough evidence of political interference to warrant dropping the charges shortly before the elections.[8]

My sources in the police and prosecuting authority have always maintained that the evidence of corruption against Zuma in the public domain was just the tip of the iceberg. But despite several attempts by the Democratic Alliance to haul him back to court, Zuma's Stalingrad strategy paid off. It would be years before he was forced to face the music.

In 2014, my colleagues at the *Sunday Times* and I obtained a treasure trove of documents confirming just how deep in Thales' pockets Zuma was. The documents were transcripts totalling 1358 pages of testimony before retired judge Phillip Levinsohn at confidential arbitration hearings in a fee dispute between Pretoria lawyer Ajay Sooklal and Thales.[9]

Thales had hired Sooklal as a fixer to use his political connections to get the charges against the French arms maker withdrawn. Thales had already retained the services of Deneys Reitz, but the law firm didn't have Sooklal's contacts, which included the then defence minister Mosiuoa Lekota, justice minister Penuell Maduna, and Schabir Shaik's brother Mo Shaik, who became head of the secret service when Zuma took power. Sooklal's job was to travel the globe lobbying presidents, cabinet ministers, party leaders, defence company officials, prosecutors and lawyers in an increasingly desperate bid to get Thales and Zuma off the hook.

The transcripts detail how Sooklal arranged flights, fancy clothes, legal fees and lavish hotel stays in Europe for Zuma when he faced corruption charges linked to the arms deal, all paid for by Thales. They also contain new details implicating Zuma and the ANC in corrupt dealings related to the arms deal that hadn't come out during the Shaik trial. An amusing example is that Zuma had used the codeword 'Eiffel Tower' to signal his acceptance of Thales' R500 000-a-year bribe in return for political protection in the arms deal probe and to secure future business for the company.[10]

On one occasion in 2006, Sooklal recalled driving Pierre Moynot, who had replaced Thetard as Thales' local director, to the home of ANC treasurer Mendi Msimang in order to hand him a cheque for €1 million as a donation to the party.[11]

When I had occasion to ask Moynot about Sooklal's allegations, he was at pains to discredit him. 'It's true we hired him for his political connections,' he explained. 'We realised very soon he was not a proper guy – he would do anything for money.'

Moynot went on to confirm virtually everything Sooklal had said, downplaying the impropriety of an international company bankrolling the future president in order to secure protection against prosecution and future contracts from the South African government. 'You must understand that we wanted the prosecution of Zuma to be stopped as soon as possible. If he had lost, the company would have had a lot of problems in his country and we would have had to leave.' I asked him about the clothes, the trips, the legal fees: did Thales pick up the tab for all those expenses? 'He had no money at the time,' Moynot conceded. 'That's why we helped him.'

Moynot was equally unabashed about Thales' €1-million donation to the ANC. 'A lot of companies want to have good relations with the ANC and give them money from time to time,' he said.

I asked him to confirm whether the amount donated was indeed €1 million. In a heavy Gallic accent he acknowledged that it was 'something like that'.

When the charges against Zuma and Thales were eventually dropped by Mpshe in April 2009, Sooklal travelled to London and Paris to brief his bosses. Moynot treated him to a celebratory dinner on his return to South Africa. 'A lot of champagne, French champagne, was consumed,' Sooklal recalled. 'Moynot asked me to buy a piece of cloth to cut a suit for Mr Zuma now that he was heading to become the president.'

Throughout the time Sooklal spent jetting around the world with Zuma, he worked as a fixer for Thales, helping the French arms company secure deals in South Africa. On one occasion, Sooklal even lobbied the South African government to support Thales' bid to secure a contract to supply a missile system to Venezuela ahead of a rival bidder from Russia. Now that Zuma was president, government business started coming Thales' way. This included a R100-million contract for the Gautrain's electronic ticketing system, a R95-million air-traffic-control maintenance contract and a R1.9-billion rail-signalling contract in the Western Cape. In comparison, the fancy suits, caviar and champagne came cheap.

Like Van der Walt's KPMG report, Sooklal's testimony, which he has agreed to repeat on the witness stand when Zuma finally goes on trial, provides a devastating account of a man willing to sell his country to feed his appetite for the finer things in life; of a president for hire.

* * *

Zuma, Nzimande and Vavi landed at Malabo Airport, Equatorial Guinea, on the afternoon of Friday 10 October 2008 and were immediately whisked off to the presidential palace eight kilometres away on the eastern side of the Bay of Malabo. The only person granted an audience with Obiang was Zuma.

The Independence Day proceedings kicked off on Sunday, but for most of the population there was little to celebrate. Thanks to its abundant oil reserves and small population of just one million people, the country boasts the highest per capita income in Africa, yet it ranks 138 out of 188 countries on the Human Development Index and is cursed with some of the worst indicators in the world for health, nutrition and education.[12] The reason for these disparities is that most of the country's wealth is looted year on year by a parasitic elite, especially by the family of the man with whom Vavi, Nzimande and Zuma had come to celebrate Independence Day. According to Human Rights Watch, the country earns about $4 billion a year from oil revenues but spends only $140 million on education and $92 million on health care. Eighty per cent of its budget is spent on massive infrastructure projects, with most contracts awarded at inflated prices to senior officials, including Obiang and his family.[13]

Obiang's son Teodorin Obiang, who is vice president, has become notorious for his playboy lifestyle, flaunting the wealth he's been accused of looting from his impoverished countrymen. Over a decade ago, French and US prosecutors charged Teodorin with money laundering, corruption and embezzlement. Since then, the authorities have confiscated his $30-million villa in Malibu, a six-storey $200-million mansion in Paris with gold-leaf bath taps and original paintings by Degas and Renoir hanging on the walls, a $120-million seventy-six-metre yacht and nine supercars, including a Ferrari, a Porsche, a Bugatti and a Maserati auctioned for $3.6 million.[14] Teodorin also owns a R50-million mansion overlooking Fourth Beach in Clifton. In 2017, a French court found him guilty of corruption and money laundering and handed down a three-year suspended jail sentence.

In Vavi's account of the trip, he and Nzimande were at first impressed by the royal treatment they received, but the novelty soon wore off. They'd come to talk to Zuma about whom he planned to appoint to cabinet and various government posts. Instead, they found themselves sitting idly on the veranda of the presidential palace while Zuma was locked in discussions with Obiang behind closed doors. On Sunday, the monotony of their stay was broken by attending the Independence Day ceremony. They'd been told that their meeting with Zuma to discuss the future of South Africa would take place the next morning. But after breakfast they found themselves back on the veranda, twiddling their thumbs, bored and frustrated. At 10 a.m., to their astonishment, Duduzane Zuma and Tony Gupta, the youngest of the three Gupta brothers, waltzed in. Duduzane was twenty-six years old at the time, Tony thirty-six. They said that they'd been 'doing business' in the Central African Republic and Angola. Before Vavi and Nzimande could enquire further, the youngsters were shepherded into the room where Zuma and Obiang were holding their umpteenth private discussion. They locked the door behind them and only emerged three hours later. By then it was time to fly home.

* * *

A decade later, Zwelinzima Vavi told me that both he and Blade Nzimande were incensed that 'these young people were prioritised over the alliance'. They'd flown halfway across the continent with Jacob Zuma but hadn't had a single discussion about the future of the country. Zuma clearly had other priorities. Even before becoming president of South Africa, he was facilitating business deals for the Guptas that his family would benefit from – a pattern of patronage that his host Obiang was well acquainted with.

'I don't know who they met in Angola or in the Central African Republic,' Vavi said, 'but I know that in Equatorial Guinea, the third leg of their African safari trip, they met the head of state in the presence of the ANC president. Why else would the president introduce his son and his business associate to the leader of another country?' Even then, Zuma was 'opening doors in foreign lands' to further the business interests of the Guptas, and by extension his own.

Vavi was also perturbed that Duduzane Zuma and Tony Gupta had just been to Angola, another oil-rich country with a fabulously wealthy ruling elite and a population languishing in poverty. The ruling party, the People's Movement for the Liberation of Angola (MPLA), had fought a successful liberation war and ruled the country since 1975 but had 'lost credibility', as Vavi put it, because of former president José Eduardo dos Santos's family's corrupt accumulation of wealth. 'The daughter of Dos Santos is one of the richest women in the continent and everybody knows that this is not because of her business astuteness but because of the proximity to the father,' Vavi said.

It was a model that would soon be replicated back home, with Duduzane Zuma and his Gupta business associates inveigling their way into every corner of the government machinery, ultimately being awarded the cream of state contracts and mining deals.

3

The DRC Moment

At 10 a.m. on 2 March 2010, President Jacob Zuma and his fifth wife, Thobeka Madiba-Zuma, touched down at Heathrow Airport in *Inkwazi*, the presidential jet. Zuma looked dapper in a sombre suit and navy-and-burgundy striped tie as he walked down the boarding stairs with his new bride by his side. She was wearing a turquoise dress with matching shoes and jacket embroidered with a paisley pattern and holding a clutch bag. As they stepped onto the red carpet, they were met by officials from Buckingham Palace. The formal proceedings of Zuma's state visit would only kick off the following day, when he would be welcomed by Queen Elizabeth and Prince Philip at the Horse Guards Parade and attend a state banquet at Buckingham Palace, where he would receive an honorary knighthood.

But first he had some important business to attend to. Zuma and his wife were driven to the Dorchester hotel, where they were put up in the presidential suite. Their entourage comprised twelve cabinet ministers and their staff and over 200 'business leaders', as the Presidency called them. It was the biggest delegation that had ever accompanied a state visit by a South African president.[1] Among them were Cynthia Carroll and Chris Griffith, chief executives of Anglo American and its iron-ore mining subsidiary, Kumba Iron Ore, as well as Nonkululeko Nyembezi-Heita, chief executive of the South Africa division of steel giant ArcelorMittal.

Nyembezi-Heita was in a funk when she arrived. Two weeks earlier Kumba had informed her that it was cancelling a preferential pricing agreement for ore supplied to ArcelorMittal South Africa from its Sishen mine in the Northern Cape. The agreement dated back to 2001, when the decision was taken to unbundle state-owned Iscor into separate steel and mining businesses. The steel business later became ArcelorMittal South

Africa and the mining business was bought by Kumba. The agreement stipulated that ArcelorMittal would retain the rights to a 21.4 per cent share of Kumba's Sishen mine, which was obliged to provide the steelmaker with 6.25 million tons of ore a year at the cost of production plus 3 per cent. By 2010, this pricing formula amounted to a discount of R5 billion a year. Sources said Nyembezi-Heita believed that there must be a political solution to the pricing-agreement impasse; she wanted Zuma to sort it out. After all, the deal had been negotiated by the government in the first place when the state-owned company was unbundled.[2]

Sources briefed by Presidency staffers said that Nyembezi-Heita pushed for an urgent meeting with Zuma to discuss the issue and was eventually granted one at the Dorchester, in the presence of Atul Gupta. Six months later, a report appeared in *Business Day* confirming this meeting: a senior Kumba employee told the newspaper that Zuma had held 'informal conversations' in London about the Kumba–ArcelorMittal pricing issue with Nyembezi-Heita, Carroll, Griffith and Atul Gupta. Zuma wanted a win-win outcome for everyone involved. 'There is political pressure for us to settle this thing,' the Kumba source reportedly said.[3] Meanwhile, I heard from another source who was briefed by someone on the trip that the Guptas and Duduzane Zuma were seen visiting the presidential suite at 'odd hours' that evening – a privilege cabinet members were denied.

The content of those discussions is unknown, but it appears that Zuma busied himself at the Dorchester cooking up a deal with the Guptas to turn his son Duduzane into an instant billionaire. Within weeks of the Dorchester meetings to find a 'win-win political solution', the Guptas hijacked ArcelorMittal's 21.4 per cent share of the Sishen mine, the richest in the country with estimated reserves worth R800 billion. At the same time, Duduzane Zuma and the Guptas were included in a black empowerment deal at ArcelorMittal worth R9 billion. It later emerged that ArcelorMittal was prepared to buy back its hijacked share of the Sishen mine for R800 million. It seemed the only winners in this game were the Guptas and the president's son.

The ArcelorMittal deal, clinched just ten months into his presidency, was set to become one of the biggest corruption scandals to dog Zuma since the arms deal. It was soon dubbed South Africa's first 'DRC moment', a cynical reference to the Democratic Republic of Congo, where back-room deals that flout due legal process and benefit President Joseph Kabila and his family have become the norm. Many felt that South Africa had reached a tipping point.

* * *

At the heart of the ArcelorMittal–Sishen scandal was Imperial Crown Trading, a company with no history of doing business in the mining sector but with strong connections to the ANC.

Initially, the company wasn't linked to Zuma or his family at all. Its first directors, appointed in December 2008, were Archie Luhlabo and Prudence 'Gugu' Mtshali. Luhlabo was a senior official in the Mineworkers Investment Company, the investment arm of South Africa's largest mining union, the National Union of Mineworkers (NUM). Mtshali was the part-ner (and later wife) of caretaker president Kgalema Motlanthe, the man who'd just taken over from Thabo Mbeki after the latter resigned in the wake of the Polokwane conference that elected Zuma president of the ANC.

Working behind the scenes for Imperial Crown was a man named Phemelo Sehunelo. He'd previously been a housing director for the ANC-led Northern Cape provincial government and then served as Kimberley's municipal manager until 2005, before being appointed to a ministerial task team on mining procurement in the Northern Cape.

In hindsight, it's clear that Sehunelo and his partners planned to use their connections to secure the Sishen right and then flip it to the highest bidder.

Their opportunity came with a change in government policy stipu-lating that all mining companies had to convert old order rights to new order rights by 30 April 2009. Historically, old order prospecting and mining rights allowed for individual ownership of minerals. With new order rights, all minerals belong to the state. They are mined under licence from the state, with new conditions attached. To convert the rights, companies had to meet black empowerment targets, including 26 per cent black ownership, or risk losing their mining rights altogether. If a company failed to apply for its rights on time, the rights would lapse and revert to the state. This left the door open for a lot of dealmaking across the mining industry. Those with the right connections and access to inside information stood to profit most.

Kumba converted its share of the Sishen mine to new order rights in good time. But with the 30 April deadline looming, it became common knowledge that ArcelorMittal wouldn't be able to convert the rights to its 21.4 per cent share in Sishen in time, as it hadn't yet completed an empowerment deal. This prompted Kumba to apply for ArcelorMittal's mineral rights. Imperial Crown Trading applied too. When Kumba gained access to Imperial Crown's application, it looked remarkably similar to its own. Imperial Crown appeared to have cobbled it together in haste, allegedly crudely photocopying bits of Kumba's application and supplementing it with forged documents, and tampering with the submission dates to make it look as though both arrived on the same day. Simultaneous applications are automatically awarded to the company with the highest black empowerment credentials, which in this case was Imperial Crown Trading.[4]

When it later emerged that Sehunelo was close to an official in the Department of Mineral Resources' Kimberley office – the office that received the mineral rights application – suspicions were raised that he had been tipped off about Kumba's application.[5] He'd been accused of similar dealings before. In one case, a Northern Cape farmer claimed that Sehunelo had obtained prospecting rights to his land illegally. In another case, he was embroiled in a dispute over ownership of a manganese mine amid claims of fraudulent share certificates.[6]

Sehunelo disputed these claims, but a senior manager at an Australian mining company, Aquila Resources, told me about a similar experience he'd had with him. Soon after Aquila had applied to the same Kimberley office for manganese prospecting rights to twenty farms in the Northern Cape, the Aquila manager received a call from Sehunelo, who told him that he'd already acquired the rights to five of the farms and offered to sell them. 'When we refused and said we'd rather wait and see how our application goes for the other farms, he said: "Don't worry, I can get those for you too. Easy."'

Kumba's objection to the Imperial Crown application fell on deaf ears. The company tried several times to meet the official responsible for the application – the then deputy director-general at the Department of Minerals and Energy Jacinto Rocha. In October 2009, Rocha told the mining company to stop 'lobbying' him. A month later, he awarded the prospecting rights to Imperial Crown.[7] Kumba would have to fight all the way to the Constitutional Court to hold on to the rights.

However, Imperial Crown was not in the clear yet. The political landscape was changing fast. Sehunelo and his accomplices may have snatched the Sishen rights from Kumba, but they were about to find out that they'd need new partners to hold on to their prize.

* * *

Four days after Imperial Crown lodged its application for the Sishen rights, Jacob Zuma was sworn in as post-apartheid South Africa's fourth president.

Within weeks of his inauguration on 9 May 2009, some of the shareholders of Imperial Crown Trading were invited to a meeting 'in Saxonwold', according to a source who was briefed by someone present at the meeting. 'They thought it meant the Saxon Hotel, but it turns out it was the Gupta residence in Saxonwold,' the source said. The Guptas told the Imperial Crown shareholders that they needed to relinquish '90 per cent of your company' in return for a slice of one of South Africa's largest black empowerment deals to date: the sale of 21 per cent of ArcelorMittal South Africa worth over R9 billion. 'The Guptas kept on saying it was "orders from above", meaning the newly elected president,' the source said.

This account is lent some credence by a report that appeared in the *Sunday Times* in 2017. The article stated that Jacinto Rocha, the official who had approved Imperial Crown's application, was called to a late-night meeting at Zuma's official residence in Pretoria, Mahlamba Ndlopfu, soon after he became president. Tony Gupta was in attendance. 'Duduzane is my only child involved with money,' Zuma reportedly told Rocha. 'I will appreciate it if you help him wherever you could.'[8]

Rocha resigned from the Department of Minerals and Energy in January 2010 after he'd awarded Imperial Crown the prospecting rights and before the Guptas officially became involved in the company. He claims the two events are unconnected. However, the Guptas were clearly no strangers to him. After he left government, Rocha started a mining consultancy that boasted the Guptas as clients, and he has admitted publicly that Tony Gupta and Duduzane Zuma recruited him to become an advisor to the soon-to-be-appointed transport minister Ben Martins in June 2012, shortly before one of Zuma's many cabinet reshuffles.

The ArcelorMittal empowerment deal the Guptas were eyeing had been in the works since 2008. The frontrunner was initially a consortium involving ANC stalwart Tokyo Sexwale and national chairperson of the ANC Baleka Mbete. Negotiations being handled in London by a close confidant of steel magnate and ArcelorMittal chief executive Lakshmi Mittal had ground to a halt by the end of the year amid the global financial crisis. By the time they resumed in earnest the following year, Zuma was president. According to two of its members, the consortium was soon put under pressure from ArcelorMittal's head office in London to include the Guptas. By 2010, the consortium had decided to walk away, leaving the way clear for the Guptas to clinch the ArcelorMittal BEE deal.

Rocha's decision to grant ArcelorMittal's lapsed prospecting rights to Imperial Crown gave the company a powerful bargaining chip in price negotiations with Kumba – one for which it was willing to pay dearly. This bargaining chip would soon be in the hands of the Guptas and Duduzane Zuma.

After the Dorchester meetings, events unfolded with dizzying speed. On 12 March 2010, a week after Zuma and his wife returned to South Africa, a company called Pragat Investments secured a 50 per cent stake in Imperial Crown. On paper Pragat Investments was owned by Jagdish Parekh, a hitherto unknown Johannesburg businessman. The *Mail & Guardian* later reported that he was holding the shares on behalf of JIC Mining Services, owned by the Guptas and Duduzane Zuma.[9]

Within a fortnight, ArcelorMittal announced that it had resumed discussions to sell a 21 per cent stake to black empowerment partners. Nonkululeko Nyembezi-Heita later said that these discussions had been with the Guptas and Parekh.[10]

On 10 August 2010, ArcelorMittal dropped a bombshell. The steel giant announced that it would sell 21 per cent of its shares to a consortium that included Duduzane Zuma, Gugu Mtshali, the Guptas' Oakbay Investments and their proxy, Parekh. At the same time, ArcelorMittal would buy Imperial Crown and its prospecting rights for R800 million in cash, payable once it was converted into a full mining right. Analysing the deal, investigative journalist Stefaans Brümmer calculated that just eighteen months after Duduzane Zuma's father was elected president, the twenty-eight-year-old had been allocated shares with a face value of R916 million. In addition, through the sale of Imperial Crown, Parekh stood to make an extra R400 million for the Guptas and Duduzane Zuma. All told, the president's son had become a billionaire overnight.[11]

* * *

South Africa's 'DRC moment' immediately generated a firestorm of opposition. It wasn't just the mainstream press and opposition parties that denounced it as cynical and corrupt. Institutional investors soon began voicing their disapproval too, starting with RMB Asset Management, followed by Sanlam. In October 2010, the Public Investment Corporation (PIC), which held a 9.1 per cent stake in ArcelorMittal, said it would vote against the deal. The PIC raised concerns about the controversy surrounding the Sishen right awarded to Imperial Crown Trading and questioned why ArcelorMittal had failed to protect its business by letting the right lapse. In effect, this had given Imperial Crown and its politically connected shareholders the gap they needed to extort R800 million from the steelmaker.[12] A year later, ArcelorMittal would bow to pressure and cancel the deal.

South Africa had pulled back from the brink – for now. But the Guptas had already set their sights on their next targets: coal contracts with Eskom and locomotive orders for Transnet. During his State of the Nation Address in February 2012, Jacob Zuma unveiled Transnet's 'market demand strategy'. The government would spend over R300 billion on modernising South Africa's rail, ports and pipeline infrastructure to stimulate the economy and meet the anticipated demand for freight transport. By then, Brian Molefe had been head of Transnet for a year. Soon, he would be in charge of Eskom too.

4

What the Driver Saw

Security guard and driver John Maseko watched the car enter through the steel double gate that opens onto Saxonwold Drive. It drove past an ornamental garden and pulled up at the entrance to the mansion. A man stepped out, walked up the half-moon stairs to a colonnaded portico and disappeared inside.

'22/01/2011: Brian Molefe – BEE,' Maseko scribbled onto a palm-sized card he kept in his pocket whenever he manned the gate. This entry was followed by: 'Majola, SA cricket.'

The Gupta compound comprises four mansions, one with its own helipad, in the affluent suburb of Saxonwold, just around the corner from Johannesburg Zoo. A cricket pitch and swimming pool are nestled amid the manicured gardens and lawns.[1]

Maseko worked for the Guptas for six months, from November 2010 to April 2011 – a time when Gupta allies were being deployed to the state entities from which the family scored lucrative contracts. When he wasn't chauffeuring the Guptas around town, he stood guard at the entrance to the family's palatial home, meticulously recording the comings and goings of their visitors. In the evenings, he transcribed his entries into a diary, along with observations on what had transpired during the day.

'I transported Atul's son to Pretoria for passport. He was accompanied by the woman who works for Sahara who is always there with other drivers transporting Indians,' he wrote. 'Majola visited Ajay Gupta.' The next day, he noted that Ronnie Mamoepa 'visited Ajay Gupta at 11h04'. He drove a Mercedes S600. Maseko captured his vehicle registration number. At the time, Mamoepa was the spokesperson for the minister of home affairs, Nkosazana Dlamini-Zuma. She made an appearance herself in the same month, 'driven by her bodyguards. Maroon Lexus. Registration not captured.'

Ten days later, on 3 February, Maseko spotted Nomvula Mokonyane, the premier of Gauteng, paying a visit to Ajay Gupta. 'Time 19h25. Escorted by marked police vehicle with two officers,' he noted. Malusi Gigaba, minister of public enterprises and in charge of almost all state entities, visited the Gupta compound 'during December or January. Date and vehicle registration not captured.'

Maseko also described how the Guptas sought to wrest control of Ward 117, which includes Saxonwold, from the DA before the local elections in May: Atul Gupta asked his drivers and security guards to bring people in from the townships 'to come and register at Saxonwold so that the ANC must win the ward'. On one occasion, Maseko drove 'Atul Gupta and his PA' to the ANC's regional offices in downtown Johannesburg.

In his diary, Maseko documented the 'exploitation of workers by the Guptas' and their racist attitudes towards their support staff. 'Atul Gupta told me black people are stupid, they can't think, that is why they are poor.' He also made security guards 'stand in the rain with umbrellas, not allowed inside the guard house, and they must be visible to cameras even if there is no shade'. Leaked emails later revealed that Tony Gupta had called a security guard 'a monkey' and had insisted that the butlers and waiters at his niece's wedding in Sun City be white.

Maseko noted that 'J Zuma visited Ajay Gupta' the day before the president left for the G20 summit in Seoul, held on 11 and 12 November 2010, as well as 'the day after he came back before he was to address the South Africans and the media'. Zuma later denied this.

Ironically, one of the reasons Maseko was enthusiastic about working for the Guptas was that he'd heard Zuma visited them often and he wanted to discuss tender corruption at his local municipality with the president. At the time, Maseko chaired a local chapter of the South African National Civic Organisation in a township south of Johannesburg. 'Zuma was always saying we must report corruption, so I wanted to raise these issues with him,' he recalled when I met him at a drab petrol station close to Vereeniging. Maseko never got his wish. 'He drove in and out in his convoy and just waved to us when he got out the car,' he told me, a look of disillusionment on his face.

Another prominent visitor to the Gupta compound was Mzwanele 'Jimmy' Manyi, who popped in on 2 February 2011, just weeks before the Presidency announced his appointment as cabinet spokesperson and director-general of the Government Communication and Information System (GCIS), effectively making Manyi the chief government mouthpiece.

Manyi's visit to the Guptas at this critical juncture is significant: in his new appointment he replaced the highly competent and respected Themba Maseko, who was unaccountably moved sideways to the Department of Public Service and Administration. By contrast, Manyi's career was dogged by controversy. In 2010, he was suspended from the Department of Labour after Norwegian diplomats complained that he had tried to solicit private business during an official meeting, although Manyi denied this. Themba Maseko later revealed that in November 2010 Ajay Gupta had called and threatened to speak to his superiors to 'sort him out' when he'd refused to shift the government's entire R600-million annual advertising budget to Gupta-owned media companies ahead of the launch of their newspaper, *The New Age*. Maseko said that two months later, in January 2011, Zuma had instructed the late Collins Chabane, who was minister in the Presidency at the time, to 'redeploy me or terminate my contract'.[2]

Again, Zuma issued his customary denials. 'It is unfortunate that Mr Maseko wants to drag the president into matters he thinks are related to the end of his tenure at GCIS,' his spokesperson Bongani Ngqulunga told *City Press*. 'The appointment of directors-general is delegated to ministers. The president has no knowledge of the allegations that Mr Maseko is making.'

The Gupta leaks would reveal that Manyi, who bought the Gupta media companies ANN7 and *The New Age* in 2017 and later renamed them Afro Worldview and *Afro Voice*, was implicated in the Guptas' state capture project. On one occasion he told a former colleague that Eskom and Transnet were looking for new board members and then forwarded her CV, together with his own, to the Guptas.

When the *Sunday Times* asked Manyi if it was a coincidence that he'd been given the job as top government spin doctor in 2011 shortly after his visit to Saxonwold, he insisted that the two events had nothing to do with each other. 'My appointment came after I spoke to late minister Collins Chabane,' he said. 'It is absolutely rubbish that the Guptas had any role in my appointment.'[3]

Gupta driver John Maseko looked dejected as he flipped through his diary, recounting the fall from grace of the party and leaders he once revered. In one entry, he lamented that 'the ANC is not dealing with corruption' in its ranks. 'If you can't catch corruption within your cabinet you too are corrupt.'

John Maseko would become one of the whistleblowers who approached Public Protector Thuli Madonsela when she was compiling her report on state capture. He supplied her with his diary and an explanation of the stream of prominent visitors he had documented entering and leaving the Gupta compound. It only became clear much later that one of the most significant visitors was Brian Molefe.

* * *

As far back as I can remember, I'd considered Brian Molefe one of the good guys. From the time he'd spent at Treasury and the Public Investment Corporation, I'd formed a picture of Molefe as highly qualified and skilled, progressive, dynamic, competent and courageous. I had no reason to believe he was corrupt.

Former colleagues I'd spoken to, even after his reputation lay in tatters, recall being in awe of his dynamism, razor-sharp intelligence, passion and courage harnessed in the service of social justice.

When Molefe ran the PIC, in charge of government pension funds worth R1.8 trillion, he earned the reputation of a fearless, principled civil servant who cut through the cant of white-dominated corporations paying lip service to transformation. At the helm of Transnet and later Eskom, he boldly slashed red tape with a vigour rarely seen in state enterprises. At Transnet, he drove a huge public infrastructure programme – the most ambitious since Nelson Mandela's government started building hundreds of thousands of houses for the poor in 1994.

When he joined Eskom at the height of the load-shedding crisis in 2015, I remember thinking – with relief – that someone competent was finally in charge.

This sentiment wasn't entirely unjustified, or uncommon. Molefe certainly had the right qualifications for all the positions he held: he'd completed a commerce degree and a master's in business leadership at Unisa, leadership courses at Harvard Business School and a postgraduate degree in economics from the University of London. He boasted the right political connections and credentials too – crucial qualities for a man who held the purse strings of large public corporations. In a perceptive biographical sketch written in 2017, when Molefe was tipped to become finance minister, then *Sunday Times* deputy editor S'thembiso Msomi described him as a man with impeccable struggle credentials who'd cut his teeth in the student activist movement in Limpopo province in the 1980s. In 1990, Collins Chabane, who would later serve as minister in the Presidency in Jacob Zuma's first cabinet in 2009, inducted Molefe into the inner sanctum of the ANC. Chabane had just served six years on Robben Island on terrorism charges, together with ANC heavyweights Popo Molefe, Kgalema Motlanthe and Tokyo Sexwale. When Chabane was released from prison, he became the ANC's provincial secretary in Limpopo and gave Molefe a position as a party functionary.[4]

Msomi points out that the ANC earmarked Molefe for deployment in strategic areas of the economy when the party readied itself to take power. In 1995, he became chief director of strategic planning in Limpopo premier Ngoako Ramatlhodi's administration before joining Treasury as director of intergovernmental relations in 1997. Molefe and his economist wife Portia, who became director-general of public enterprises in 2005, were seen as a 'fairytale couple' driving Thabo Mbeki's vision of growing South Africa's economy while transforming its racially skewed wealth base.[5] At Treasury, Molefe joined director-general Lungisa Fuzile and Reserve Bank governor Lesetja Kganyago. They were seen as playing key roles in ensuring the state had the capacity to manage the economy while transforming the white-dominated corporate sector. The PIC, which had billions in government pension fund money invested in listed companies, wielded the financial muscle to force change.[6]

Molefe's epic battles at the PIC, which he joined six years later in 2003, were the stuff of legend. In 2004, he launched a withering attack on Sasol for refusing to appoint the PIC's nominee, Imogen Mkhize, to the petrochemical multinational's board. The PIC owned 13 per cent of Sasol, so Molefe felt it had the right to insist on the appointment, especially as Sasol's ownership and management was overwhelmingly white. Sasol backed down and Molefe became a hero of the type of black empowerment that Mbeki championed. However, he did not find much favour with the trade unions. Organised labour said that Molefe was merely replacing white captains of industry with their black counterparts instead of driving true economic transformation.[7]

Shortly before Mbeki was removed in December 2007 in the bloodless internal ANC coup, Molefe scored another victory for transformation. In January that year, he set his sights on industrial giant Barloworld. The PIC was Barloworld's largest shareholder, with an 18 per cent stake, and therefore had a lot of clout. Molefe objected to the fact that the company, founded in 1904, had never had a single black executive director and was planning to reappoint Warren Clewlow, the father-in-law of new chief executive Clive Thomson, as chairperson. Like Sasol, Barloworld buckled. Shortly afterwards, Isaac Shongwe (who will make a cameo appearance later in this tale) became the company's first black executive. Clewlow stepped down as chairperson and was replaced by advocate Dumisa Ntsebeza in an acting capacity.[8]

Barloworld then fudged the internal shuffle. In June 2007, the company made Ntsebeza the company's first black chairperson, but it promptly appointed a white man, Trevor Mundy, as his deputy – a position that the company had not had for a decade. Molefe rightly branded this as racist and patronising. Barloworld was forced to back down a second time and Mundy quit his position.[9]

Molefe did have a blemish on his record at the PIC, though – one that was in hindsight a portent of things to come: the partial privatisation of Telkom. In 2004, a US–Malaysian joint telecoms venture decided to sell its 15.1 per cent stake in Telkom worth R9 billion. The winning bidder, the Elephant Consortium, was headed by Andile Ngcaba, a man who had just quit as Mbeki's director-general of telecommunications, a position in which he wielded considerable power to influence the deal. Another Mbeki man on the Elephant Consortium team was ANC head of the Presidency Smuts Ngonyama, who once famously boasted that he hadn't joined the struggle against apartheid to be poor. Ngcaba was accused of abusing his position as telecoms director-general to craft policy and regulations that protected Telkom's monopoly at the expense of consumers and favoured the Elephant Consortium deal, which would benefit him personally.[10]

When the Elephant Consortium failed to raise the capital in time to clinch the deal, Molefe controversially stepped into the breach, in much the same way that he would allegedly help the Guptas secure last-minute finance to clinch the Optimum deal twelve years later. In November 2004, Molefe announced that the PIC had bought the US–Malaysian stake of Telkom for a discounted price of R6.6 billion and would 'warehouse' the shares for six months to give the Elephant Consortium time to get its act together. The move raised eyebrows. Until then, the PIC had never 'warehoused' shares for anyone. In the end, the PIC sold two-thirds of the shares to the Elephant Consortium, partially funding the purchase and keeping the remaining 5 per cent. By the time the Elephant Consortium exited the deal in 2010, it had raked in R3 billion from the sale of its shares and earned another R1.4 billion in dividends. It's not clear how much profit the consortium made from the deal, though, because a large chunk of its earnings was used to pay off debt. The amount Ngonyama and Ngcaba pocketed remains a mystery too, but one source close to the deal told IT newsletter TechCentral in 2010 that it amounted to 'a bloody fortune'.[11]

Molefe was able to justify the deal because it had made the PIC a healthy profit of R1.5 billion. In hindsight, it carried a strong whiff of the Gupta corruption scandals to come. Molefe used his influential position to advance the business interests of friends of the president, a pattern that would be repeated under the Zuma administration. It would seem that old habits die hard.

* * *

The first inkling I had that I'd got Brian Molefe completely wrong came in 2011 when my colleague Mzilikazi wa Afrika and I went to meet Zwelinzima Vavi at COSATU House, the federation's low-key headquarters in central Johannesburg, to talk about the Guptas and their relationship with Jacob Zuma. Vavi had originally been a Zuma praise singer but had become disillusioned by the corruption scandals that dogged the president. We figured that he would have plenty of dirt to dish. We weren't disappointed.

As we walked down the corridor to his office, I remember being struck by the number of Zapiro cartoons on the walls, even ones lampooning Vavi. 'I've always admired his sense of humour,' he said with an impish smile.

Vavi shared some anecdotes about his experiences with Zuma and the Guptas that he said left him feeling queasy and should have alerted him to the fact that the president was in the Gupta family's pocket. The first was when he'd travelled with Blade Nzimande to Equatorial Guinea in October 2008, where they'd seen Duduzane Zuma and Tony Gupta arrive together from a dealmaking safari to Angola and the Central African Republic and be given preferential access to Equatorial Guinea president Teodoro Obiang Nguema Mbasogo in Zuma's presence.

During the 2010 FIFA World Cup in South Africa, Vavi gained a deeper appreciation of the power wielded by the Guptas. He'd just watched the nail-biting Germany vs Spain semifinal at Moses Mabhida stadium in Durban. Vavi was a member of the local organising committee, which had flown from Johannesburg in a private jet to watch the game. Vavi had an urgent meeting that night and needed to fly back, but the rest of the team were set on staying in Durban. He asked fellow committee member Essop Pahad for help. Pahad had a long-standing relationship with the Guptas dating back to his time as a minister in the Presidency in Mbeki's cabinet. When Pahad returned to Vavi, he had Ajay Gupta in tow.

'Here's the man who can help you,' he said.

Shortly after this introduction, Vavi and his wife were tearing through the streets of Durban with the Guptas to King Shaka International Airport, escorted by a police VIP protection unit, or so-called blue light brigade.

'They blocked the traffic and robots, sirens blaring. We were there in no time,' Vavi recalled. At the airport they were whisked through the VIP section. 'The gates just opened for us.'

At Lanseria Airport in Johannesburg, Vavi and his wife saw the Guptas disappear into the night escorted by a cavalcade of blue lights. 'I thought: wow, these guys must have power,' he said. 'It feels like you're travelling with the president.'

Vavi finished his story, then turned to us with a glint in his eye.

'Have you looked at Brian Molefe?'

We hadn't.

'He did good work at Treasury, didn't he?' I volunteered. 'I can't recall hearing anything bad about him.'

'Brian faced a lot of allegations of pillaging at the PIC,' he said. 'He gave deals to his comrades.'

Wa Afrika and I looked at each other.

'Our members did a proper investigation into this,' Vavi continued. 'Workers put together a dossier. Names, dates, amounts, the lot. You should look into it.' Corruption leads involving the Guptas, Zuma and now Molefe? We were in.

'We'd like that dossier!' Wa Afrika exclaimed. In that moment, we half expected Vavi to call his PA to fetch it from the room next door.

'I'm afraid not, gents,' Vavi said. 'I gave it to Number One. We never kept a copy.'

* * *

For seven years, Brian Molefe had been one of the most powerful chief executives in the country. But with his contract at the PIC coming up for renewal in April 2010, he suddenly found himself isolated and vulnerable.

Molefe had been at the coalface of implementing Thabo Mbeki's neoliberal vision of economic transformation, much to the chagrin of the unions, the SACP and factions of the ANC that had put Zuma in power. His timely intervention in the Telkom deal, which turned some of Mbeki's closest cronies into multimillionaires, had made Molefe many enemies in the new ruling elite. Now that Jacob Zuma was in power, they expected a purge of Mbeki loyalists. Molefe was high on their list. In March

2010, the ANC's deployment committee decided that Molefe's contract at the PIC would not be renewed. It looked as though his high-flying career as a top civil servant was over. But then something happened to change the rules of the game: Zuma did not follow the script he'd been handed, and Molefe got to stay on at the PIC for another three months.

It's been speculated that Zuma called the PIC chairperson, then deputy finance minister Nhlanhla Nene, to ask that Molefe be kept on to ensure that the PIC loaned the Guptas and Duduzane Zuma the $37 million they needed to buy Dominion uranium mine, later renamed Shiva, in the North West province.

The only economic rationale for buying the mine in 2010 amid a worldwide slump in uranium prices would be if South Africa were planning a huge nuclear build programme, which now appears to have been Zuma's plan all along. Under Zuma, South Africa's 2010 energy plan recommended that nuclear should represent 13 per cent of the country's energy mix by 2030. To achieve this target, the country would need to spend R1 trillion to build eight nuclear plants. Treasury officials repeatedly questioned the rationale of adding 9 600 megawatts to the power grid when Eskom was already spending over R300 billion on two new mega power stations at a time when electricity demand was at its lowest level since 2007. But Zuma was a strong supporter of the plan and appeared from the outset to favour Russia as the supplier. Since taking office in 2009, he had held numerous private discussions with Russian leaders Dmitry Medvedev and Vladimir Putin. Nuclear power was always on the agenda. Putin in particular was intent on expanding the global footprint of Russian nuclear company Rosatom and the political influence that came with it. Russia's lobbying to be awarded the contract is said to have included election campaign donations to the ANC.

The conundrum for the Guptas and Duduzane Zuma was that they couldn't exactly take the president's enthusiasm for a nuclear deal with the Russians to the bank. They would need to obtain funding from a state lender such as the PIC that was willing to bow to political pressure.

In the end, another state lender, the Industrial Development Corporation, stumped up the money.

Another reason the Guptas may have wanted to keep Molefe at the

PIC, if they had indeed 'captured' him by this time, was that his contract expired at a critical time for a much larger deal they were hatching: the hijack of ArcelorMittal's share of Kumba's Sishen mine in order to extort an R800-million cash payment and shares worth R3 billion from the steel-maker. Negotiations between the Guptas and ArcelorMittal began in earnest at the end of March 2010, shortly after the alleged late-night meeting between Zuma and the Guptas in the Dorchester hotel in London and just before Molefe was due to vacate his post. As the PIC held a 9.1 per cent stake in ArcelorMittal, it would be in a powerful position to veto or promote the deal. The PIC ended up voting against it three months after Molefe left.[12]

A commonly held belief is that the Guptas approached Molefe when he was vulnerable so as to facilitate 'a rapprochement between the out-of-favour Molefe and Zuma's ANC' and groom him for his future role as their dealmaker.[13] Sources have told me that Molefe held several dis-cussions with the Guptas in 2010. During this time, he is said to have held two private meetings with Zuma: one at the Union Buildings and one at the ANC headquarters at Luthuli House.

That Molefe was meeting with the Guptas at this critical juncture in his public service career is lent credence by a statement issued by COSATU spokesperson Patrick Craven in early 2011. Craven said that during a meeting with COSATU leaders to discuss allegations that the Guptas were using their political connections to enrich themselves, Ajay Gupta and Duduzane Zuma admitted to being 'friends of Molefe'.[14]

Despite his alleged 'rapprochement' with Zuma, Molefe took a low-key position on the board of Investec's property fund after he finally left the PIC in July 2010. I've heard it said that Investec CEO Stephen Koseff was grooming him to take over the bank – a position that would have suited Molefe's desire to wield power and influence again – but Molefe felt the process was taking too long and began casting around for a govern-ment job.

In any case, by the end of the year, Molefe's name was being bandied about for a key parastatal post and the Guptas were back in the picture.

On 7 December 2010, *The New Age* published a story that said the newspaper 'has it on good authority that Molefe will be appointed CEO' of Transnet. The article also predicted the appointment of three new Transnet board members: Mafika Mkwanazi, Don Mkhwanazi and Ellen Tshabalala. Mafika Mkwanazi later reportedly admitted to having a personal relationship with the Guptas and said he'd held 'exploratory talks' about doing business with them. Tshabalala was known to be close to Zuma and served on the president's newly established BEE advisory council together with Don Mkhwanazi.[15]

On 8 December, the day after the story was published, public enterprises minister Malusi Gigaba appointed all three to the Transnet board, with Mafika Mkwanazi as chairperson. They were joined by Iqbal Sharma, a close associate of Gupta business partner Salim Essa.

No proof of Molefe's discussions with the Guptas in 2010 has come to light, but thanks to their driver John Maseko's meticulous note-taking, we know that Molefe visited the family at a critical moment in Transnet's executive recruitment process. On 26 January 2011, four days after Maseko saw Molefe drive through the gate at Saxonwold, Transnet posted its first advertisement for the position of chief executive since the departure of Maria Ramos in 2009. Candidates were given just five working days to respond. The way the process unfolded from there suggested that it was a sham, with a predetermined outcome. Despite the five-day notice, sixty-three applications were received. These were vetted in record time, and on 16 February 2011 Gigaba announced that Molefe had got the job. A senior executive described his appointment as 'miraculously quick'.[16]

In April 2011, barely two months after his appointment, Molefe presented Gigaba's new board with an ambitious plan to modernise Transnet by buying 776 new locomotives. It was rubber-stamped. Four months later, in August 2011, the order was increased to 1 064 locomotives. Molefe had set the wheels in motion for South Africa's biggest corruption scandal since the arms deal.[17]

5

Trains and Planes

Transnet has its origins in the amalgamation of the Cape and Natal railways in the 1870s when the Durban and Cape Town harbours were linked in one network. Today, its freight rail division, which was previously known as Spoornet, transports 220 million tons of cargo over 30 000 kilometres of track – 80 per cent of Africa's total network.[1]

In February 2012, Jacob Zuma unveiled Transnet's R300-billion 'market demand strategy'. The new mantra amid a global economic downturn was that state spending on public infrastructure would drive growth, create jobs and reverse racial inequalities inherited from apartheid. Transnet would play a key role in realising the new strategy.

There's no doubt that properly functioning ports and railways would have positive spin-offs for the broader economy. In 2010, National Chamber of Milling director Jannie de Villiers illustrated the broader ramifications of a collapsing rail infrastructure, reporting that members of the chamber were already forced to pay 20 to 30 per cent more to transport maize by road than rail.

'We may ask for two wagons and only get one. Then there may be no driver or no locomotive. And if the load is transported, only half arrives at its destination because the wagon door is damaged,' he explained, warning that the result was rising food costs.

Poor rail infrastructure was also forcing the mining industry to switch from rail to road. By 2012, 87 per cent of the total freight being transported in South Africa was travelling by road, putting the network under intolerable strain. Trucking sixty million tons of coal from mines to power stations and export terminals in Richards Bay or Maputo every year was particularly damaging to the roads.[2]

The new stategy promised to stimulate the economy by revamping the country's transport infrastructure with the expectation that this would increase the demand for freight rail. The risk that the new deal could accelerate the looting of state coffers unless clean governance was prioritised was largely ignored.

* * *

In 2012, the world's largest rail industry trade fair, InnoTrans, was held in Berlin from 18 to 21 September. This biennial event, more than any other on the global calendar, is where mega rail deals are clinched. A South African businessman was there. He does not want his identity to be made public because he fears his story will cost him government contracts, so we'll call him Garfield.

Garfield's business interests have expanded steadily over the years. Established in 2001, his company has grown to more than eight divisions, expanding into rail, construction and logistics. By 2011, it was becoming increasingly apparent to businessmen like Garfield that government plans to revamp the country's rail infrastructure would present lucrative opportunities. Public enterprises minister Malusi Gigaba had signalled as much during a rail investment conference in Dubai in March that year. Massive capital investment by Transnet, whose locomotive and wagon fleet was twenty-six years old, would become a 'major driver for economic growth', he told delegates. Then he added the clincher: 'Much attention and effort is being given to increasing local spend and to use this capital expenditure programme to entrench world-class technologies, suppliers and service providers in South Africa.'[3]

This was a golden opportunity for Garfield. Transnet would place locomotive orders with global rail corporations, but to win contracts these corporations would need local black partners – like Garfield. He ultimately partnered with Canadian plane and train manufacturer Bombardier, a company that would come to enjoy an uncomfortably close relationship with the Guptas.

In June 2011, Gigaba's Transnet board approved issuing a tender to buy ninety-five electric locomotives for R2.7 billion. This was a stopgap measure 'to mitigate the immediate shortage' of trains, according to an internal document, and was completely separate from a much larger contract for 1064 locomotives still awaiting approval from Gigaba and the Transnet board.[4]

Garfield's company and Bombardier worked hard to put together a rock-solid bid by the time the tender closed in February 2012. They came out on top with the highest overall score, followed by China South Rail. Then Transnet took the unusual step of asking both companies to make oral presentations. The presentations turned out to be remarkably similar. This led Garfield to suspect that officials at Transnet could have supplied China South Rail with Bombardier's bid documents, although he wasn't able to provide any proof. In August that year, Garfield heard that China South Rail had closed the scoring gap and that Transnet would award the tender to the Asian firm. Bombardier decided to let it go, with an eye on the bigger prize of the order for 1064 locomotives still to come.

Another executive on his way to the InnoTrans fair in Berlin was Lucky Montana, the controversial head of South Africa's passenger rail agency, PRASA, which was also planning a massive revamp of its coach fleet. Montana later told Parliament that the day before he was due to depart, he received a curious phone call from Ben Martins, the minister of transport.[5] You may recall that a few months earlier, in June 2012, Martins had been summoned to the Gupta compound two days before his appointment was announced and introduced to his new advisor, Jacinto Rocha. Rocha was the minerals department official who'd helped the Guptas and Duduzane Zuma temporarily hijack the Sishen mining rights and subsequently squeeze an R800-million cash payment out of ArcelorMittal.

Martins invited Montana to his ministerial residence in Delphinus Street in the upmarket Pretoria suburb of Waterkloof. Montana had deep respect for Martins – he was an intellectual, a freedom fighter and a published poet who took his friend and comrade to visit art galleries on weekends, where he'd give impromptu lectures on the artworks and painters. For about half an hour, Montana and Martins exchanged pleasantries over tea. Then, to Montana's surprise, Duduzane Zuma and Tony Gupta walked in. Martins introduced them to Montana and told him that they wanted to take part in PRASA's R51-billion fleet-renewal programme. Montana offered to take up the conversation on his return from Berlin.[6]

As Garfield tells it, he arrived in Berlin on 17 September 2012 and met up with Chris Antonopoulos, the vice president for sales at Bombardier's train division, which is headquartered in the same city. During the trade fair, Garfield received a call from one of his executives – an acquaintance of Salim Essa.

'There are some people from South Africa who want to see you and Chris urgently,' he told Garfield. 'It's about the Transnet tender. They want to meet in Zurich.'

Garfield was given the name of a hotel in Zurich overlooking the river. It was a crisp autumn afternoon when he and Antonopoulos arrived. As arranged, they went to a private boardroom on the upper level. They whiled away the time watching ducks and boats drift past below. Then two men walked into the room and introduced themselves. One was Essa, the other Iqbal Sharma. Garfield claims that throughout the exchange, Essa and Antonopoulos did most of the talking, while he and Sharma merely observed.

'You should have won the ninety-five locomotives contract, but you are with the wrong crowd. We have the right connections,' said Essa, pointing to Sharma. 'He is on the Transnet board. We control a budget of R4 trillion. Broadband Infraco, Transnet, Eskom. We can work with you for the 1 064 locomotives contract but we take 20 per cent.'

In Garfield's telling, Antonopoulos almost fell off his chair, not because of the proposal per se but due to the price. 'It's way too high,' he said.

'We'll make it easy for you,' said Essa. 'The money doesn't have to go to South Africa. It goes straight to Dubai.'

'What about doing it through black empowerment partners?'

'We don't care about localisation. The 20 per cent is above that,' said Essa. He didn't want anything Bombardier chose to share with its BEE partner to come out of the Gupta kickback.

Then he seemed to hit on a novel idea: 'Don't you make aeroplanes?'

Antonopoulos confirmed that Bombardier did. 'But that's a separate division.'

'Why don't you give us a discount and claim that you sold it to us second-hand?'

According to Garfield, the Bombardier executive appeared lost in thought for a moment. He didn't agree to the proposal, but nor did he object. The meeting ended on an inconclusive note and the parties agreed to a follow-up meeting in South Africa.

Apparently, Garfield and Antonopoulos weren't the only bidders the Gupta team approached. Montana told Parliament that when he arrived in Berlin, he received a flood of complaints from train manufacturers. They alleged that they'd been called to a series of meetings in Zurich chaired by Essa, who claimed to be working for 'President JG Zuma, Minister Ben Martins and Lucky Montana' and had asked for kickbacks to be paid into a bank account in Dubai.[7] Montana later confirmed to me that Garfield and Bombardier's head of sales for sub-Saharan Africa, David Anglin, were among those who'd approached him to complain.

Garfield and Montana were spitting mad by the time they left Europe.

* * *

The InnoTrans fair ended on Friday 21 September 2012. On his way back to South Africa from Berlin, Montana called his friend and culture guru Ben Martins and asked him to arrange an urgent meeting at his Water-kloof house that weekend with Tony Gupta and Duduzane Zuma. They arrived with a man named Piyoosh Goyal.

Goyal is a colourful scrap-metal dealer from India who is described in a report by amaBhungane as a 'senior devotee' and 'midday meal director' at a Krishna temple in New Delhi. In 2015, he was charged with corruption for allegedly bribing a State Bank of India official to approve a Rs750-million (R120-million) loan. He also happens to be one of the alleged Gupta money launderers who reportedly funnelled hundreds of millions in kickbacks via accounts held in Dubai from companies that secured train and crane deals from Transnet.[8] Goyal has persistently denied that he conducted himself in any unlawful way.

In his telling, Montana let rip at Tony Gupta and Duduzane Zuma, berating them for using his and President Zuma's name to 'extort' money from the rail companies. Unperturbed, the two offered to collect Montana's cut and also funnel it to a secret account in Dubai if he ensured PRASA's rail contract went to China South Rail. When he angrily refused, accusing them of wanting to break the law, they turned to Martins and reminded him that he'd convinced them Montana was his 'comrade'. The meeting ended with Tony Gupta informing Montana that the Guptas would no longer approach rail companies for kickbacks and henceforth would work solely with China South Rail. Goyal would be their middleman. 'He will contact you if we have any issues,' said Tony Gupta, clearly hoping that Montana would still consider contracting with China South Rail.[9]

In a statement submitted to Parliament, Montana said Goyal had contacted him soon afterwards for a meeting at the Park Hyatt hotel in Rosebank, Johannesburg, which – along with the African Pride hotel in Melrose Arch – is a favourite haunt of tenderpreneurs cutting deals with state enterprise officials. Goyal handed Montana the CVs of Salim Essa and Iqbal Sharma, who'd just been appointed chairperson of Transnet's acquisitions and disposals committee. Montana said Goyal had demanded that they be appointed to the board committee that would be evaluating PRASA's rail tender. When Montana refused, Essa complained to Ben Martins.[10]

When PRASA's evaluation committee released its shortlist of candidates for the tender, China South Rail was not included. Montana claimed the Guptas were angry and demanded that he cancel the process and start from scratch, but he refused. Then they demanded that the rail agency's annual general meeting convened by Martins be postponed so that they could appoint new directors.[11]

I obtained a copy of the Guptas' preferred list of candidates that was handed to Martins' advisor Jacinto Rocha. Sharma is there, along with Jimmy Manyi who, as you may recall, took over as cabinet spokesperson and director-general of the GCIS in February 2011, shortly after he was spotted visiting the Gupta compound. He replaced Themba Maseko following Maseko's refusal to shift government advertising contracts worth R600 million to Gupta companies. The Guptas wanted Manyi to be appointed chairperson of PRASA. Also on the list is an Indian national, Ashok Pavadia, who served as a joint secretary in India's Department of Public Enterprises.

In the end, Martins did postpone the AGM and obtain a legal opinion to justify refusing to reconfigure the board with Gupta proxies. China South Rail lost out on the tender. This decision, and his refusal in 2013 to allow the Guptas to commandeer O.R. Tambo Airport to host a reception for the family's wedding guests, no doubt contributed to Zuma's decision to move Martins out of the transport portfolio. He had served in the position for just one year.[12]

In 2018 Montana testified before a parliamentary inquiry into public enterprises that his repeated refusal to do the Guptas' bidding was the reason he was finally ousted from PRASA in 2015.

* * *

Garfield says that soon after returning from Europe in September 2012, he, Sharma, Antonopoulos and Essa held a follow-up meeting at the African Pride hotel in Melrose Arch. Essa asked Antonopoulos again if he'd thought about their 20 per cent stake in the locomotives contract. Without waiting to hear the answer, Garfield decided to walk away. 'I realised, no, let me go and build things from the ground up,' he told me afterwards. 'At least I know that what I have made is mine.'

Leaked emails would later reveal that shortly before the tender was awarded, Bombardier had offered the Guptas a 'revised price' of $52 million to buy one of its ultra-long-range executive jets, the Global 6000, which sold for about $60 million at the time. To sweeten the deal, Bombardier threw in credit memos worth $1.35 million, along with extras and 'special customisations' for the jet worth $2 million.[13]

On 19 February 2014, Trevor Lambarth, Bombardier's vice president for aircraft sales in Europe, emailed Ajay Gupta thanking him for the 'hospitality and kindness' he'd shown him and Bombardier's Africa sales director, Hani Haddadin, during their visit to South Africa a few months earlier. He concluded by expressing the hope that clinching the deal would 'lead to further opportunities for our organisations to explore working together, whether on infrastructure or aviation-related business'.[14]

Barely a month later, Transnet announced that Bombardier was one of four bidders to win a slice of its tender for 1 064 locomotives. By then the total cost of the tender had increased from R38 billion to R54 billion. The price that Bombardier would be paid to supply 240 locomotives increased from R8 billion to R13 billion.

Montana told me afterwards that he believed Bombardier won the contract because Garfield had been 'edged out' and the company had 'started talking to the Guptas'.

* * *

Lucky Montana has himself been accused of being involved in corruption at PRASA, which has raised questions around his credibility. But, to my mind, the fact that he sent a contemporaneous account of the alleged Zurich shakedown to Sfiso Buthelezi, who at the time chaired the PRASA board, lends credence to Montana's version of events. It has also never been disputed by Salim Essa, Duduzane Zuma or the Guptas. And there's no denying that the Guptas never gained a toehold at PRASA while Montana was in charge.

Ben Martins confirmed the main thrust of Montana's parliamentary testimony too. He submitted a letter to the parliamentary inquiry a day later admitting he'd arranged two meetings at his house with Montana, Duduzane Zuma and Tony Gupta. Martins gave both meetings a different spin to Montana, though. He said that the first came about after Tony Gupta called him about the PRASA tender and threatened to take the passenger rail agency to court after being told it had already run its course. Martins suggested he should 'first seek clarity' from Montana before going to court and offered to set up a meeting at his official residence for this purpose.

'I saw nothing untoward in arranging this meeting between Mr Tony Gupta and Mr Lucky Montana as its aim was to clarify and give answers to the questions that Mr Gupta had posed to me,' Martins said in his letter. 'I did not at any stage ask Mr Montana to unduly, irregularly or illegally assist Mr Gupta. There was no unlawful and/or malicious intent on my part in facilitating the meeting.'[15]

Martins said that before Tony Gupta and Duduzane Zuma arrived for the meeting, he and Montana had discussed rumours that the PRASA chief executive and his chairperson would be removed from the rail agency. Martins assured Montana he would resist pressure to fire them.

Martins also confirmed that Montana had called him after the

InnoTrans conference. Montana said he was shocked that the Gupta brothers were going around telling train makers that they worked for President Zuma, Martins and himself, and that he'd demanded a meeting to confront Tony Gupta and Duduzane Zuma about it. 'Upon his return from Germany, such a meeting took place,' Martins said. He recalled that Montana 'sternly rebuked Mr Tony Gupta for abusing the name of the president, myself and that of Mr Montana. The meeting ended acrimoniously.'

Martins stressed that the meetings ultimately didn't result in China South Rail, the company the Guptas were batting for, being awarded the PRASA tender or in Montana or Buthelezi being replaced on the rail agency board by Gupta proxies.

I have no reason to doubt Garfield's version of events in Zurich. Over the years, he has related the same story to me several times. In each telling there is little difference in the details. Besides, Garfield has an unblemished record as a business leader and entrepreneur who has built his group of companies from the ground up, without relying on dubious partnerships or paying backhanders to politicians. He has no discernible motive to make up the whole episode in Zurich. The other alleged participants – Antonopoulos, Essa and the Guptas – have all ignored requests to be interviewed about the incident.

* * *

Bombardier is itself no stranger to corruption allegations. In December 2017, Canadian newspaper the *Globe and Mail* published the results of its year-long investigation into Bombardier's alleged practice of making 'controversial side payments' to secure contracts. A former Bombardier employee told the newspaper that he'd personally taken part in preparations for bids in South Africa, Malaysia and South Korea in the early 2000s. This was before Transnet's 1064 locomotives tender was issued, but it establishes a systemic pattern of how the company does business.

Bombardier termed these payments 'success fees' because they were only paid out on the successful conclusion of a contract. 'What is a "success fee"? It's a bribe,' the whistleblower told the *Globe and Mail*.

'It's money that gets paid to an agent – but do you get paid $8 million to $15 million just because Bombardier wins a contract? No, that money gets passed around.' The whistleblower added that the fees ranged from 5 to 6 per cent of the contract value. 'All we had to do was fill in the percentage,' he said. 'Someone in the sales department would come and say this is what the percentage was.'[16]

A Bombardier spokesperson admitted to the newspaper that the company paid success fees to middlemen but said these were 'perfectly legal and provided for in the commercial codes of many countries, and used by many Canadian and international companies in a variety of industries'.

I asked Bombardier about the accusation that it had incentivised the Guptas to help the company win a state contract in South Africa. The company strenuously denied there was any connection between selling the Guptas a jet and being awarded the Transnet tender. The plane and train manufacturer bridled at the suggestion that the Guptas had been given a substantial discount on their Global 6000. The $52-million 'revised price' they paid was 'well within a "normal" sales price range for Global 6000s sold that year', company spokesperson Mark Masluch said in an email. 'Any suggestion otherwise is entirely false and lacks any factual basis.'

However, an article that appeared in *Flying Magazine*, a trade publication in the US, appears to refute this claim. In 2013, editor Robert Goyer, who happens to be a pilot, took this type of aircraft for a test flight. He described it as an 'ultra-long-range wonder', 'staggeringly beautiful' and 'the very picture of elegance' with superb technical capabilities. Interior features include a private stateroom in the back complete with a toilet and shower, high-speed internet, and HD displays throughout the cabin. The aircraft also boasts the latest high-tech avionics and displays, cutting-edge safety and monitoring systems, and one of the best autopilots Goyer had ever flown. 'This kind of beauty and capability comes, not surprisingly, with a breathtaking price tag – the Global 6000 starts at about US$58.5 million, a bit more if you want the shower,' Goyer gushed.[17]

As for the R5-billion price hike of Bombardier's locomotives, Masluch said that this could be explained by the fact that it had been asked to quote for supplying 599 locomotives, but Transnet had reduced this number to 240. 'Bombardier Transportation had to adjust its price accordingly, including amortising the development cost over a much small number of locomotives,' he said.

Asked about the accusation that Salim Essa had solicited a bribe from Bombardier in Zurich on behalf of the Guptas, Bombardier's spokespeople repeatedly dodged the question. The company's vice president for external relations Olivier Marcil's last word on the subject did not address the accusation that Chris Antonopoulos had attended meetings at which bribes were discussed. The company had won the contract 'solely on the basis of our proposal, which included fair pricing and our unmatched technical ability to deliver a high-quality product and fully meet the local content requirements', Marcil declared.

When I put the allegations to Iqbal Sharma, he flatly denied that he had attended any meetings with Essa and Tony Gupta in Zurich or Melrose Arch, let alone been party to soliciting bribes. 'That never happened. Travel records say I wasn't even in the country. I would have no reason to go.'

When I put Sharma's denial to Garfield, he let out a deep belly laugh. 'He was there, I tell you,' he insisted. 'To this day I can still smell that man's perfume.'

* * *

Iqbal Sharma has the distinction of being the man who introduced Salim Essa to the Guptas. More than anyone else outside the family, Essa's fortunes are inextricably linked with those of the Guptas. In fact, he is often referred to as 'the fourth Gupta brother'. They share deeply intertwined business interests in mining, defence, financial services, business consulting, telecoms, IT and logistics, often together with Duduzane Zuma. In most cases, their joint business ventures are either dependent on state approvals or have earned revenue or commissions from large state contracts. Crucially, Essa was often the Gupta family's proxy in their dealings with state entities. The evidence suggests that more often than not he served as their conduit for stashing offshore kickbacks.

In 2016, I was sent the iPhone call log of a Transnet board member. He listed Essa's mobile number under the codename 'Aladdin', the character in *The Arabian Nights* who finds a magic lamp that unleashes a powerful genie, which helps turn the feckless boy into a fabulously rich sultan fit to marry a princess. It was an apt epithet for the man who magically got money taps flowing at state entities.

The evidence is overwhelming that Essa built a powerful network of relationships with executives and board members at Eskom, Transnet and state arms maker Denel who would ensure suspect tenders and payments to Gupta-linked companies were approved. The evidence – contained in the Gupta leaks, parliamentary testimony and submissions, and documents supplied by whistleblowers – suggests Essa would also act as a middleman between the Guptas and multinationals seeking to clinch lucrative state contracts – such as consulting firm McKinsey, software maker SAP, IT company T-Systems and train manufacturer China South Rail – in return for substantial kickbacks. In return for a hefty 'commission' or 'success fee' – often shorthand for bribes – Essa would allegedly offer to ensure that the multinational would be awarded the contract. If there's one man outside the Gupta family who holds the darkest secrets of their alleged criminal enterprise, it's Essa.

Essa was born in Polokwane in Limpopo, but he moved to Johannesburg at an early age with his mother and two siblings, Shehzaad and Nabeel, after his parents divorced. After a short stay in the Muslim neighbourhood of Azaadville near Krugersdorp, they moved to the upmarket suburb of Houghton, Johannesburg. Essa's father, Aziz Omar Essa, who passed away in March 2018, remained in Polokwane, where he ran a successful building supply company that expanded into wholesale food distribution and property investments. Essa's first cousin, Polokwane businessman Muhammed Noor Hussain, married local lawyer Nazia Carrim, who was later appointed to the Eskom board.

After Essa graduated with a BCom from the University of the Witwatersrand, he worked as a trader for his father's company and considered joining the business full-time but decided to branch out on his own, pursuing a range of business ventures in telecoms, renewable energy and finance.

He married Zeenat Osmany and the couple bought a house in New Forest Road in the Johannesburg suburb of Forest Town, a few blocks from Zuma's former residence in Epping Road, which the president continued to visit occasionally after his inauguration in 2009. Forest Town lies next to Saxonwold, where the Gupta compound is situated. Duduzane Zuma lived just around the corner from the Guptas, in a house on Griswold Drive.[18]

Essa and his wife also bought a luxury apartment overlooking the twelfth hole of the Houghton golf course where, in 2017, a penthouse went on the market for R78 million.

Sharma, the dapper nephew of anti-apartheid struggle stalwart Fatima Meer and husband of Bollywood starlet Tarina Patel, met the eighteen-year-old Essa for the first time in 1996. They got to know each other through mutual friends and became close. After several forays into business, Sharma joined the Department of Trade and Industry in 2001. Two years later, he met Atul Gupta at a social function that was held at the residence of the Indian consul-general in Johannesburg. They hit it off because Sharma was fluent in Hindi and Atul Gupta's English was poor. Sharma rose through the ranks in the department, reaching the level of deputy director-general and chief executive of its export-promotion wing, Trade and Investment South Africa. During that time he also got to know the other Gupta brothers, Ajay and Tony, mostly through attending Indian social and religious functions, including Diwali celebrations. He left the department in October 2010, shortly before joining the Transnet board.

Sharma insists that he only started exploring business opportunities with Essa and the Guptas in 2011 – after he resigned from his post in the civil service – and that there is therefore no truth to the allegation that the Guptas planted him on the Transnet board in December 2010 to swing big contracts their way.

This may be true on paper, but I find it hard to imagine that Sharma never held a single discussion with the Guptas or Essa about business opportunities during his time as a civil servant, especially after he'd made the decision to resign. Sharma's claim is also difficult to square with the fact that Malusi Gigaba, a regular attendee at Diwali functions at Saxonwold, sought and failed to promote Sharma to chairperson of the Transnet board in mid-2011, and that Sharma chaired the acquisitions and disposals committee meeting in August 2012 that recommended negotiating with Gupta-linked China South Rail for the tender to supply ninety-five locomotives – the contract that Bombardier had expected to get.

Either way, Sharma says that in 2011 he started exploring business opportunities in 'resources, manufacturing and services' with the Guptas. By then he had already gone into business with Essa, working on renewable-energy projects. Later that year, during 'a casual encounter' at the Guptas' Oakbay offices on Katherine Street in Sandton, Sharma introduced Essa to the youngest Gupta brother, Tony. By then, Tony Gupta was already close friends with Duduzane Zuma, who'd been courted by the Guptas and given a job seven years earlier when he was down and out, with his father facing arms deal corruption charges.

Duduzane Zuma, Tony Gupta and Salim Essa soon became an insepar-able trio. Over the next five years, they would end up wielding enormous power to swing state contracts, influence who would sit on the boards and executives of the country's biggest state entities and, in a move of breathtaking arrogance that eventually led to their downfall, even pick cabinet ministers.

Sharma and Essa's first significant joint business venture was a partner-ship in 2012 with a Chinese firm called Daqo, which manufactures solar panels. By then, in Sharma's telling (Essa declined to be interviewed), Essa was already cosying up to Duduzane Zuma as his new business partner.

The next company Sharma and Essa partnered in was VR Laser, a steel-cutting concern in Benoni that served the defence industry and would become embroiled in a R100-billion arms deal scandal involving the Guptas. In 2008, the founder and original owner of VR Laser, John van Reenen, announced an empowerment deal worth R81 million that saw black businessman Benny Jiyane acquire a 26 per cent stake in the company. VR Laser said the transaction meant it would now be eligible to tender for lucrative state contracts with Eskom, Transnet and arms maker Denel.

'In light of South Africa's power crisis,' Jiyane told *Engineering News* at the time, 'the business we can gain from Eskom will be very signifi-cant, as it will be for its capital programme, and the maintenance of its existing power stations.'[19]

Another state entity that VR Laser aggressively targeted was Transnet, hoping to supply it with precision-cut steel to assemble locomotives. 'The company is expecting a significant amount of business from Transnet off the back of the company's refurbishment programme, which would run into a significant cash flow over the next fifteen years,' Jiyane declared.

In early 2013 – when Sharma and Essa approached Van Reenen to buy the rest of his company – Sharma was a member of the Transnet board, which was deliberating a R54-billion deal for new locomotives that VR Laser could potentially benefit from. Sharma insists their approach had nothing to do with Transnet or locomotives. Instead, he says, they were eyeing 'the defence sector and export markets as I had good leads on potential opportunities in the Middle East'.

He says negotiations kicked off in March 2013 and concluded in November that year, with Jiyani, Van Reenen's original BEE partner, retaining his shares. Sharma says that Essa then proceeded to cut a deal with the Guptas behind his back. Early in 2014, without Sharma's knowledge but with Essa's connivance, Jiyane sold his shares to Duduzane Zuma and Tony Gupta. Sharma says that when he found out, it led to a falling-out between him and Essa, and the pair parted company. Sharma took Essa's stake in Daqo in return for his shares in VR Laser. That, according to Sharma, was the end of his dealings with Essa, VR Laser and the Guptas.

This telling of the VR Laser narrative leaves a few issues unresolved. First, the Gupta leaks reveal that Sharma received a R20-million loan in December 2012 from Gupta-owned company Aerohaven. This happened at a time when China South Rail was paying the Guptas alleged kickbacks for smaller locomotive contracts from Transnet, raising the possibility that Sharma's 'loan' may have been a bribe to facilitate these deals.

Sharma rejects this suggestion. The money was nothing more than 'a loan' to buy VR Laser's properties, he says. 'I subsequently resigned as a director and shareholder and the entity continued to repay the loan.' The Gupta leaks also reveal – perhaps more damningly – that on at least two occasions in October 2013 Sharma forwarded sensitive information from Transnet to Tony Gupta. This was a critical juncture for the 1064 locomotives contract, coming less than six months before the largest slice of the deal was awarded to China South Rail, which would allow billions in alleged kickbacks to flow back to the Guptas through a company Essa would set up in Hong Kong called Tequesta.

But Sharma is adamant he did not send the emails to Tony Gupta. 'While the veracity of the leaks has yet to be tested, I can confirm that at least two emails attributed to me were not sent by me,' he says.

Lastly, there's the question of why Sharma's CV should appear in the hands of alleged Gupta money launderer Piyoosh Goyal, who demanded that Sharma be put on the PRASA board. Sharma's response is that he can't comment on something he knows nothing about.

Despite these disquieting questions, Sharma continues to insist he's been given a raw deal and smeared because of his innocent association with the Guptas and their henchman, Essa. He points out that none of his planned partnerships with the Guptas panned out and that he cut ties with Essa before he became embroiled in any of the highly publicised Gupta scandals.

* * *

The other key players in charge of Transnet's massive fleet-renewal plan were Gigaba's new choice for chief executive, Brian Molefe, and chief financial officer Anoj Singh – a man who would later gain notoriety at Eskom for bending over backwards to ensure that the business interests of Essa and the Gupta brothers were catered for while they wined and dined him in Dubai. All that remained was to come up with a solid business case for spending tens of billions of rands on a large fleet of freight trains when there wasn't enough demand for cargo transport to justify the expense. Essa knew just the right people for the job.

6

Sharing the Spoils

The metals and mining division of global consulting firm McKinsey & Company long prided itself on making accurate predictions based on complex modelling of global commodity trends. A company such as Transnet would happily pay for such information – it was, after all, in the business of transporting ore from mines to ports in an export-driven economy.

Although freight volumes were declining, Jacob Zuma's 2012 announcement that over R300 billion would be set aside to modernise South Africa's transport infrastructure meant things were looking up. Of course, spending that kind of money on upgrades would be risky, given the effect that fluctuating commodity prices would have on demand for freight rail. If Treasury was going to help fund such a plan, Transnet needed a solid business case. McKinsey stepped up to provide it.

'Following a change in government policy towards the objectives of the "developmental state" – and under the leadership of the new CEO at the time, Brian Molefe – Transnet decided to embark on a new strategy to stimulate demand by investing in infrastructure projects without confirmed orders from customers,' David Fine, the senior McKinsey partner in charge of the Transnet project, explained during the parliamentary inquiry into public enterprises. 'Such a strategy requires detailed projections of freight demand based on realistic assumptions of global growth and demand.'

McKinsey used its 'proprietary models' to forecast the potential increase in commodity volumes needing rail transport over the next seven years. It identified opportunities to export more coal, manganese and chrome to Asia; strong growth in local demand for iron ore, coal and cement; and the potential to shift the transport of goods containers from road to rail. McKinsey predicted that annual volumes would more than double from 84 million tons to over 170 million tons by 2019.[1]

It turned out that these predictions were wildly optimistic. In 2015, the Chinese economy, which accounted for 45 to 55 per cent of the world's steel and coal consumption, experienced an unprecedented slowdown. This had a negative impact on global commodity prices 'and ultimately on the demand for South African mining exports that help drive demand for freight capacity', Fine said. But by then it was too late. In March 2012, Transnet officials, with substantial input from Fine's team of consultants, submitted a business case to Transnet's capital investment committee to buy 1 064 locomotives at a total cost of R38 billion. Two months later, a consortium led by McKinsey submitted a bid to provide an array of advisory services to grease the wheels of the deal.

* * *

By the time Transnet and McKinsey had developed a business case for buying 1 064 locomotives, the Gupta looting machine had already kicked into gear with a smaller contract for ninety-five electric locomotives worth R2.7 billion. The tender was issued in June 2011, shortly after Malusi Gigaba's new board – under freshly installed chief executive Brian Molefe – had approved the company's fleet-renewal plan. This was the contract that Bombardier and the firm's BEE partner, Garfield, had expected to get. Instead, it went to China South Rail in a handy test run for skimming the cream off Transnet's mega deal.

The Gupta leaks later revealed that in January 2012, a month before that tender closed, the South African representative of China South Rail, Wang Pan, sent Molefe an email asking to visit Transnet sites. Wang forwarded his email to a director of alleged Gupta money launderer Piyoosh Goyal's scrap-metal company, Worlds Window. From there it was forwarded to Goyal's assistant and the Guptas.[2]

In August 2012, a board tender committee meeting chaired by Salim Essa's business partner, Iqbal Sharma, recommended that China South Rail be awarded the R2.7-billion contract.[3] Shortly after the InnoTrans fair in September 2012, when the Guptas and Essa were allegedly attempting to extort kickbacks from bidders, the deal was finally signed.

From documents contained in the Gupta leaks, teams of journalists and researchers in different parts of the world were later able to piece together the complex money flows from China South Rail to a constellation of Gupta-linked entities in the UAE, China, India and South Africa. The documents include a consulting contract with Salim Essa, payment tables, ledgers, and a spreadsheet detailing astronomical 'advisory fees' of 20 to 21 per cent of the contract values – the same cut that Essa had allegedly asked Bombardier for. One ledger shows that in December 2012, two months after the R2.7 billion Transnet contract for ninety-five locomotives was signed, the first payment of $6 million was paid by China South Rail to Century General Trading, a scrap-metal company in the United Arab Emirates. This was followed by payments to another UAE scrap-metal dealer, JJ Trading. The documents show that between December 2012 and January 2015 the scrap-metal traders, both with links to Goyal's scrap-metal company Worlds Window in Delhi, received R1.4 billion in 'advisory fees' from China South Rail for various Transnet deals. After retaining a small percentage for themselves, these companies funnelled the rest from their accounts at HSBC Bank in the UAE to Gupta-controlled companies in the UAE and India. An exact replica of the scheme was used in 2013 with a R4.4-billion contract to supply 100 locomotives to Transnet, which was once again awarded to China South Rail. For these two smaller contracts alone, China South Rail earmarked a total of R1.5 billion in suspected kickbacks for the Guptas and their alleged money launderers.[4]

After disguising the origin of these suspected kickbacks through split payments to and from a convoluted network of front companies, with fixed deposits often used as collateral for loans and intercompany loans or advances used for bogus transactions, the Guptas used the money to fund their increasingly lavish lifestyles and property empires in Dubai, India and South Africa, while sharing some of their largesse with politicians with whom they needed to curry favour. This included paying for a house for one of Jacob Zuma's wives, Bongi Ngema-Zuma.[5]

The smaller Transnet locomotive contracts of 2012 and 2013, which were rushed through without going out to tender on the pretext of an emergency shortage, were only dress rehearsals for the main act to come. It wouldn't be so easy to slip through the deal for 1064 locomotives without following proper procurement processes. It was critical for the looters to control the brokers, consultants and advisors all hungrily circling the deal for their cut. In the end, only those willing to share the spoils got to eat.

* * *

The original consortium for the plum contract of advising Transnet on the mega locomotive deal consisted of McKinsey and its black empowerment or so-called 'supplier development' partner Letsema Consulting, Advanced Rail Technologies and Nedbank. McKinsey would lead the consortium and expand on its market demand strategy work to 'validate the business case'; Nedbank would provide deal structuring and funding advice; Letsema was responsible for overall project management; and UK-based Advanced Rail Technologies would provide the technical expertise. The McKinsey-led consortium was awarded the contract in January 2013 and expected to start work in March that year.[6]

Letsema, South Africa's first black-owned and managed consulting firm, was founded by Isaac Shongwe in 1996. It had first partnered with a previous incarnation of New York–headquartered management consultancy Oliver Wyman before joining forces with McKinsey in 2005. Over the years, the rail and port sector became one of Letsema's specialities. By 2012, its work with McKinsey generated about 80 per cent of the firm's total income, almost half of this with Transnet. Managing the 1 064 locomotives contract would be an important feather in Letsema's cap. What Shongwe wasn't aware of at the time was that a rival consultancy, Regiments Capital, was already waiting in the wings, ready to take Letsema's place.

Regiments was founded in 2004 by politically connected businessman Litha Nyhonyha, former Investec trader Eric Wood and Niven Pillay. By 2012, the company had some impressive gigs under its belt but was struggling to enter the big league. What it needed was the magic of Aladdin's lamp.

What happened next remains a matter of intense dispute, including in opposing papers filed by Nyhonyha, Wood and Pillay after a spectacular falling-out between the co-founders that landed up in court. Based on internal spreadsheets and emails from Regiments, publicly available court documents and parliamentary testimony – as well as confidential discussions over several months with former and current employees and executives at McKinsey, Regiments and its Gupta-linked offshoot Trillian, and sources previously close to the Guptas or their associates – I've pieced together what is, in my opinion, an accurate reflection of how McKinsey and Regiments came to work together on the Transnet contract.

In December 2012, shortly before McKinsey was awarded the consulting contract, Regiments director Pillay and his old friend Kuben Moodley teed off at the Houghton golf course, where Essa owned a swish pad overlooking the twelfth hole. As they strolled down the fairway, Moodley turned to Pillay and asked if he was happy about where Regiments was going. 'What you need is a heavy-hitting international partner to take it to the next level,' Moodley supposedly told him.

A few weeks later, Moodley arrived at Regiments' offices, an intimidating glass-fronted edifice on Ferguson Road in Illovo with spectacular views of northern Johannesburg from its rooftop canteen. Pillay ushered Moodley and his companion into a boardroom. 'Let me introduce you. This is my friend Salim Essa,' said Moodley.[7]

The deal they proposed was simple. Moodley would be paid a 5 per cent 'finder's fee' for bringing along Essa, who in turn brought McKinsey and its business. Moodley has always denied he was involved in any unlawful activity involving the Guptas, insisting he was paid for performing a legitimate service. What that service consisted of, apart from indirectly bringing McKinsey and Regiments together through Essa, remains unclear. Essa's job, unbeknown to Letsema, was to ensure that Regiments replaced the company as McKinsey's partner. For this, Essa would be paid 50 per cent of the proceeds of whatever earnings the partnership generated. Whether Essa hoped to pull it off through his connections at McKinsey, Transnet or both was anyone's guess. Leaked emails show that Essa later became close to McKinsey senior partner Vikas Sagar, who managed the consultancy's relationship with Regiments from the start. Testimony in Parliament from former Regiments executive Mosilo Mothepu, leaked emails, other internal documents and several confidential sources also attest to Essa's close relationship with Transnet and later Eskom chief financial officer Anoj Singh and Transnet board member Stanley Shane.

Sure enough, in December 2012, shortly after Moodley had brought Essa to Ferguson Road, and just in time for the 1 064 locomotives contract to land on Singh's desk, McKinsey signed up Regiments as its supplier development partner. According to David Fine's testimony, this was done at Transnet's behest.

Regiments, as a junior partner in the McKinsey-led consortium, initially only stood to earn about R10 million off a consulting contract worth R35.2 million. But the consulting fees grew to over R500 million in the next four years, with the lion's share going to Regiments after McKinsey was relegated to a supporting role.

Regiments' miraculous good fortune also appeared to translate into a windfall for Essa and Moodley. This is suggested by two documents. The first is a company table in the court filings, showing that 55 per cent of what Regiments stood to earn from its parastatal work with McKinsey, including at Transnet, was allocated as a 'business development fee'. The second document is a spreadsheet released by a whistleblower in 2017 containing a general ledger for a nine-month period in 2015. The ledger shows that every time Regiments invoiced for its Transnet work with McKinsey, 55 per cent of its fees were paid to its 'business development partners' Albatime, Forsure and Fortime. Albatime, which received 5 per cent, belongs to Moodley, who had brought his associate and sometime golfing partner Salim Essa to the Regiments table. Forsure and Fortime, which were paid the remaining 50 per cent, are letterbox companies linked to Essa and the Guptas.

The 1 064 locomotives contract turned out to be the thin end of the wedge. Pretty soon Regiments was partnering with McKinsey at a range of parastatals, for a total of about twenty contracts over four years. This came as a great shock to Letsema, McKinsey's stalwart supplier development partner for the past seven years.

In 2013, Letsema directors Derek Thomas and Aldo Sguazzin were called to a meeting with Garry Pita, the chief procurement officer at Transnet. He told them that the firm could no longer work on the 1 064 locomotives contract because its founder and chairperson, Shongwe, was indirectly serving one of the bidders, General Electric. At the time, Thomas was happy to give Pita 'the benefit of the doubt', he told me

66

during an interview at the company's Melrose Arch offices in 2017 that was also attended by Sguazzin and Shongwe.

Sguazzin said: 'This was the start of kicking Letsema out of Transnet. Suddenly Regiments was injected into the McKinsey relationship. From then on we were sidelined.'

Soon, Letsema's earnings from Transnet fell to 10 per cent of total revenue before drying up altogether. 'Transnet should have been proud to use a local company with our track record,' said Shongwe. Instead, they had the rug pulled from under them. 'It almost destroyed us.'

The next McKinsey partner to go was Nedbank, which announced in May 2013 that it had decided to opt out because it wanted to help finance the deal. Transnet was quick to suggest that Regiments should step into the breach.

Financial advisory services on the contract were soon expanded to include sourcing funds for the deal, which came with a hefty commission. Court filings show that Transnet paid Regiments R166 million to negotiate a $2.5-billion loan to fund part of the locomotive deal from China Development Bank and another R230.2 million for conducting ten interest rate swaps, some to hedge risk for the locomotives project.

In addition, Transnet increased Regiments' advisory fee on the locomotive contract from R10 million to R89 million, reportedly because it had demonstrated it could save money by splitting the order between four bidders for faster delivery, which would allow Transnet to grow its freight volumes more quickly and earn more revenue sooner.[8]

This took the total value of fees Regiments earned from a contract originally worth R10 million up to R485 million. The Regiments table and spreadsheet suggest that half of this probably flowed straight to Essa, and some to Moodley, even though neither provided Transnet with any discernible services.

* * *

Kuben Moodley is a complex character. He was born in 1971 and grew up in the impoverished working-class suburb of Chatsworth near Durban. He's built like a prize fighter, swears like a trooper – including at journalists who cross him – and likes to party hard. One former colleague described him as 'a toughie who loves strip clubs'. Others were impressed by his work ethic. By his mid-thirties, Moodley was managing Telkom's prepaid division, where one of his corporate clients described him as 'an efficient manager' and 'a very good guy'.

During his time at Telkom, Moodley got to know the executives at telecoms company Blue Label. According to my sources, he struck up a close friendship with its chief operating officer Mark Pamensky and introduced him to Salim Essa. Pamensky would play a key role in the Gupta looting machine after he left Blue Label to serve on the boards of both Eskom and Gupta company Oakbay Resources and Energy.

Moodley left Telkom around 2010, and in October 2012 he became the sole director of Albatime. Within five years he'd built up a substantial portfolio of business interests. His web only began to unravel in 2016 after Public Protector Thuli Madonsela's report on state capture and the Regiments court proceedings implicated him in several Gupta-related scandals.

Moodley has disputed the Public Protector's findings and has always insisted that he isn't linked to the Gupta family or their business network in any way, describing Essa as merely someone 'known to me from social circles'. However, available evidence suggests that he has a case to answer.

Banking records and documents contained in the Gupta leaks show that Albatime made three suspicious payments to Gupta-owned company Sahara Computers in July and August 2015 totalling R87 million as part of a two-year contract worth R139 million. The contract and an invoice from Sahara stipulate that the payments are for 'IT services'.

Albatime is a small business brokerage situated in a drab Johannesburg office park in Fourways across the road from a late-night carwash. I wondered how on earth this firm could justify spending that much money on 'IT services'. The only possibility, if this was a legitimate transaction, was that it had acted as a broker to other companies for Sahara's products. But when I asked Moodley what services Sahara had performed to justify such large payments, he dodged the question. Instead, he referred me to a news report, which quoted him saying that Albatime had paid for 'the procurement of IT equipment and services in the same fashion as numerous corporates, wholesalers, and resellers who acquired IT services from Sahara'.[9]

AmaBhungane and Scorpio have pointed out the fact that Albatime's underlying agreement with Sahara was only created five days after the first payment of R52 million was made, and that income from the contract was reflected in Sahara's books at zero cost, suggests the deal could have been a simulated transaction to disguise a commission paid to the Guptas.[10]

Court proceedings brought against Regiments in 2017 by Transnet's pension fund provide further clues as to where the money Transnet paid to Regiments landed up. The fund alleged that R50.7 million of the R230.2 million Regiments was paid for interest rate swaps was transferred to Albatime in five tranches from December 2015 to April 2016. The remaining R179.5 million was transferred to Trillian, an offshoot of Regiments formed by Essa and Eric Wood, who had fallen out with Niven Pillay and Litha Nyhonyha.

The timing of these payments is particularly intriguing. Subsequent investigations by Madonsela and audit firm Deloitte found that Trillian, which was majority owned by Essa, had contributed R235 million towards the Gupta purchase of Optimum coal mine in April 2016 and that Albatime had contributed R10 million. A report drawn up by Deloitte, which had been asked to investigate the payments by the Reserve Bank, found that Albatime and Trillian had issued instructions for the money to be used as collateral for a loan to Gupta company Tegeta that went towards buying the mine. However, Moodley continues to insist the deposit had nothing to do with the Optimum transaction.

What all these transactions appear to show is that, in effect, the Guptas were benefiting directly from the inflated fees Transnet was paying Regiments.

Forsure Consultants, the second 'business development partner' to which Regiments was diverting a large chunk of its Transnet fees, provides further clues suggesting that these could have been kickbacks being diverted to the Gupta network. The company headquarters is a small yellow house surrounded by a white security palisade located at 103 St Fillans Avenue in the working-class suburb of Mayfair, south of Johannesburg. When I visited the place, I found letters strewn among dry autumn leaves, and a Toyota Yaris with a learner driver sticker in the window parked in the driveway. The neighbours assured me that the house has been occupied for years by an Ethiopian trader who sells his wares at the nearby China Mall. A Google Maps photograph taken in 2009 shows that the house was previously the location of Angel Beauty Salon, which offered 'hair cutting, waxing, bleaching, threading, pedicure – ladies only!' The St Fillans Avenue property also happens to be the registered physical address of Homix, a suspected Gupta money-laundering front linked to Essa.

In 2015, the *Mail & Guardian* reported that telecoms company Neotel had paid R66 million in kickbacks to Homix – R30 million in April 2014 and R36 million in February 2015 – to secure contracts from Transnet worth R2.1 billion. It turned out that Homix was being run by Ashok Narayan, the former managing director of Gupta IT company Sahara Systems.[11]

It later emerged that half a dozen companies, including Regiments and Neotel, had made over seventy payments to the company at the house in Mayfair in 2014 and 2015, totalling at least R250 million. Of this, R185 million was immediately transferred to an equally obscure company called Bapu Trading. Reporters who visited its registered address at a small shopping mall in Erasmia, east of Pretoria, found no sign of the company.[12]

However, an investigation by the Reserve Bank's financial surveillance department found that Homix had used R65 million to buy foreign currency to pay two companies in Hong Kong for imports. The investigators also found that the customs documents for the imports were fake, but by then most of the money had already been transferred. One of the Hong Kong companies, Morningstar International Trade, shares the same registered address as three other companies Essa registered in Hong Kong: Tequesta, which was set up to receive R3 billion in suspected kickbacks from China South Rail after it won the largest contract of the 1 064 locomotives deal; VR Laser Asia, the company the Guptas sought to use to clinch a R100-billion arms deal with Denel in India; and Regiments Asia.[13]

Fortime, the third Regiments 'partner' listed in the ledger as receiving tens of millions from Transnet, is registered to a modest suburban home on the outskirts of Mthatha in the Eastern Cape. This address is also shared by another entity called Birsaa Projects that received suspect payments from Gupta-linked deals with international software giant SAP, which later admitted to paying kickbacks of R100 million for contracts worth R1 billion from Transnet and Eskom.[14]

Pillay and Nyhonyha say that they only found out about the payments to Homix after Wood left the firm, and they had never heard of Regiments Asia. Wood says this is rubbish and that all three directors signed off on all the payments.

Either way, the fact that Regiments had diverted astronomical sums from its Transnet fees to Gupta-linked letterbox companies and individuals who performed no discernible services for the parastatal suggests that these 'commissions' were little more than kickbacks paid to the Guptas and their associates in return for using their influence at state-owned entities to keep the money taps flowing.

Testimony by former Regiments executive Mosilo Mothepu to the parliamentary inquiry into public enterprises in 2017 supports this contention. Mothepu described how she'd returned to Regiments in 2015 after a five-year absence and encountered a company that had grown from 'humble beginnings' to a McKinsey-sized consultancy with a staff of 270 working on 'blue-chip' public sector contracts. When she asked her colleagues what had changed since she left, she was told that 'Salim Essa and Kuben Moodley brought these contracts'.

'Every single SOE we dealt with, either Denel, SA Express, Transnet, Eskom, Salim had a relationship with either a board member there, or the executive, or the chairman,' she explained. 'He is the guy that brings in the contracts. What facilitates the process is [that] the executives and boards of SOEs have to approve certain things and pressurise lower management to execute them.'[15]

A whistleblower statement released by former Trillian executive Bianca Goodson tells the same tale. Goodson explained that the company's business model was to secure work 'through Essa's relationships'. Trillian secured the contracts but didn't do the work itself. The firm simply passed it on to 'internationally recognised companies and acted as the supplier development partner of choice, with roughly a 50 per cent share in revenue'.[16]

In the end, the expensive advice dispensed by Regiments, with half its fees siphoned off as 'commissions' to Essa to secure the work, didn't save Transnet any money at all. In fact, it had the opposite effect. David Fine told the parliamentary inquiry that McKinsey had calculated, based on data provided by Transnet's freight rail division and 'expert input' from Advanced Rail Technologies, that the total cost of 1064 locomotives should not exceed R38.6 billion over seven years, including hedging costs. McKinsey withdrew from the project in February 2014 shortly before the tenders were awarded and played no role in evaluating the bids or determining the final price.[17]

On 17 March 2014, Brian Molefe announced that the contract had been split among four winning bidders. General Electric and China North Rail would supply 233 and 232 diesel locomotives respectively, and Bombardier would supply 240 electric locomotives. The biggest order, for 359 electric locomotives, was placed with China South Rail. The total price tag for the whole package came to R54 billion.

Fine said that when he enquired with Transnet as to why the price had increased by 40 per cent, the parastatal's chief financial officer, Anoj Singh, told him that 'Transnet had done new calculations based on funding costs, exchange rates and inflation and had come to the conclusion that it was better to secure the deal that they did'.

In other words, Singh had paid Regiments R485 million for advice that had contributed to the total contract value going up by almost R16 billion. It was a blueprint for looting that would soon be replicated. A year later, Singh and Molefe would move to the next feasting table: Eskom. But first, a few good men had to be moved out of the way.

7

Indecent Proposal

Brian Dames is an Eskom company man through and through. He joined the utility in 1987 to work at Koeberg nuclear power station near the West Coast fishing village of Melkbosstrand. That was during the dark days of apartheid. Because Dames was black, he wasn't allowed to live with his colleagues in the whites-only residential suburb nearby, join their medical aid or pension scheme, or even share a meal in the same canteen.

Despite this, for the twenty-two-year-old nuclear physicist, working at Koeberg with top scientists in the field was hugely inspiring. Besides, political change was in the air. Eskom, perhaps seeing the writing on the wall, had launched a training programme for young black university graduates, grooming them for future leadership positions. This process accelerated three years later with Nelson Mandela's release from prison and with the advent of democracy in 1994.

By then, Eskom had become one of the world's largest power utilities. In the 1960s and 1970s, the apartheid government, obsessed with the desire for self-sufficiency, went on a power station building spree. Soon, large coal-fired plants sprang up all over the Mpumalanga Highveld, where coal is plentiful and cheap. Many of these plants consisted of six identical units, the so-called 'six-packs', with tall boiler houses and cooling stacks towering over the bleak flatlands east of Johannesburg. The power stations were built next to mines so that coal could be transported to furnaces on conveyor belts at minimal cost. Long-term contracts guaranteed Eskom a secure supply of low-cost coal, providing consumers with some of the cheapest electricity in the world.[1]

However, under apartheid the homes of most black South Africans were not electrified. One of the great successes of post-apartheid reconstruction was providing these homes with electricity. Professor Anton Eberhard, who founded the Energy and Development Research Centre at the University of Cape Town, points out that Eskom deserves credit for this remarkable achievement.

'It's worth remembering that in 1994 all white South Africans had access to electricity, even white farmers who lived in very remote areas, but less than a third of black South Africans had access,' he told Parliament. 'That figure now stands at 90 per cent. South Africans have achieved one of the fastest electrification rates in history.'[2]

During this exciting and dynamic period of expansion, Dames was rapidly promoted. After several years at Koeberg, he joined the utility's power generation section and was later appointed as manager of Duvha power station in Mpumalanga. Built in the late 1970s, Duvha is one of the largest coal-fired plants in the country and was once considered the flagship of Eskom's fleet. Its six boilers are capable of producing 3 600 megawatts – about 10 per cent of the current coal-fired capacity. 'The manager at the time told me that you can either take the easy assignments at Eskom or you can take the difficult assignments. And I took the difficult one, which was Duvha,' Dames recalled in his testimony before the parliamentary inquiry into public enterprises.[3]

After four years at Duvha, Dames returned to the Cape to head Eskom's nuclear division, which included Koeberg. Next, he was put in charge of Eskom's investment arm, which involved managing projects throughout Africa, and joined a team of executives in 2004 that was tasked with expanding the utility's generation capacity.

By then, the bleak prospect of a supply crisis was staring Eskom in the face. Since 1994, South Africa had experienced a decade of steady economic growth. During this time, Eskom had pursued its aggressive electrification drive without building any new plants. Some of the older plants, built as a result of over-optimistic predictions of economic growth by apartheid planners, had been mothballed. In December 1998, Eskom warned that the demand for power would outstrip capacity by 2007. But Thabo Mbeki's government placed a moratorium on building new plants, wanting the gap to be filled by independent power producers. Eskom was only given the go-ahead in 2004, but by then it was too late. Four years later South Africa was plunged into darkness, partly thanks to the moratorium. Mbeki later apologised for this.

As stopgap measures, Eskom built two new diesel- and gas-powered plants: Gourikwa near Mossel Bay on the Southern Cape coast and Ankerlig in Atlantis near Cape Town. Both were completed in 2007 and designed to supplement the grid during peak-hour emergencies. Previously mothballed power stations Camden, Grootvlei, Arnot and Komati were also upgraded and brought back into service between 2008 and 2012.

In the meantime, construction began on three new mega power stations: Ingula, a pumped-storage hydroelectric plant on the escarpment of the Drakensberg mountains; Medupi on a large coalfield near the Botswana border in Limpopo province; and Kusile ninety kilometres east of Johannesburg. Once completed, Kusile and Medupi would add 4 800 megawatts each to the grid and Ingula just over 1 300 megawatts.

As with Transnet's R300-billion rail, port and pipeline expansion plan, Eskom's so-called 'new build' programme offered ample opportunity for graft. Anecdotal evidence soon surfaced that Eskom officials received kickbacks for anything from laundry contracts to securing multibillion-rand loans. It would only be much later that the true extent of the rot, along with the names of the top executives implicated, came to light.

By then, costs had spiralled out of control. In Eskom's 2005 annual report, the utility said it expected to spend R93 billion to build four new power plants. By 2007 this had increased to R160 billion for just three plants – Kusile, Medupi and Ingula. By 2018, the price tag had skyrocketed to R337 billion. This money had to be borrowed on international capital markets, most of it guaranteed by the government. However, an investigation by law firm Dentons later cited corruption as a major cost driver. In effect, the taxpayer was used to underwrite grand-scale larceny.[4]

Eskom's new build was too little, too late. By 2007, the reserve margin – the difference between peak demand and excess generation capacity – had shrunk to 8 per cent, compared with an international standard of 15 per cent. This left Eskom with little room for planned maintenance and resulted in an increase in breakdowns because power plants were being run too hard.

The power utility had also allowed coal stockpiles at its power stations to run down to dangerously low levels despite being given ample prior warning. In mid-2007, US energy consultant Susan Olsen had written a report for Eskom warning that incompetence at its coal supply division was placing the entire utility at risk. For years Eskom had neglected negotiating new long-term coal supply contracts that delivered the right quality coal at reasonable prices. Mining companies were running rings around the utility, supplying marginal-quality coal at inflated prices. Olsen urged immediate remedial action to avert disaster.[5]

Jacob Maroga, the chief executive at the time, fired Olsen and ignored her report. In January 2008, the country found itself in the grip of rolling blackouts that would last for several months. The economy was hit hard, with mines being forced to close for a week at a time when global commodity prices were at record highs. By one estimate, the mines lost R600 million a day in export revenues, with the national economy losing up to R2 billion a day.[6]

Subsequent investigations revealed that corruption at Eskom's coal division, not merely incompetence, was a major cause of the crisis.

Dames was put in charge of fixing the problem. 'One of my first tasks was to visit all the power stations,' he recalled. 'I did it over a weekend, I visited each and every power station and their teams. When I flew over the power stations it was very clear for me that there was no coal.'

Stockpiles that should have been 'as high as trees' had been reduced to brown sand.

South Africa was getting critically close to hosting the FIFA World Cup in July 2010. Determined the honour would not be snatched from the country owing to fears that its power utility couldn't handle the influx of 500 000 visitors, Dames launched Eskom's 'keeping the lights on' campaign. He went on an aggressive coal-buying drive that included trucking coal from mines far from power plants, which doubled the cost of restoring Eskom's stockpiles. Next, he implemented a power-saving strategy by getting key customers, including the mines, to cut back on consumption. Scheduled plant shutdowns for maintenance were deferred until after the World Cup.

On 1 July 2010, Brian Dames, then forty-four, became the youngest chief executive in Eskom's history. The final whistle of the World Cup blew ten days later. South Africa had successfully hosted the tournament without a single power outage. After twenty-three tumultuous years at Eskom, Dames had grown more than a few grey hairs and thought he'd seen it all. But the worst was yet to come.

* * *

One of the first items on Dames's to-do list in his capacity as chief executive was replacing six steam generators at Koeberg. In line with international best practice, the nuclear power plant subjected itself to external peer review every two years. A review in 2010 concluded that the generators were nearing the end of their lifespan. Eskom decided they should be replaced during a planned reactor shutdown in 2018 and issued a tender in 2010 for their replacement. What Dames didn't know was that political machinations under way in the background would soon put paid to even the best-laid plans.

In May 2009, President Jacob Zuma appointed the respected anti-apartheid veteran Barbara Hogan as his first minister of public enterprises, a critical position that provides political oversight to all the most important state entities, including Eskom and Transnet. Almost a year later, in February 2010, Zuma announced that Hogan and his first finance minister and former close comrade, Pravin Gordhan, would conduct a review of state enterprises. The purpose was to examine their financial models and their role in Zuma's new 'developmental state'.

Three months later, in May 2010, Zuma surprised everyone by hand-picking a panel of relative unknowns to do the same job. Gordhan and Hogan's review was summarily shut down. At the time, both downplayed the move.[7] But there were soon rumblings that Hogan's attempt to clean up the corruption that plagued parastatals had put her on a collision course with the president. Her outspoken stance in seeking to curb conflicts of interest, such as ANC investment arm Chancellor House benefiting from Eskom's new build contracts, and her efforts to rein in lavish bonuses and pay packages for executives, made her many enemies.[8]

Hogan's refusal to play ball with the Guptas didn't endear her to the president either. By then, the Gupta family were ramping up their efforts to infiltrate key state entities, including Transnet, Eskom and SAA, to secure large contracts or concessions for themselves or multinationals from which they could extract suspected kickbacks. Hogan later told Public Protector Thuli Madonsela that she became concerned at the influence the Gupta family wielded over the president, which became apparent during a state visit to India in June 2010, where they 'took control of the proceedings' and appeared 'to be directing the programme'. During the trip, Hogan was pressured several times to meet the chief executive of Mumbai-based Jet Airways. The airline had been lobbying SAA to discontinue its flights between Johannesburg and Mumbai so that it could service the route. She refused.

Hogan also noted that Zuma had taken a particular interest in the appointment of board members at Transnet and Eskom.

Former ANC MP Vytjie Mentor told Madonsela that in October 2010, four months after Zuma's India trip, the Guptas offered her Hogan's job. As Mentor tells it, during a meeting at the family's Saxonwold home, she was told she had to cancel SAA's Mumbai route and give it to Jet Airways if she wanted the job. When she refused, Zuma suddenly emerged, as though he'd been listening from the room next door. 'It's okay *ntombazane* [girl], take care of yourself,' he allegedly murmured as he escorted her outside, showing no anger that she'd rejected the proposal.[9]

A week later Zuma fired Hogan, and on 1 November 2010 thirty-nine-year-old former ANC Youth League president Malusi Gigaba became his second minister of public enterprises.

Gigaba lost no time in making his mark. His speeches were immediately peppered with talk of state entities driving Zuma's agenda of a developmental state. Parastatals couldn't simply focus on the bottom line; theirs was a higher purpose. Their role was to develop the country's infrastructure, stimulate the local economy and galvanise domestic industrialisation. Government would play a 'much more hands-on, robust, strategic leadership role' to ensure these objectives were met.[10]

For Dames, this wasn't good news. Eskom hardly needed lecturing on its obligations to fulfil a developmental mandate. Throughout the Mbeki years, when state-owned companies were expected to fend for themselves without government bailouts, the power utility had expanded its reach to poor townships where payment default rates were high.

After a period of upheaval that saw Dames's predecessor Jacob Maroga and then chairperson Bobby Godsell at each other's throats over strategic direction, including the mismanagement of coal procurement that led to the 2008 blackouts, Eskom had settled into a period of leadership stability. This was critical at a time when Eskom had just embarked on its largest power plant construction drive since the 1970s and was borrowing over R300 billion to fund it. Dames and his highly competent team wanted to be left in peace to get on with the job, which was to stay in business to provide affordable power that would grow the economy.

Gigaba had other ideas. He'd brought with him a host of inexperienced advisors – young, brash and eager to stamp their authority on the technocrats running Africa's largest power utility. A former Eskom manager who'd been close to Dames described what it was like being subjected to the whims of Gigaba's kindergarten: 'They treated senior executives with decades of experience – including Brian [Dames] – like dirt,' the manager told me. 'They expected them to be at their beck and call because they worked for the minister. They had no idea about lines of accountability, that the executive reported to the board and the board reported to the minister. They acted like they were in charge. Brian did his best to resist them, but it was hell.'

One member of Gigaba's team was a thirty-six-year-old director at law firm Edward Nathan Sonnenbergs named Siyabonga Mahlangu. The Gupta leaks later revealed that in December 2010, shortly after Gigaba appointed him 'special counsel', Mahlangu had travelled to India with Duduzane Zuma and another Gupta business associate, Tshepiso Magashule, the son of the current ANC secretary-general Ace Magashule.[11]

Mahlangu earned notoriety when the *Sunday Times* reported in March 2013 that he was present at a meeting in Saxonwold at which Tony Gupta allegedly offered the then chairperson of SAA, Vuyisile Kona, a R500 000 bribe to do the family's bidding. Kona reportedly said 'no' and left. Mahlangu confirmed introducing Kona to Gupta company Sahara, but denied any knowledge of the bribe.[12] Mahlangu was also accused of strong-arming SAA into buying more copies of Gupta newspaper and Zuma mouthpiece *The New Age* than it needed, although he denied this, and he later bought a R5-million house from the Guptas in the Johannesburg suburb of Birdhaven.[13]

During his testimony in 2017 before Parliament's inquiry into public enterprises, Dames recalled receiving a call from Mahlangu that had made him irate. Mahlangu told Dames he wanted him 'to meet with some people', without elaborating.

In Dames's telling, a few days later he found himself at the headquarters of Sahara Computers in Midrand. Mahlangu introduced him to one of the Gupta brothers, who told him: 'We've decided we can work with you.'

Dames said there were three items on the agenda. The Gupta brother asked Dames to arrange a coal contract at Lethabo power station near Sasolburg in the Free State; he wanted Eskom to build a new mega power station that the Guptas would be able to supply with coal; and he wanted the utility to sign a contract to buy thousands of copies of the *The New Age*. There were several problems with these proposals: Lethabo had a secure coal supply contract; Eskom had already started building Medupi and Kusile and wouldn't need another mega plant for decades to come; and buying newspapers was hardly a job for the Eskom chief executive. 'After this meeting I was very angry,' Dames said. 'I actually called Mr Mahlangu and said to him: "You will not bring these people to me again."'[14]

Dames did refer the Guptas' *New Age* proposal to Eskom's media procurement team. The Gupta proposal included a request for Eskom to sponsor the newspaper's so-called business breakfasts. These events would later provide a win-win scenario for all the looters involved. The Gupta-owned newspaper raked in tens of millions in sponsorships from state entities and sold table tickets to government officials and business leaders at R800 a head. Parastatal bosses, cabinet ministers and Zuma were guaranteed plenty of airtime to promote themselves during the forty-five minute monthly events, which were broadcast for free on the SABC – something that should have cost *The New Age* about R800 000.

On top of this, government departments took out lavish front-page advertisements in *The New Age* to publicise the events. It was a licence to print money, and Dames knew it.

'Follow the normal governance rules and be consistent,' he told his media procurement team. They soon came back with the answer: 'This is not wanted. What do we do?' Dames instructed them to 'close the mandate'.

It was a small but significant victory for Dames in his efforts to stop the president's benefactors from looting the power utility. However, stopping the president from getting his way when it came to the Koeberg generators wouldn't be so easy.

* * *

By the end of 2010, Eskom's executive procurement committee had evaluated bids for the generators and concluded that the bulk of the work should go to Westinghouse, a Japanese-owned, US-based nuclear company. Westinghouse had done the original design for the type of reactor built under licence at Koeberg by French nuclear company Framatome, predecessor of Areva.[15]

In January 2011, the Eskom board approved the procurement committee's recommendation. But two months later, in March 2011, President Zuma went on an official visit to France. During the visit, he signed a co-operation agreement with Areva.

By then, Eskom had already informed Westinghouse that it had won the lion's share of the work. In April 2011, with the Westinghouse team in South Africa to sign the contracts, Gigaba convened an urgent board meeting to cancel the tender. The Westinghouse team went home empty-handed and Eskom was left red-faced.

Since Gigaba's appointment as minister in November 2010, the Eskom board had sought several meetings with him but had been rebuffed because of his unhappiness with its handling of the Koeberg tender. In June 2011, Gigaba orchestrated the biggest shake-up at Eskom in a decade. In one fell swoop, and without informing them beforehand, he announced that he'd sacked eight out of ten non-executive directors at the power utility.[16]

The man Gigaba chose to head Eskom's board would later become mired in controversy. Zola Tsotsi was an obscure mid-level Eskom engineer who'd gone off to head Lesotho's electricity authority for a while. He soon irritated Dames by appointing two Eskom staffers to work in his office when the norm was for the chairperson and chief executive to share an assistant.

Although Tsotsi enjoyed a close relationship with Gigaba, he raised hackles among executives for engaging directly with Eskom suppliers and spending time at Megawatt Park, the sprawling Eskom headquarters in Johannesburg, running his own companies that did business with Eskom. When Tsotsi was appointed, he was a director of a company called RPP Pipe Supports & Bellows, which had active contracts with Eskom. He was also a director of Torre Technologies, an empowerment company with a stake in Steinmüller Africa, an engineering firm that won contracts to supply boiler parts to Kusile and Medupi. Tsotsi told the *Financial Mail* at the time that he planned to resign from the RPP but would remain a director of Torre and would simply 'declare that situation'.[17]

It turned out that Tsotsi's greatest attribute was his willingness to take orders from the president.

Tsotsi was joined on Gigaba's new board by then Transnet chairperson Mafika Mkwanazi, who later admitted to having had exploratory talks about doing business with the Guptas, and Chwayita Mabude, whose name was on a list of people the Guptas wanted on the board of Airports Company South Africa (she was subsequently appointed).[18]

Gigaba's most controversial new board appointment was Collin Matjila, the former head of COSATU's investment arm Kopano Ke Matla. The Financial Services Board previously implicated Matjila in the financial mismanagement of COSATU's pension fund. He was also accused of losing the trade federation millions in suspect property deals, including one involving Gupta lieutenant Salim Essa, although Matjila claimed he did not benefit personally from the transactions.[19]

Like Iqbal Sharma at Transnet, Matjila was put in the critical post of chairperson of the board tender committee, where he began meddling in multibillion-rand contracts, including for the Koeberg steam generators.

After Gigaba had thrown a spanner in the works in April 2011 by canning the Westinghouse deal, the Koeberg tender was reissued in June 2012, with bids to be submitted four months later in October. By December 2012, only Westinghouse and Areva remained on the shortlist. After evaluating their bids, a committee of technical experts at Eskom came to exactly the same conclusion reached over a year earlier: Westinghouse should be awarded most of the work. The technical committee passed its findings on to the executive procurement committee, which in January

2013 made the same recommendation to the board tender committee, at which point it landed on Matjila's desk.

Matjila immediately set about undermining the technical experts' work. Ignoring corporate governance rules that prohibit board members from interfering in operational matters, especially the hiring of contractors, Matjila appointed Swiss company AF Consult to run a parallel process to evaluate the bids. The Swiss advisors reported directly to the board. Eskom executives tasked with making recommendations on the tender weren't even invited to the briefings. This ratcheted up tensions and mistrust between the Eskom board and the utility's top executives.[20]

Court proceedings would later show that, in its report submitted to the Eskom board in July 2013, the Swiss consultants recommended that 'strategic considerations' that weren't part of the original bid specifications – such as a plan for local skills development in building nuclear plants – should be used to decide who won the contract.

In Dames's telling, Matjila took the report straight to the Eskom chief executive and confronted him. 'We've told the team we are not gonna talk to them any more, we're gonna talk to you as the chief exec,' he told him. 'Here's the independent report, we would like you to change a recommendation of the tender.'

Dames was unfazed. 'Not a problem,' he said. 'Give it to me. I'll deal with it.'[21]

Dames asked the Koeberg technical experts and legal team to check each and every recommendation in AF Consult's report. They reached the same conclusion as before: the original process and decision that recommended Westinghouse was sound. He submitted these findings to Matjila and Tsotsi.

A few weeks later, an angry Matjila marched into Dames's office, handed him a handwritten note, and left. Dames stared at it in disbelief. It was an instruction to change the process of awarding a R5-billion nuclear tender, scribbled on a scrap of paper. 'I can remember it clearly; it was a white piece of paper with I think blue writing,' he told Parliament later. 'I was amazed.' In his twenty-six years at Eskom, he'd never seen anything like it.[22]

After Dames composed himself, he wrote a formal letter to Matjila. 'I disagree with your process,' he said. 'If this is an instruction of the board tender committee, I'll ask the team and the head of generation to meet with you and you can tell him what it is that you'd like.' He left it at that.

On 3 December 2013, Eskom asked the nuclear vendors to submit new bids. Ten days later, Matjila's board tender committee went on a four-day junket to France, hosted by power utility Électricité de France, which enjoys close ties to Areva. One committee member, Neo Lesela, posted pictures on social media of the truffles, pastries and tarts she was indulging in at the Hôtel de la Marine in Normandy, where the party was staying. 'I think I've died and gone to heaven,' she enthused.[23]

* * *

The cavalier way in which Gigaba's board and advisors rode roughshod over corporate governance rules eventually made it unbearable for Dames and some of his best executives to stay on at Eskom. The utility's highly rated finance director Paul O'Flaherty, who together with Dames was credited with bringing financial stability to the company at a time of crisis, was the first to go. In November 2012, he announced that he would leave after the annual general meeting in July 2013. Dames decided his time was up too, handing in his resignation in February 2013. 'It became very difficult to vouch for the governance of Eskom,' he explained. 'I think Paul and I got to the same conclusion at the same time.'[24]

At first, Tsotsi wouldn't accept Dames's resignation, but he later changed his mind when Dames presented him with a list of demands aimed at improving governance at Eskom. In the end, Dames was persuaded to stay on until the end of March 2014 to give the appearance of an orderly leadership transition.

Behind the scenes, the Guptas were plotting to plant their man at the helm. On 22 March 2014, with a week to go before Dames vacated his post, Salim Essa emailed Collin Matjila's CV to Tony Gupta and Tony's then twenty-year-old nephew Srikant Singhala. From there it was forwarded to Duduzane Zuma. Ten days later, Matjila became the acting chief executive of Eskom. Dames had been the last line of defence against the looters; with him gone there was nothing stopping them.[25]

8

Making Hay

Public enterprises minister Malusi Gigaba's crew didn't wait long for Eskom's new finance director, Tsholofelo Molefe, to settle in before making their move.

Molefe took over in January 2014 from Caroline Henry, who'd filled in as Eskom's acting finance director since Paul O'Flaherty's resignation six months earlier. Barely a fortnight after Molefe's promotion, she received a call from Gigaba's chief of staff, Thamsanqa Msomi.

In Molefe's telling, Msomi explained that Gigaba's ministry had received complaints that Eskom 'wasn't transforming from a procurement perspective'. He hoped that she, as a black finance director, would understand the need to accelerate the implementation of Eskom's 'transformational objectives'.

Eskom spent R140 billion a year on anything from laundry services to buying coal. It would be completely unjust, let alone contrary to government policy, for a parastatal such as Eskom to spend most of this money on white-owned companies.

'That's always been the strategy of the board,' Molefe said. 'We will obviously drive transformation in the company. This has been the case for a while.'

Msomi wasn't so easily placated.

'Black suppliers are complaining that Eskom isn't providing them with contracts,' he persisted. 'They would like to meet and lay their complaints.'

Molefe tried to explain that the issue should be taken up with the procurement division, which she no longer headed, but that she was willing to meet with the suppliers to explain the correct channels to follow.

'I'll make the arrangements,' Msomi told her. Soon afterwards, he brought 'the supplier' to meet her. It was Salim Essa.

Then things got weird. When Molefe asked Essa who he worked for, he refused to say.

'I work with various black-owned companies who complained,' he said. He explained that her predecessors 'always went for white companies'. He told her that he also worked with McKinsey. 'We get results,' he said.

After the fifteen-minute 'introductory meeting' with Essa to outline 'the challenges' of working with Molefe's predecessors, Msomi asked her several times for a follow-up meeting, but she refused. Instead, Molefe asked Eskom chairperson Zola Tsotsi to tell Msomi to stop harassing her.[1]

The Gupta leaks later revealed that when Msomi moved with Gigaba to the Department of Home Affairs in 2014, he worked as a fixer for the Guptas, personally helping them fast-track visas for workers and business associates from India.

* * *

Tsholofelo Molefe's most pressing task after taking over as finance director was to present Eskom's new financial plan at the utility's next board strategy session, after which it would go to the minister of public enterprises for approval.

At issue was how Eskom could survive financially without being allowed to charge 'cost-reflective' tariffs while servicing debts of over R300 billion for its new build programme. In 2013, the National Energy Regulator, the government body that sets electricity prices, said Eskom could only increase tariffs at 8 per cent a year until 2018, which was half of what it had asked for. Top of Molefe's agenda at the board strategy session would be a request for more government support, followed by plans for cutting costs and reducing maintenance backlogs on Eskom's ageing power station fleet to improve generation performance.

Molefe presented her plan to the board chaired by Zola Tsotsi in April 2014, shortly after Gupta deployee Collin Matjila replaced Brian Dames as interim chief executive.

In Molefe's account to the parliamentary inquiry, the board wasn't impressed with the plan. Tsotsi said it wasn't 'robust enough' to get Eskom out of trouble and would need to be beefed up before it was presented to the minister. Whether Tsotsi and Matjila were colluding in this is hard to prove. But the fact is the chairperson's stance gave the interim chief executive just the gap he needed.

'What Eskom needs is the right advice,' he declared. 'I know some people who can help.'[2]

The company Matjila had in mind had done some balance-sheet optimisation work for Transnet and SAA. He offered to arrange a meeting that weekend in order to report to the chairperson on Monday.

Molefe thought it odd that Matjila insisted on having the meeting on a Sunday. Alarm bells started ringing when Essa, the mystery man whom Gigaba's chief of staff had introduced her to three months earlier, walked through the door. This time Essa came clean. The company he was punting, for a 50 per cent cut in the proceeds, was called Regiments Capital.

Molefe was hardly a new kid on the block. A qualified chartered accountant, she'd started her articles with Coopers & Lybrand before completing a bachelor's degree in accounting and finance in the UK. After that, she'd worked in internal auditing and risk management at IBM, Liberty, Absa and FNB before joining Eskom as a finance manager in 2005. During a decade at the utility, she'd worked closely with several financial advisory firms, but she'd never heard of Regiments. She left the meeting with a distinct sense of disquiet.

Molefe told Parliament that Essa arranged a meeting at Eskom for the next day with Regiments director Eric Wood. In attendance were Molefe, Matjila and renewable energy division head Steve Lennon, an Eskom stalwart who'd joined the utility in 1983 and would quit amid the increasing chaos six months later.

Wood was asked if Regiments had the capacity to provide financial advice to a company as large as Eskom. His reply was the same as Essa's, when Molefe had first met with him and Gigaba's chief of staff: 'We don't normally work alone,' he said. 'With most of our contracts we partner with McKinsey.'

The meeting ended with Matjila asking Wood to draw up a proposal for the services Regiments could offer Eskom.

Molefe and Lennon left the meeting feeling decidedly queasy. During a huddled discussion, they decided that if the board and the minister insisted that Eskom obtain external financial advisors, then the job, which would attract lucrative fees, should be put out to tender. Molefe went to Matjila's office to convey the message.

'There are other financial services companies that have been lining up for work at Eskom,' she told him. 'We would have to follow a very fair and transparent process.'

But Matjila would have none of it – Eskom was facing a financial crisis; this was an emergency and there wasn't any time to waste by going through the laborious process of testing the market. He insisted that the job should go to Regiments, brushing aside her objections that Eskom would be breaking Treasury rules on procurement.

'If you're not comfortable signing an agreement with Regiments, I'll do it myself,' he said.

A fortnight later, Regiments sent Molefe a draft agreement containing a range of proposals. One of them advised selling Eskom's non-core real estate. Another was to monetise the parastatal's coal contracts, for which Regiments wanted a fee of R500 million.

Matjila tried several times to bully Molefe into signing the Regiments agreement but she refused, outlining her reasons in a memo to the Eskom board. She explained that the contract had not followed due process and offered no clear financial value to Eskom.[3]

Instead of backing her, Zola Tsotsi accused Molefe of 'wasting time with long-winded procurement processes'.[4]

In the end, the board did not approve the deal, but it asked Molefe's team to conduct a desktop analysis of the ten to fifteen proposals Regiments had sent to Eskom. The team concluded that they were either not viable or were already being implemented. Eskom had no need to hire Regiments.

That's where the matter supposedly ended. But just over a year later, when Brian Molefe took over at Eskom, Regiments would be reborn as Trillian and the proposals would be resurrected.

* * *

The next item on Collin Matjila's to-do list was bulldozing through a contract with Gupta media outlet *The New Age* that his predecessor, Brian Dames, had successfully blocked.

The Guptas wanted Eskom to sign a one-year contract to sponsor their so-called business breakfasts at R1.2 million per monthly event. Matjila instructed Eskom's legal, corporate affairs and enterprise development divisions to make it happen. Enterprise development head Erica Johnson was tasked with drawing up a business case to justify blowing virtually the entire sponsorship budget on one event a month. The rationale for doing so was ostensibly because the breakfasts would allow Eskom 'to engage key decision-makers and opinion-shapers and shift the understanding around Eskom's long-term sustainability'.[5]

But as Matjila's first month at the helm of Eskom wore on, he changed the contract length from one year to three years, with the cost going up to R43 million. Presumably aware that the contract would be revoked once he was replaced by a permanent chief executive, he also demanded that an exit clause be removed from the document. This meant that his successor would be legally bound to honour the Gupta contract whether he or she liked it or not.

At this point, Johnson and the legal and corporate affairs divisions objected. Because of the contract's three-year duration, it legally required the finance director's signature. Tsholofelo Molefe refused to sign, but Matjila simply batted away any suggestion that the deal should go through the regular channels. On 30 April 2014 he committed Eskom to a three-year contract with the Guptas worth R43 million. To sweeten the deal, he threw in a three-year subscription of 4000 copies a day of *The New Age* newspaper for another R4 million.[6]

Eskom's auditors later picked up the R43-million contract as a reportable irregularity because Matjila wasn't authorised to sign it. But by then he was long gone; no action could be taken against him and the Guptas had already got the money.

* * *

One of Collin Matjila's last acts during his six-month stint in 2014 as interim chief executive at Eskom was to stitch up the Koeberg tender.

You may recall that Matjila, as head of the board tender committee, had engaged in a running battle with then chief executive Brian Dames over who should be awarded the R5-billion contract to supply Koeberg with new steam generators. Over a period of four years, a team of technical experts had repeatedly recommended Westinghouse. But ever since Jacob Zuma visited France in 2011 and signed a cooperation agreement with Areva, Matjila had stubbornly favoured the French company.

With the 2018 deadline looming, the procurement team was getting anxious at the endless delays. They had spent the past year regularly placing the Koeberg deal on the board tender committee's agenda but were never invited to present their findings, which consistently favoured Westinghouse. Instead, the board members held secretive discussions about the deal among themselves.

In January 2014, Areva and Westinghouse submitted new bids and the technical team again recommended Westinghouse, which was accepted by the executive procurement committee. Once again the recommendation went nowhere.

By the time Dames left Eskom in March 2014, the issue had still not been resolved. But within a month of taking the helm, Matjila sprang into action.

Court documents in subsequent litigation launched by Westinghouse reveal that in May 2014 Matjila appointed a new parallel subcommittee, which reintroduced the 'strategic considerations' brought up by AF Consult in 2013 that would end up becoming the deciding factor.

Final offers were submitted in July 2014, with Westinghouse being rated the top bidder again. This recommendation was sent to the board tender committee, which Matjila had previously headed. Now that he'd been seconded to head the executive, he was replaced by Neo Lesela who, just months earlier, had been gushing about the truffles she ate at the Hôtel de la Marine in Normandy during a junket arranged by the French power utility close to Areva. Lesela's committee rejected the recommendation.

Matjila then roped in a new ally. On 4 August 2014, he and Matshela Koko, the head of Eskom's technology and commercial division, prepared a revised recommendation that said the contract should go to Areva.

Eskom's head of generation, Thava Govender, refused to sign this submission because he saw no basis for changing the recommendation. A special procurement committee meeting held two days later raised further concerns about Areva because it used a subcontractor that had only worked in China, and projected costs might therefore be higher than initially stated. For the umpteenth time, the procurement committee recommended to the board that the contract should go to Westinghouse.

None of these objections made any difference. On 12 August 2014, the board awarded the tender to Areva. In a letter from Lesela and Tsotsi to newly appointed public enterprises minister Lynne Brown, they admitted Westinghouse's bid was R140 million cheaper but said that Eskom had been swung in favour of Areva by 'strategic considerations' not in the original bid criteria. Most notably, Areva had offered to 'study the feasibility' of manufacturing nuclear valves in South Africa and thereby promote local industrialisation and job creation.

The court didn't buy this argument, concluding that the board's reliance on criteria not specified in the tender without giving the companies the chance to amend their bids was unlawful. In the end, though, the Constitutional Court ruled in favour of Areva on procedural grounds.

The looters had won again.

9

Turn Off the Lights

When Tshediso Matona arrived at Eskom, he walked straight into a shitstorm.

It was October 2014. He'd been seconded from the Department of Public Enterprises, where he'd served as the director-general for three years. He found a company in disarray, just as it was about to enter the worst load-shedding crisis since the summer of 2008.

For the past six months, acting chief executive Collin Matjila had reaped a whirlwind of chaos – he'd dished out irregular media contracts to the Guptas, bullied the procurement team to disregard expert advice on a nuclear tender and tried to sneak in a Gupta-linked company through the back door to earn billions in consulting fees. Board members and executives were at each other's throats. Matona's job was to fix the mess.

One of the first things he was asked to do was find Matjila another job at Eskom so that he could stay on at the parastatal. Matona refused Matjila's request, making an instant enemy of a man who was rumoured to be a member of the president's inner circle.[1] This was just the beginning – Matona's enemies were about to multiply.

Chairperson Zola Tsotsi was running Eskom like an operational manager rather than a non-executive chair. He wrote letters to Japanese supplier Sumitomo committing Eskom to make payments to the company, asked energy minister Tina Joemat-Pettersson to authorise Eskom to negotiate power deals with three private companies (including for a floating power plant) and allegedly started putting pressure on officials to buy coal from Gupta mines that didn't have water licences or environmental approvals, although he denies this.[2]

One of these was Vierfontein colliery, near the town of Ogies in

Mpumalanga, owned by Gupta mining company Tegeta. The Guptas had been pressuring Eskom without success since 2012 to sign a coal supply deal with Vierfontein worth R500 million a year, even though they were mining there illegally without a water-use licence or environmental approvals. In mid-2014, shortly after Eskom officials had rejected the contract again, Tsotsi called a staff meeting berating them for 'failing to speed up procurement transformation'. The officials deemed it highly irregular for the chairman to address them directly. They believed they were being asked to approve the Vierfontein deal, which was the only contract of those being assessed at the time that was rejected. In the end the deal did not go through.[3]

When I asked Tsotsi about this incident, he denied he'd been trying to bully the Eskom officials into approving the Gupta deal. 'I admonished them for dragging their feet on the part of black junior miners – it had nothing to do with the Guptas.'

Ironically, although Eskom was insisting that its coal suppliers were 51 per cent black owned, the Gupta mines rarely had more than 30 per cent black ownership and most of these shares were usually held by Duduzane Zuma and Salim Essa.

Another mine that had tried without success to supply Eskom with coal since the Guptas bought it in 2011 was Brakfontein, near Delmas in Mpumalanga. Eskom managers had repeatedly rejected signing a contract with Brakfontein because it produced poor-quality coal, didn't have a water licence and flouted environmental laws. For a long time, the Saxonwold family's efforts to secure the deal fell on deaf ears. But leadership upheavals at Eskom would soon favour the Guptas and set them on the road to becoming major players in a coal market worth R50 billion a year.

First, however, disaster struck at Eskom. On 1 November 2014, exactly a month after Matona arrived at the parastatal, a coal storage tower collapsed at Majuba power station, near Volksrust on the border between KwaZulu-Natal and Mpumalanga. The silo held 10 000 tons of coal and supplied all six units of the power station, which generates about 10 per cent of South Africa's electricity. The 'catastrophic failure' forced Eskom to initiate rolling blackouts the next day.[4]

For the next ten months, South Africa was subjected to regular load shedding, recording ninety-nine days of power cuts in the first seven months of 2015. Once again, the economy was hit hard. Mining, agriculture and manufacturing all declined, and GDP contracted by 1.3 per cent. This was described by one economist as the equivalent of losing one major industry. The loss to the economy in one year was estimated at R170 billion.[5]

Rain-soaked coal stockpiles and the collapse of the coal silo were clearly catalysts for load shedding rather than its underlying cause. The real fault lay with a ten-year delay in building Medupi and Kusile, maintenance on Eskom's ageing coal-powered fleet being postponed for the 2010 FIFA World Cup and 2011 local government elections, and corrupt or badly managed coal contracts.

But with disaster came fresh opportunity.

* * *

Eskom's diesel- and gas-powered plants in the Cape were designed to be used for a few hours a day during peak consumption when its fleet of old coal-fired plants couldn't meet demand. The power crisis in 2014 forced the utility to run them for up to twelve hours a day. Diesel costs shot up to over R1 billion a month.

This suited some Eskom officials. When international law firm Dentons was hired in 2015 to investigate the root causes of Eskom's energy and financial crisis, it found anecdotal evidence that employees had used family members to set up companies fronted by friends or relatives to be awarded diesel contracts.

Investigators identified several red flags. Companies with no track record in the fuel supply industry had been set up solely to benefit from the new diesel contracts, amounts invoiced exceeded purchase orders, and the same companies provided different bank accounts for different invoices. Some companies used remarkably similar invoice templates and the same turns of phrase on their websites, suggesting they were different iterations of the same compromised players.

Investigators estimated that Eskom lost R200 million in two years from these contracts by failing to use its purchasing power to negotiate discounts.[6]

Abuses in Eskom's coal division, with a R50-billion annual budget, were even worse. The Dentons report described it as a 'black hole': there was no transparency on how contracts were awarded, price negotiations were kept secret, and most short- and medium-term contracts were not put out to public tender.

Ted Blom, a coal analyst and former Eskom employee, dates rampant corruption in the coal unit to 2001, when a colliery dedicated to supplying Majuba power station closed because of geological problems. This forced Eskom to buy coal on the open market and transport it by truck or rail to the plant on an emergency basis with no public tender.

'Eskom didn't have proof of delivery mechanisms, didn't have weighbridges, didn't have labs to assess the stuff,' Blom told Parliament. 'They immediately started buying stuff from the open market with no control mechanisms in place, without even written documents. A lot of the stuff was just done verbally and that opened up the space for corruption.'

Blom said that with the collusion of its own officials, Eskom ended up paying tens of millions of rands for 'fictitious coal purchases as well as fictitious transport arrangements'.[7]

He went as far as suggesting that the 2008 and 2014 energy crises were engineered 'to keep the gravy train running' at Eskom. 'With hindsight, it becomes clear that this crisis was also fabricated to open up coal supply agreements for Gupta suppliers,' he concluded in a report submitted to Parliament on behalf of the Organisation Undoing Tax Abuse (OUTA).[8]

Although no hard evidence of an orchestrated conspiracy exists, the power crises did provide a handy justification for emergency coal contracts that didn't need to go out to tender. In the decade after the Majuba colliery was shut down in 2001, and especially after the 2008 load-shedding crisis, there was a dramatic rise in the use of short- and medium-term contracts. These increasingly replaced the long-term contracts Eskom had signed with mines in the 1970s and 1980s that generally ran for forty years.

Long-term contracts are either fixed-price or 'cost-plus' agreements. With the former, Eskom and the mine agree on a fixed price and annual escalation, with the mine allowed to export surplus coal. With cost-plus mines, Eskom and the mining company share the initial outlay costs but Eskom is responsible for providing the capital to keep the mine going. The price Eskom pays for coal is based on the cost of running the mine plus a management fee and an agreed return on the capital that the mining company originally invested in the mine. The advantage for Eskom is that it is entitled to all the coal produced by the mine, guaranteeing security of supply. Cost-plus mines also produce the cheapest coal.[9]

Short- and medium-term contracts hold the advantage of allowing black miners to gain a foothold in the lucrative coal supply game dominated by a handful of traditionally white-owned mining giants. The disadvantage is that these contracts are much more expensive, mostly because of high road-transport costs. They also result in thousands of coal trucks clogging up the Mpumalanga roads, posing a major safety hazard.[10]

Because most of the deals were made on an emergency basis without going out to tender, opportunities for corruption multiplied. It later became apparent that in many cases emergencies were manufactured to ensure that lucrative coal deals could go to politically connected companies, including those belonging to the Guptas, often in return for kickbacks or other gratifications.

The lurid picture Blom painted of graft at Eskom's coal unit is supported to some extent by Dentons' 2015 investigation. Despite the time allocated for its investigation having been cut drastically short on the instruction of public enterprises minister Lynne Brown, Dentons found evidence of rampant corruption, especially in the coal supply chain. Its report details coal vendors signed up under loose arrangements, a lack of checks and balances to identify fraudulent documentation, and fuel-sourcing managers granted unchecked negotiating powers, thus encouraging kickbacks for contracts. In some cases, Eskom signed contracts with vendors who didn't have an agreement with a coal mine; the terms of coal deals sometimes changed from offer letter to final contract; and large coal contracts were arbitrarily awarded, amended or cancelled without board approval. When Eskom's legal division did actually review contracts, their advice was routinely ignored or fraudulently misrepresented to the board.[11]

Dentons found that the same pattern was repeated with lucrative transport contracts, which were arbitrarily awarded to favoured suppliers without going out to tender, often at fraudulently inflated prices. Eskom officials cashed in on the spoils. The report cited examples of 'senior executives seeking opportunities ostensibly for the benefit of themselves at the expense of Eskom' by 'making deals with suppliers outside of the formal procurement process and/or turning a blind eye to expensive contract breaches'.[12]

A former executive at Eskom told me he suspected some of his managers were taking kickbacks from coal suppliers to negotiate favourable deals. The rot spread throughout the chain of command. Eskom officials at power stations would be bribed to falsify slips after weighbridges mysteriously broke down during night deliveries, while stockpile attendants were bribed to not give the game away. Some vendors bribed Eskom lab technicians to falsify test results when they delivered poor-quality coal. This meant that Eskom was paying a premium for substandard coal that damaged its boilers.

Both the Dentons report and Eskom executives I've spoken to said these tricks proliferated at Medupi and Kusile thanks to inexperienced contract managers and a lack of integrated upfront planning. Widespread looting became a major contributor – together with labour unrest, poor performance by boiler and turbine suppliers, and ratings downgrades – to projected costs ballooning from R150 billion when construction began to what will amount to more than R300 billion by the time both plants are fully operational.

Everyone seemed to be enjoying the party – everyone, that is, except South African taxpayers.

* * *

In October 2014, the government announced an extensive bailout package for Eskom.

Treasury would sell off state assets, which turned out to be its stake in Vodacom, to provide the utility with a R23-billion cash injection. This was followed a few months later by a write-off of R60 billion loaned to Eskom during the height of the 2008 energy crisis. Taxpayers would effectively foot the bill for Eskom's R83-billion bailout.

Eskom management tried to justify the need for the bailout by explaining that the utility wasn't allowed to charge 'cost-reflective tariffs'. It used the same argument to ask for a 16 to 25 per cent annual price increase. (In 2013, the energy regulator granted it an annual increase of just 8 per cent for the next three years.)[13]

The Dentons report poured cold water on this argument. It pointed out that Eskom had itself to blame for its financial woes. The utility was paying far more than it should for coal and diesel, its decision not to invest in 'cost-plus' mines and to rely increasingly on expensive short-term contracts was 'sub-optimal', and little had been done to contain spiralling costs at Medupi and Kusile.

'If management's energies are centred on leveraging Eskom's considerable buying power for self-interest, rather than to drive efficiencies, the notion that the tariff is not cost-reflective loses all credibility,' the report remarked dryly.

In effect, the money that taxpayers were being asked to pour into Eskom's coffers was being looted out the back door.

But things were about to get worse.

10

Tsotsi in the Boardroom

On 10 December 2014, cabinet held a meeting that would greatly accelerate the Gupta project to take control of Eskom.

Topping the agenda was the electricity crisis, which the government said was caused by Eskom providing electricity to twelve million new homes without building any new power stations. There was no mention of how corruption was bleeding the utility dry and hobbling efforts to fix the problem.

In a statement issued the following day, cabinet outlined its plan to tackle the crisis. It included the launch of a programme for coal-fired power to be supplied to Eskom by private companies, improving maintenance on Eskom's ageing fleet of power stations to reduce unplanned outages, stabilising the utility's finances, and converting its emergency diesel-powered generators to run on cheaper gas.[1]

Cabinet also reaffirmed government's commitment to renewable energy, which had attracted R140 billion from private investors since 2011 and would soon generate more power than Medupi or Kusile.[2]

A 'war room' of technical experts and government and Eskom officials led by then deputy president Cyril Ramaphosa was set up to implement the plan.

The cabinet announcement ushered in sweeping changes to the Eskom board. New public enterprises minister Lynne Brown appointed nine new board members, five of whom – Ben Ngubane, Nazia Carrim, Romeo Kumalo, Viroshini Naidoo and Mark Pamensky – to a greater or lesser extent had ties to the Guptas or their business associates.

Ngubane's first allegiance was to the president. Their relationship dates to their peacekeeping efforts in KwaZulu-Natal in the 1990s, when Ngubane was a moderate Inkatha Freedom Party premier and Zuma the provincial ANC leader. After a stint as ambassador to Japan, Ngubane crossed the floor to join the ANC in 2006. When Zuma became president in 2009, he deployed Ngubane to various parastatal boards, starting with the SABC in December 2009 and the Land Bank the following year. Ray Hartley, a former editor of the *Sunday Times*, called Ngubane 'Zuma's corporate hatchet man'. Zuma had sent Ngubane to state enterprises to realign them 'with the larger project, which we now know was the capture of these entities by the Zuma family and their business allies', said Hartley.[3]

The Gupta leaks later revealed that Ngubane was involved in a failed 2013 oil deal in the Central African Republic with Gupta lieutenant Salim Essa. Ngubane and Essa's company, Gade Oil and Gas, tried to secure exploration rights to a lucrative oil concession from the Seleka rebel regime four months after its forces had killed fifteen South African soldiers.[4]

Polokwane lawyer Nazia Carrim is married to Essa's cousin Muhammed Noor Hussain. Public Protector Thuli Madonsela flagged the connection in her report on state capture. Madonsela pointed out that Carrim had attended board meetings at which decisions were taken that helped the Gupta-owned company Tegeta buy Optimum coal mine. Essa held a stake in Tegeta.[5]

When I asked Carrim about this after Madonsela released her report in October 2016, she said she had 'no idea' that Essa part-owned Tegeta and that she and her husband hardly spent any time with him. 'The last time I saw him was two years ago,' she said. That he had benefited from board decisions she was party to was, in her words, 'a coincidence'.

Her husband, Hussain, said he was 'shocked' to hear that he'd been linked to the Guptas. 'Me and Salim, we hardly talk,' he said. 'We meet Salim maybe twice a year at Eid or something. We're not in business together. We're not in cahoots.'

Romeo Kumalo and Essa were co-directors of a company called Ujiri Technologies. Kumalo pointed out that the company never traded and has no links to the Guptas, but his proximity to Essa raised a red flag for Madonsela.

Another new director, Viroshini Naidoo, was linked to Essa and the Gupta business network through her husband Kuben Moodley. He was the business broker who, according to court filings and whistleblower documents and testimony, had been paid a 5 per cent 'finder's fee' for bringing his golfing partner Essa to financial advisory firm Regiments. That introduction by all accounts resulted in Regiments and its offshoot Trillian winning lucrative consultancy work from Transnet and Eskom. Documentary evidence exists that Moodley's company, Albatime, contributed to the purchase price of Optimum, although he continues to deny that it did. Moodley also served as an advisor to mining minister Mosebenzi Zwane, who played a direct role in negotiating the sale of the mine to the Guptas.

Perhaps the most compromised member of the new Eskom board was Mark Pamensky, who'd joined Gupta company Oakbay Resources and Energy three months earlier. His intricate entanglement with the Gupta business empire while heading Eskom's investment and finance committee was laid bare when emails between him and Atul Gupta were retrieved from the server of Gupta-linked Sahara Computers and leaked to the media.

Questions were also raised about the suitability of the skill sets of the new board members. Brown had appointed four chartered accountants, including Pamensky, but only one electrical engineer – Pat Naidoo – to the governing body of Africa's largest power utility.

The only two directors to survive the purge (for now) were Chwayita Mabude, who had previously been deployed by the Guptas to the board of Airports Company South Africa, and Zuma's man at Eskom, Zola Tsotsi.

* * *

If Zola Tsotsi hadn't figured out by then why he'd been deployed to Eskom, he was about to find out.

In Parliament Tsotsi testified that a few days after the cabinet announcement, he received an email from Salim Essa. It contained a list of people the Guptas wanted on the board's subcommittee, including the chairperson. These subcommittees would grant final approval for large coal, infrastructure and consulting contracts worth billions. It was a crucial step in taking control of the parastatal.

Essa told Tsotsi to forward the list to Lynne Brown as though it had come from Tsotsi.

If this is indeed what Essa did, it was an audacious play for a private businessman to dictate to the chairperson of Eskom whom he should recommend to the minister to sit on his subcommittees. Tsotsi told Parliament he 'changed the list based on what I thought it should be' before sending it to Brown, but when she sent it back 'it had been changed to what it was when I got it from Essa'.

Tsotsi recalls that when he refused to rubber-stamp Essa's list, Brown asked him to meet her at her official residence at Bryntirion Estate in Pretoria.

Bryntirion is a 107-hectare residential precinct near the Union Buildings with ministerial mansions dotted around expansive lawns, a nine-hole golf course, fifteen tennis courts and a landscaped rotunda. A terraced garden leads to the president's official residence, Mahlamba Ndlopfu, built on the highest point of the estate.

In Tsotsi's telling, when he arrived at Brown's residence, the minister was engrossed in conversation with Tony Gupta and Essa. 'We've been discussing the list of board members,' Essa told Tsotsi, handing him a sheaf of papers. 'This is what we came up with.'

Tsotsi stared at the document in disbelief. To dispel any doubts, Brown weighed in: 'This is the final list,' she told him. Tsotsi didn't stick around to argue or even sit down to join them. Barely five minutes later he was driving home.[6]

* * *

This version of events, which Zola Tsotsi relayed under oath to Parliament's inquiry into public enterprises in November 2017, was contested by Lynne Brown in her own testimony just hours later.

DA MP Natasha Mazzone got the ball rolling. 'Ms Brown, why were Salim Essa and Tony Gupta at your house when Mr Tsotsi arrived?' she asked.

'Mr Essa and Mr Gupta were not at my house when Tsotsi arrived,' she replied. 'In fact, I really deny that. Mr Tsotsi must please tell me which day it is so that I can verify it. But at this stage I do not know that Mr Essa and Gupta came to my house.'

Asked what would motivate Tsotsi to lie about the encounter, Brown said: 'I don't know. I was not here. I cannot tell why he was lying.'

Mazzone left it at that. But the EFF's Floyd Shivambu soon weighed in. 'I don't think that Mr Tsotsi ... can come and lie about your meeting at your house, with Salim Essa and Gupta. I don't think if we have to choose who to believe between you and Tsotsi, we must believe you.'

'You believe what you want to believe, Mr Shivambu,' was the minister's reply.

When I put it to Tsotsi that either he or the minister must have been lying under oath, he said he stuck by his story. I asked him why he hadn't refused to implement Essa's list. 'What was I going to say?' he shrugged. 'She's the boss, giving me instructions.'

* * *

The destruction of Eskom's top tier had a profound effect on the power utility, resulting in an exodus of employees with essential skills at the height of the country's load-shedding crisis and opening the sluice gates for billions to flow into the pockets of the Guptas and their fellow looters.

By January 2015, emboldened by their hand-picked board at Eskom and with billions in suspected kickbacks for the Transnet locomotives deal with China South Rail already starting to flow to their front companies in Dubai, the Guptas ramped up their efforts to get in on the R50-billion-a-year coal-buying action at Eskom.

First, they had to remove executives who were proving an impediment to their ambitions.

Topping their list was chief executive Tshediso Matona, who'd started talking about launching an investigation into all contracts over R10 million concluded in the past three years, and finance director Tsholofelo Molefe, who'd refused to sign off on their R43-million media sponsorship deal and prevented Eskom from appointing Regiments Capital as a financial advisor.

Having the Regiments deal fall through in 2014 must have been particularly galling for the Guptas. The financial advisory services the company was offering, which included work on coal contracts and selling off unused buildings worth R10 billion, could have earned it billions in fees. Given the apparent kickback arrangement that Regiments already had in place at Transnet, it's fair to assume that up to half this money was likely to flow directly to Gupta dealmaker Salim Essa and from him to Gupta front companies and bank accounts in Dubai and Hong Kong.

These numbers are not as far-fetched as they first appear. A year later, Trillian, the offshoot of Regiments majority owned by Essa, was having discussions with McKinsey on how to carve up R9.4 billion in fees that the firms were expecting to earn for consulting work at Eskom.

The Regiments advisory work would hold the considerable added advantage for the Gupta network of giving them an inside track on deals and opportunities at Eskom worth hundreds of billions. These would range from coal, gas and diesel contracts to sourcing finance and suppliers to refurbish or maintain power stations. As they had proved at Transnet, the Gupta-linked companies could then either secure the deals for themselves or act as gatekeepers for multinationals bidding for Eskom contracts, using their political muscle to ensure those who paid them hefty kickbacks won the contracts.

Another thorn in the Guptas' side was Eskom's head of group capital, Dan Marokane. The urbane, articulate and highly competent petrochemical engineer was seen as the natural successor to Brian Dames, the chief executive who'd repeatedly rebuffed the Saxonwold family's overtures until he finally threw in the towel in March 2014.

One Eskom executive told me that Marokane posed a threat to the looters' ambitions because he was too good at his job. 'He played an important role in dealing with the load-shedding crisis. We were just beginning to stabilise, which is what they didn't want,' the executive said. 'Then they wouldn't have an excuse to bring in Brian Molefe and the others. So Dan had to go.'

But the Guptas also knew that decimating Eskom's top decision-making tier and replacing executives who blocked their ambitions with pliant puppets wasn't going to be easy. They'd need to enlist the president's help.

* * *

Senior sources at Eskom told me that as soon as Lynne Brown's new board was appointed, things started looking up for Brakfontein, the Gupta-owned coal mine near Delmas.

Since Tegeta had bought the mine in 2011, the company had received a string of rejection slips from Eskom officials because Brakfontein didn't have a water licence, produced poor-quality coal and had been fined for contravening environmental regulations. There was also allegedly pressure from Zola Tsotsi to use Brakfontein as a supplier, but if so, even this failed to do the trick.

On 22 December 2014, less than a fortnight after cabinet announced the new Eskom board and at a time when most people were on holiday, Brakfontein 'miraculously' received its water licence, according to a senior Eskom official who was involved in the negotiations.

'Suddenly there was pressure from above to conclude this contract urgently,' the official said.

Some hard haggling followed. The Guptas initially wanted to be paid R350 a ton but Eskom was only prepared to fork out R240 for Brakfontein's low-grade coal. Minutes of a meeting on 30 January 2015 show that when Tegeta chief executive Ravindra Nath tried to justify the company's price increases by citing the need to fund new black empowerment partners and comply with environmental laws, Eskom negotiators refused to back down, informing Tegeta that if 'they are unable to review their price, Eskom would have to look at alternative suppliers'.[7]

The Eskom sources said this prompted Nath and his team to storm out of the negotiations. Heated arguments between Nath and Eskom officials were heard down the passage before he returned with a revised offer for a five-year contract worth R1 billion to supply Majuba power station with 65 000 tons a month at a compromise price of R277 a ton, which Eskom accepted. This was by no means the end of the negotiations though, as the Guptas would soon demand a higher price.

* * *

Zola Tsotsi testified in Parliament that he was summoned to another meeting with Lynne Brown in Cape Town shortly before Jacob Zuma delivered the State of the Nation Address on 12 February 2015. This time, he said, she accused him of interfering in the day-to-day running of Eskom.

'I have received complaints from management and board members,' she told him. 'Please refrain from doing so, because if you don't, I shall have to find someone else to do your job.'

The chairperson was aghast: the new board was appointed shortly before the Christmas holidays; they'd barely had the opportunity to get to know him – how could they object to his leadership style? 'Most board members hardly know what I look like,' he told her. 'As for management, if scrutinising their decisions and behaviour and calling them to account constitutes interference with management, then I will happily continue doing so. If you had acceded to my request that we have regular briefing sessions, even this meeting would not have been necessary.'

'You go and do what you have to do. I will go and do what I have to,' was Brown's curt reply. 'There is no reason for you and I to talk about anything.'

With that, the meeting ended.

Tsotsi recalls that later that afternoon he received a call from Tony Gupta asking for an urgent meeting in Cape Town. 'Chairman, you are not helping us with anything,' Tony Gupta told him. 'We are the ones who put you in the position you are in. We are the ones who can take you out!'[8]

Tsotsi told Parliament that he had received similar threats from Tony Gupta before. On one occasion, the Guptas wanted a gas contract likely to be worth billions a year to supply the converted diesel-powered emergency generators in the Cape. But by then, the energy department had already signed a memorandum of understanding with another company. 'When I discovered this, I informed them that the matter was out of the hands of Eskom as there was the MoU,' said Tsotsi. 'Mr Gupta later returned to me, complaining that we are dealing with *uBaba*'s enemies.'[9] *uBaba* was a reference to Zuma.

On another occasion in 2014, Tony Gupta asked Tsotsi to attend to the issue of Collin Matjila being investigated for irregularly signing the R43-million sponsorship deal with *The New Age*. 'He asked me why I couldn't just make this problem go away,' Tsotsi said. 'I told him the organisation has processes and these processes are being followed. That was the first time that he kind of threatened that I'm not delivering for him.'

Tsotsi said that by the time Tony Gupta threatened to have him removed as chairperson during their encounter in Cape Town in February 2015, he thought Tony Gupta 'had had enough, because I'm not assisting with anything'.[10]

Two days later, on 12 February 2015, Zuma delivered his State of the Nation Address in Cape Town, unveiling his nine-point plan 'to ignite growth and create jobs'. Solving the energy crisis was top of the list.

'The short- and medium-term plan involves improved maintenance of Eskom power stations, enhancing the electricity generation capacity and managing the electricity demand,' Zuma said. 'The long-term plan involves finalising our long-term energy security master plan' – a mix of fossil fuels, renewables and nuclear. Government's target was to connect the first nuclear plant to the grid in 2023, 'just in time for Eskom to retire part of its ageing power plants', he said.[11]

One by one the chess pieces were lining up for the Guptas. It was time to make their next move.

* * *

Eskom's next board meeting was scheduled for Thursday 26 February, two weeks after the State of the Nation Address. The night before it was due to take place, Zola Tsotsi received a flurry of phone calls. The first was from the president.

According to Tsotsi, Jacob Zuma told him that he'd been trying to reach public enterprises minister Lynne Brown and her deputy, Bulelani Magwanishe, without success. However, he had managed to get hold of acting director-general of public enterprises Matsietsi Mokholo. Ttsotsi was told that he should expect a call from Mokholo shortly. 'The board meeting will not be taking place,' Zuma told him, without offering an explanation. 'She will ask you to postpone it.'

Tsotsi recalls that Mokholo called minutes later. 'The minister asked that the board meeting be postponed,' she said.

'Why would she want to do that?' Tsotsi demanded.

'She didn't give any reasons.'

Tsotsi had his orders. He informed his fellow board members that the meeting had been called off until further notice.

Tsotsi recalls receiving another strange phone call a week later, this time from the chairperson of South African Airways, Dudu Myeni, who enjoys a close relationship with Zuma.

'You must come to Durban for a meeting with the president,' she told him.

'What's this about?'

'I can't talk about it over the phone. Just be there.'

What follows is Tsotsi's account to Parliament of what happened after he arrived at the president's official residence in Durban on Saturday, 7 March 2015. Myeni has confirmed she attended the meeting but denied meddling in Eskom's affairs.

Tsotsi recounted that when he walked in he was met by Myeni, her son Thalente Myeni and a man named Nick Linnell, who was introduced to Tsotsi as a lawyer. Linnell was a business consultant from Zimbabwe whom Myeni had hired as an advisor to the SAA board at a fee of R167 000 a month. His main job, according to a report in *City Press*, appeared to consist of cooking up cases against executives she wanted to get rid of.[12]

According to Tsotsi, while they waited for Zuma to arrive, Myeni, who had no reason to involve herself in Eskom's business, filled Tsotsi in on the reason for the meeting: Eskom's financial crisis and poor performance warranted an inquiry. For the duration of this inquiry, she told him, three Eskom executives – chief executive Tshediso Matona, head of group capital Dan Marokane, and head of technology and commercial Matshela Koko – must be suspended.

Tsotsi was taken aback. 'There's no reason to suspend these executives,' he said. 'It will only create instability.'

Myeni was adamant. 'Even the war room is frustrated with the decline in performance at Eskom,' she retorted. 'We must have an inquiry. The suspensions won't cause any difficulties because they will be told they aren't being accused of wrongdoing, they're just being asked to give the inquiry space to do its work.'

When Zuma arrived, Myeni repeated what she'd told Tsotsi. Linnell offered to draw up a resolution he could present to the board. 'You go and deal with the board,' Zuma told Tsotsi. 'I will tell the minister.'[13]

As usual, Tsotsi followed the orders he'd been given. At 8 p.m. the following night, a Sunday, Tsotsi asked the Eskom company secretary to convene an urgent board meeting for the next morning.

On 9 March 2015, Tsotsi briefed his fellow board members about his conversation with Myeni at Zuma's official residence in Durban. Then he produced the documents Myeni's Zimbabwean business consultant, Nick Linnell, had drawn up: a single-page memo with a two-page 'board resolution' attached.

The memo began with a preamble of sorts that painted a bleak picture of how Eskom was run. Load shedding was expected to last for five years, Medupi and Kusile were years behind schedule and tens of billions over budget, and Eskom had been forced to go cap in hand to Treasury for a bailout. The impact of these failings was a national economic down-turn, the flight of foreign and domestic investment, and a 'spiral effect' of increasing unemployment.

'Until this moment, the board has been entirely reliant on the execu-tive for information pertaining to these challenges,' Linnell's memo said. 'It is abundantly clear that this in itself is part of the problem. This board has no independent and objective insight into the extent that some of our failings might be caused or exacerbated by management failure. Given the abnormal risks facing the company and its obligations to the public, this board must know the facts – as unpalatable as they might be.'[14]

Those present must have seen Linnell's memo for what it was: a flimsy justification for a purge. Reducing Eskom's current crisis to the failure of managers to convey their failings to the new board was clearly absurd.

The two-page 'resolution' that followed committed the board to appoint an inquiry to establish what had caused 'the current deficiency of generating and distribution capacity at Eskom'. A subcommittee headed by Tsotsi and comprising Chwayita Mabude and Zethembe Khoza, who later approved lucrative Gupta-linked deals, would be mandated to over-see the inquiry, Linnell's resolution said.

Tsotsi told the meeting that the president wanted Matona, Marokane and Koko suspended to ensure the board received accurate information and didn't try to influence the inquiry.

The directors present rejected the resolution. They couldn't under-stand why they were being asked to make such an important decision based on a two-page memo that contained flimsy justifications. A decision was taken that if Zuma wanted them to take such a drastic step, they needed to hear it from the minister.[15]

* * *

While Eskom's newly appointed directors were receiving shock treatment in taking orders from the president at hastily convened board meetings, Eskom employee Suzanne Daniels received a call from her boss, Matshela Koko. 'Come and meet me at Melrose Arch,' he said. 'Now.'

Melrose Arch is a shopping mall and commercial and residential real estate development situated just off the M1 highway that slices through the heart of Johannesburg. The development is self-contained, with security-controlled access points, and designed to simulate the atmosphere of a London high street, complete with outdoor cafés and restaurants, plazas, upmarket boutiques, wine bars, fancy hotels, corporate office towers and apartment blocks with penthouse suites that boast sweeping views of the city. In case anyone misses the connection, the road that cuts the precinct in half is called High Street. It's a favourite hangout of political movers and shakers, corporate climbers and dealmakers, rent-seekers and information peddlers. It's also where Salim Essa's company Trillian had offices until recently, ironically in the same building as Glencore, the mining giant swindled out of its prime coal asset, Optimum, by Essa and the Guptas.

Daniels is a qualified lawyer who joined Eskom as its chief legal advisor in 2006 and later became a contracts manager in the primary energy division before landing up as Koko's de facto chief of staff in 2014.

Koko, like Brian Dames, had spent all his working life at Eskom. When evidence of corruption began to stack up against him, he defiantly asserted that he would never resign because his blood was 'Eskom blue'.[16]

He'd joined the utility's engineer-in-training programme in 1996 as a young university graduate and was posted to Duvha power station, where he rose to the level of senior boiler consultant. He was later promoted to senior manager in various engineering units before being appointed Eskom's head of technology in 2010, which made him responsible for all the utility's engineering needs. In May 2014, during Gupta acolyte Collin

Matjila's short and disastrous stint as interim chief executive, Koko had been appointed group executive in charge of the newly merged technical and commercial divisions.

The commercial division has been described as the 'glittering prize of Eskom'. Whoever heads it is in charge of Eskom's operational expenditure of R140 billion a year. This includes R50 billion spent on coal. Koko had become one of the most powerful executives in the company, wielding influence in precisely the areas in which the Guptas were most interested.[17]

What follows is Daniels' account to Parliament of her meeting with Koko, which Koko disputes. When she arrived at Melrose Arch, she recalls, Koko wasn't there. As she sipped a cup of coffee at JB's Corner on High Street, she spotted Edwin Mabelane, a senior manager in the technology division who also reported to Koko, having lunch at a restaurant opposite her. She idly wondered at the strange coincidence of two of Koko's senior officials being at Melrose Arch at the same time.

Koko eventually arrived and he and Daniels walked across Melrose Boulevard to Essa's offices. There, Koko introduced Daniels to Essa, who told them to hand their phones to his glamorous blonde receptionist and motioned them to a glass-walled boardroom.

Essa turned to Daniels. 'People at Eskom are going to be suspended,' he told her. Then he listed them: Dan Marokane, Tsholofelo Molefe, Tshediso Matona – and Matshela Koko.

Daniels turned to Koko, who didn't register any surprise.

'Why are you telling me this?' Daniels asked Essa.

He wanted to know what procedures Eskom would have to follow to suspend them.

Her head was reeling as she tried to make sense of what she'd been told. 'How on earth could this man know something like this?' she wondered. Koko remained stubbornly silent.

Daniels told Parliament that after explaining the legal procedure to Essa, she left the meeting and drove home to Pretoria, where she called Rustum Mohamed, an old friend who had previously worked closely with Mcebisi Jonas before he became deputy finance minister.

'I've just met with a guy called Salim Essa,' she said. 'Just tell me one thing: can he do what he says he can?'

'Yes, he can,' confirmed Mohamed.

Next, she called Marokane, who happened to be playing golf at the country club near her house. 'Did you know you are about to be suspended?' she asked him when he arrived.

He'd heard rumours but nothing concrete. 'I'll tell the others,' he promised.

That evening, she had an unrelated telephone conversation with an executive at the French nuclear company Areva. The next morning, Koko confronted her: 'Why are you talking to Rustum and the French?' he demanded to know.

That's when Daniels realised something really sinister was going on. These people had access to privileged information at Eskom and must have had her phone tapped. And Koko, the man whose office she ran, was in the thick of things.[18]

* * *

The next person to be summoned to Melrose Arch for an audience with Salim Essa was Abram Masango, the project director at Kusile power station who reported to Dan Marokane.

In Masango's telling, he had just finished giving a presentation at Megawatt Park and was on his way back to Kusile when Matshela Koko called.

'Meet me at Melrose Arch,' he said.

'But I'm already halfway to Kusile,' Masango protested.

'That doesn't matter. This is important. Turn around and meet me there now.'

Masango recalls that when he arrived at Melrose Boulevard, he spotted Koko standing on the balcony of an office building. There was no company signage outside. Leaving his driver in the car, he walked up the stairs to join him.

Like Suzanne Daniels, he was immediately asked to hand his cellphone over to Essa's receptionist, which made him decidedly uncomfortable. Koko ushered him into a small office and introduced him to Essa. The Eskom executive looked nervous. 'We are going to be suspended tomorrow,' he told Masango in Essa's presence.

'Suspended for what?'

Koko ignored the question. He explained that he would be suspended along with Tshediso Matona, Dan Marokane and Tsholofelo Molefe, but unlike the others he would return to his post. Then he turned to Essa. 'This man has the potential to become the acting CEO,' he told Essa of Masango.

'Abram, you are messing up Eskom on contracts management,' said Essa. 'You guys must sort out the claims with these contractors.'

Masango thought Essa had a point. Poor project management and bad planning had resulted in contractor claims against Eskom at Kusile and Medupi running into tens of billions of rands. In fact, a claims committee meeting to be chaired by Marokane had been scheduled for the following day.

With that, Masango recalls, Essa ended the meeting.

As he headed back east across the bleak maize-covered flatlands towards Kusile, a deep sense of disquiet descended on Masango. He couldn't fathom why he'd been asked to hand in his phone to attend a meeting with Essa where a bombshell about Eskom suspensions was dropped. It was all very sinister. Like Daniels, Masango began to fear for his future.[19]

* * *

While backroom manoeuvres were under way to remove executives deemed unsympathetic to the Guptas, pressure mounted on coal negotiators to offer Tegeta a better deal.

Correspondence between Tegeta and Eskom in February 2015 reportedly shows that the Guptas weren't satisfied with Eskom's generous offer of R277 a ton for Brakfontein's low-grade coal. Now, they demanded that the amount of coal supplied be increased from 65 000 to 100 000 tons a month and the duration of the contract be extended from five to ten years.[20]

Eskom officials resisted these demands until the pressure from above became unbearable. In early March, shortly before Zola Tsotsi received his orders from the president to gut the Eskom executive, the message was made more explicit. One of the coal negotiators told me that he'd received a chilling warning: 'You guys have been dilly-dallying on Brakfontein,' his line manager said. 'Get it concluded by Friday next week. If you don't, I'll find someone else who will.'

On Tuesday 10 March 2015, the day after Suzanne Daniels was allegedly introduced to Salim Essa at Melrose Arch by Matshela Koko, who wielded overall authority over coal contracts, Eskom finalised a deal with the Guptas to supply 113 000 tons of coal from Brakfontein every month for ten years. The contract was worth R3.8 billion – almost four times the original amount agreed on.

An investigation by audit firm PwC later revealed that Eskom's own test lab in Germiston had delivered a report shortly afterwards concluding that Brakfontein's coal quality ranged from 'marginal' to 'unacceptable'. Coal quality has major cost implications for Eskom. High sulphur and ash content can damage boilers, and high moisture levels waste energy. It was simply too risky to buy Brakfontein's coal.[21] This should hardly have come as a surprise to Eskom, as the mine had failed numerous quality tests over the years. It was clear the contract should never have been signed. But by then it was too late to do anything about it: the Guptas' cronies were already in charge. Instead of cancelling the contract, Eskom instructed the Guptas to start delivering their substandard coal to Majuba.

* * *

Events now began to unfold rapidly. At 10 a.m. on 11 March 2015, a day after Eskom signed the R3.8-billion coal deal with the Guptas, Lynne Brown and her acting director-general, Matsietsi Mokholo, joined a full board meeting in Huvo Nkulu boardroom at Eskom's Johannesburg headquarters, Megawatt Park. Finance director Tsholofelo Molefe and chief executive Tshediso Matona were in attendance.

Brown stunned everyone by declaring that she was aware a bugging device had been found in Huvo Nkulu. She wanted to know where it had been planted and why no action or investigation was undertaken after it was discovered. Matona explained that he had no knowledge of an actual device being located, but that suspicions that the boardroom may be bugged had prompted him to order regular security sweeps.

'That's not good enough,' Brown admonished him. 'This matter needs to be investigated as a matter of urgency, which I am not detecting from the actions taken thus far.'[22]

According to a report by law firm Dentons and testimony to Parliament by Matona, an investigation by Eskom's security division later established there was no bug. Brown's concerns were put down to 'nothing more than paranoia' because of the regular leaks to the press of board meeting deliberations.[23]

Matona told Parliament that then, out of the blue, Brown asked him and Molefe to recuse themselves from the board meeting. They looked at each other in disbelief but left without questioning her directive.[24]

The board minutes show that Brown proceeded to paint a dismal picture of Eskom's performance, following the script written by Nick Linnell from the impromptu board meeting with Zola Tsotsi two days earlier: load shedding was continuing unabated, information that executives supplied to Cyril Ramaphosa's 'war room' was unreliable and ratings agencies were threatening downgrades. In a nutshell, mismanagement at Eskom was placing the entire economy at risk and the board needed to take drastic action to avert disaster. A forensic inquiry to get to the bottom of the rot was the best way forward.[25]

According to another board member present, Tsotsi then reiterated what he'd told the directors on Monday – Matona, Marokane and Koko should be suspended so that the inquiry could continue unfettered. Brown backed him.[26]

The board minutes show that this time, with the minister present, the objections the board members had raised just days earlier seemed to evaporate. A decision was taken to launch an urgent inquiry, which would be wrapped up in three months. The board decided that executives in charge of areas being investigated 'must step aside for the duration of the inquiry in order not to impede it'. The meeting adjourned at 11.44 a.m., after which Brown and Mokholo left the Eskom premises.[27]

After lunch, the Eskom board reconvened to discuss the meeting with Brown and resolved to implement the plan. The board's 'People and Governance Committee' was mandated to handle the suspensions. This time, Tsotsi brought Dudu Myeni's hatchet man Linnell along.

According to Tsotsi, it was during a governance committee meeting that afternoon when the issue of suspending financial director Molefe was raised for the first time by Ben Ngubane. Tsotsi and Mark Pamensky objected, saying that suspending the finance director and chief executive at the same time would spook Eskom's international investors, but Ngubane insisted the instruction had come from the minister.[28]

In Tsotsi's account, at 2.20 p.m., during a short recess, he called Brown.[29]

'Minister, what is this I'm hearing that the finance director is part of it?'

'Yes, the finance director is part of it,' she said.

'But this wasn't even raised by the president,' Tsotsi protested.

'Chairman, I am instructing you to suspend the finance director.'

'Minister, this will cause problems with our lenders.'

'Don't argue with me,' said Brown. 'Remember what I said to you in Cape Town.' With that, she hung up.

When asked about this exchange during the parliamentary inquiry, Brown said she could not recall the phone call and flatly denied adding Tsholofelo Molefe's name to the list.[30]

Matona later described the whole process as 'a farce'. Once the board had resolved to suspend the executives, they were immediately called one by one into the governance committee meeting, informed of the inquiry and that their presence would hamper it, and asked to provide reasons why they shouldn't be suspended.[31]

'When I came back into the meeting there was a letter of suspension already in front of the chairperson,' said Matona. 'I could see the outcome was pretty much predetermined.'[32]

I'm told that that night, Marokane called Suzanne Daniels. 'It's happening,' he said simply.

The next day, Tsotsi convened a press conference to announce the suspensions and the launch of 'an independent inquiry' into Eskom's financial crisis and inability to keep the lights on. He stressed the executives weren't suspected of any impropriety but had merely been asked to 'step aside' to ensure the inquiry wasn't interfered with.

Taking Matona's place at the helm would be board member Zethembe Khoza, who had previously worked with Kuben Moodley at Telkom. A senior manager in the finance department, Nonkululeko Veleti, would stand in for finance director Molefe; Kusile project manager Abram Masango took over from Marokane; and Koko was replaced by Edwin Mabelane, the man Daniels had spotted having lunch at Melrose Arch when Koko allegedly took her to meet Salim Essa.[33] The coincidences were beginning to proliferate.

* * *

It didn't take long for it to dawn on Zola Tsotsi that he had overplayed his hand.

Lynne Brown followed his announcement by stressing the suspensions were '*not* punitive'. Eskom simply wanted 'unfettered access to the information. Information is not forthcoming from Eskom.' Nobody bought this logic. Within thirty minutes of Tsotsi's press conference, analyst Charl Kocks said it would be highly irregular to suspend the executives without any suspicion of wrongdoing, as Tsotsi had claimed. 'A board does not do something this drastic, unless an executive is implicated in doing something wrong, is involved in someone else's wrongdoing or could possibly help cover up any wrongdoing,' he told *Moneyweb*.[34]

On the same day, Eskom's creditors from around the world began to phone Tsotsi demanding an explanation for the suspensions.

Eskom's claim that the suspensions were carried out in order to address the load-shedding crisis was also greeted with suspicion because the utility had failed to suspend two officials in charge its fleet of power stations: head of generation Mongezi Ntsokolo, and his predecessor in the same portfolio, Thava Govender, who now headed the transmission division. Similar concerns were raised at a meeting convened that day to explain the suspensions to senior staff.

'My questions were not answered properly,' said one manager who was present. 'It became clear to me that they were just pretending this was about load shedding.'

In an interview that evening on Radio 702, DA MP Michael Bagraim ridiculed Brown's claims that the suspensions were 'not punitive', branding her dishonest. 'By its very nature, suspending someone is punitive,' said Bagraim. 'You wouldn't see this in the private sector! Let both sides be heard! It's ridiculous and immoral how they're doing it.'

He correctly predicted litigation. 'It's an industrial relations nightmare,' he said. It wasn't long before Tshediso Matona went to the Labour Court asking for his suspension to be set aside.

The next morning, Friday 13 March, Eskom director Norman Baloyi wrote an email to the board expressing his 'shock' at the decision to suspend the executives and concern at the way the process was being handled. He said the board and public at large deserved answers to the questions raised by Bagraim and Kocks. A month later, Brown fired Baloyi. He had held the position for just five months.[35]

For a while, Tsotsi thought he was still in charge. He scrambled around setting up the inquiry, appointing Nick Linnell to coordinate it. In the meantime, he fielded dozens of calls from creditors and wrote a desperate letter to Brown asking for another government bailout for Eskom. The utility had run out of cash to pay suppliers and staff, buy coal and diesel, and repay its loans. Tsotsi warned Brown that Eskom faced a deadly spiral of debt defaults, early loan recalls and further downgrades.[36]

But by then his fellow directors were already plotting a mutiny. According to my sources and testimony in Parliament, on the morning of Saturday 14 March, at a board meeting chaired by Ben Ngubane, the Eskom directors raised a litany of complaints against Tsotsi, who was not present at the meeting. They were concerned about his poor understanding of corporate governance rules, in particular his interfering with the executive, and signing documents and engaging suppliers on Eskom's behalf. The way in which the inquiry had come about after Tsotsi's meeting with Jacob Zuma in Durban in the presence of Dudu Myeni and Linnell caused a great deal of discomfort too. A key grievance was having Linnell foisted on the board to run the inquiry without consultation.[37]

Matters came to a head the following week when ratings agency Standard & Poor's downgraded Eskom's long-term credit rating to junk as a result of the suspensions. At a heated board meeting on 19 March, it was Tsotsi who was forced to step out of the room while the board tabled a vote of no confidence in him. A week later, he was gone.[38]

Tsotsi paints a picture of himself as someone who was victimised for standing up for what was right at Eskom against those wielding power corruptly. But there are too many grey areas in his story to accept this black-and-white portrait uncritically. His own actions suggest he was complicit in the president's abuse of power by obeying an instruction from Zuma, and effectively Myeni, to gut the Eskom executive on spurious grounds that later benefited the Guptas.

When I put it to him that this indicates he was deployed to Eskom simply to further the interests of the president's family and business associates, he bridled at the suggestion. 'I was just a committed member of the ANC, supporting our leader and our government,' he insisted.

Tsotsi has also failed to offer a satisfactory explanation for going along with Brown's insistence on using Salim Essa's list for board committee chairs even though he disagreed with it.

A picture emerges of Tsotsi as someone conflicted by wanting to please the president, which ended up helping the Guptas, while chafing against their increasingly outrageous demands, which led to his removal. As Tsotsi put it: 'The president wanted me to stay for a second term but the Guptas did not want me to be there. They convinced him that I had to go.'

* * *

On the night of 30 March 2015, after a gruelling three-hour board meeting at Megawatt Park, Tsotsi agreed to step down as chairperson of Eskom. Ben Ngubane was appointed to take his place.

At 6.46 a.m., Gupta executive Nazeem Howa emailed Salim Essa. The email, contained in the Gupta leaks, reveals just how deep the Gupta network's tentacles had penetrated Eskom.[39]

'*Salim bhai*,' wrote Howa, using the Hindi word for brother. 'An amended version for your approval.'

Attached to his email was a statement from 'Dr Ben Ngubane, chairperson of Eskom, on behalf of the board'.

Howa would later become chief executive of Gupta holding company Oakbay Investments and a director of Oakbay Resources and Energy, along with Mark Pamensky, who sat on Eskom's board and also headed the utility's strategically important investment and finance committee.

Ngubane's statement expressed 'sincere thanks to Mr Tsotsi for his selfless decision' to step down. It reaffirmed Eskom's decision to launch an inquiry into the power crisis and suspend four executives for its duration – actions that were actually orchestrated with the connivance of Essa and the Guptas.

Ngubane promised to implement 'radical solutions' to clean up corruption and mismanagement at Eskom and turn the ailing utility around. The inquiry would be the first step towards this end. 'It is our express desire that the investigation determines whether the current situation was exacerbated by incompetence, ill-formed decision-making, mismanagement or untoward actions,' he said.

That Gupta associates were drafting Ngubane's first public announcements as chairperson of Eskom demonstrated just how deeply the family's tentacles had penetrated the power utility.

In the meantime, Tshediso Matona had lost his urgent court bid to be reinstated. Although the court found that his suspension was unfair, the matter was referred to an arbitration hearing. But as the process dragged on, Matona became convinced that Eskom had made up its mind to get rid of him, through protracted legal proceedings if necessary. Two months after he was suspended, Matona decided to take a golden handshake.

'I chose to walk away,' he said. 'I chose to leave that sorry and sordid episode behind me and move on with my life. And that's what I did.' He had been in the job for less than six months.[40]

Dan Marokane and Tsholofelo Molefe had come to a similar conclusion and were also in exit talks with Eskom. Matshela Koko, on the other hand, apparently continued to convene meetings with his staff as if nothing had happened, secure in the knowledge that he would return once the dust had settled.

On 8 April 2015, Eskom appointed international law firm Dentons to investigate the root causes of the utility's financial and power generation crisis, but by then it hardly mattered. The real objective of the upheavals had already been attained: the way had been cleared for Brian Molefe and, shortly afterwards, Anoj Singh to take the helm at Eskom. Soon, contracts that had been languishing for years would start rolling the Guptas' way.

11

Stacking the Deck

Brian Molefe's arrival at Eskom in April 2015 was greeted with great optimism. His tenure at Transnet hadn't yet been tainted by the R5.3 billion suspected Gupta kickback scandal, or the shady consultancy deals with Regiments and McKinsey that took place under his watch and allegedly resulted in fixer fees worth hundreds of millions of rands going to Salim Essa. At Transnet, his legacy was low debt levels, government guarantees that totalled just R3.5 billion – compared with R350 billion for Eskom – and the successful conclusion of a R54-billion locomotive deal.

Molefe hit the ground running at Eskom. He impressed fellow executives by arriving at his first meeting having read – and *understood* – his briefing packs. His grasp of the intricacies of Eskom's complex business model came as a huge relief to his new colleagues. He immediately understood that the utility's biggest challenge was being saddled with huge debts and finance costs for new power stations that would only start generating income years down the line. The urgent need, deferred for years, to spend billions on maintenance for Eskom's ageing power plant fleet, as well as electricity tariffs that didn't come close to reflecting the cost of doing business, added to the toxic mix of factors that were on the verge of bankrupting the power utility. Power cuts were merely a symptom of a much deeper malaise, one he needed to address urgently for the health of the entire economy.

I wasn't alone in thinking that if there was one person who could turn the ailing parastatal around, it was Brian Molefe.

Energy analyst Chris Yelland enthused that Molefe's appointment 'added a new feeling of confidence', as he was 'a person who comes with a significant background in large state-owned enterprises. He seems to have the confidence of the business community and of the public sector that he may be the person to lead a turnaround at Eskom.'

Yelland bemoaned the 'pressure from government' that Molefe's predecessors such as Brian Dames and Tshediso Matona had had to endure, rolling out power connections to millions of homes without building new power stations or having a proper municipal tariff collection plan, and being forced to delay urgently needed maintenance that would have caused outages during the 2010 World Cup and municipal and national elections in 2011 and 2014.

'I hope that Brian Molefe will be left alone to get on with the job' without being saddled with 'a lot of political interference and social requirements', said Yelland. 'We're seeing an improved picture, where Eskom is being left to concentrate on Medupi, Kusile and Ingula, that's the existing new build, as well as improving the performance of its existing fleet of power stations, getting rid of this maintenance backlog and getting performance and energy availability back to where it should be.' In the meantime, the private sector could step into the breach with 'new generation capacity coming from renewable energy and also from independent power producers with coal and gas'.[1]

At his first press conference the day after he was appointed, Molefe said he would prioritise improving staff morale. 'Team building is the single most important thing that needs to be done before you even deal with load shedding,' he said. 'If we can have a strong team we will be able to deal with whatever problem there is.'[2]

Enthusiasm for the new arrival didn't last long, especially among his closest colleagues. It soon became apparent to them that Molefe's fatal flaw was hubris. 'He was astute, well read and hard-working. But he has an inflated sense of self-importance,' one Eskom executive told me. 'He's arrogant and thinks he's cleverer than everyone else.'

A senior manager described an incident involving the chief executive of a major mining house that summed up the attitude Molefe would later display with coal giants Glencore and Exxaro: 'We were sitting in the boardroom waiting for Brian. He arrived ten minutes late. He didn't apologise or greet anyone. He just sat down, listened to them present their case, and said: "My team will get back to you." Then he got up and walked out.'

* * *

One of the first items on Molefe's agenda was Optimum colliery, a sprawling open-cast and underground mining complex blighting the landscape between Middelburg and Hendrina in Mpumalanga. Its relationship with Eskom dates back to 1968 when the mine, owned by a previous incarnation of BHP Billiton, was awarded a contract to supply Hendrina power station. Like all South Africa's coal-fired plants, Hendrina was built on a coalfield so that coal could be transported from the mine on conveyor belts, keeping transport costs down.[3]

In 1993, Optimum signed a twenty-five-year agreement with Eskom to supply 5.5 million tons of low-grade coal a year at R150 a ton; this amounted to about half of its output. The remaining higher-quality coal was exported.

In 2008, BHP Billiton sold the mine to a majority black-owned consortium led by its South African coal division's former chief operating officer Eliphus Monkoe, with shareholder director Mike Teke appointed as chief executive. The deal included Optimum's 7.5 per cent stake in Richards Bay Coal Terminal, along with its eight-million-ton export allocation, and a stake in the nearby Koornfontein mine, which supplies Komati power station.

In 2012, global resources giant Glencore bought Optimum from Teke and Monkoe's consortium for $780 million. Almost half of the company was owned by its thirteen directors, who together walked away with R4 billion. Cyril Ramaphosa, Glencore's black empowerment partner, provided some of the funding through his company Shanduka, but he divested when he became deputy president in May 2014.[4]

The new owners of Optimum were held to BHP Billiton's original 1993 deal to supply Eskom with half the mine's coal at R150 a ton until December 2018. Presumably Glencore and Shanduka agreed to buy the mine despite being obliged to honour these unfavourable terms because they were entitled to export half the coal mined at Optimum and Koornfontein, a total of eight million tons, through the Richards Bay terminal.

This worked out fine when international coal prices were high and Optimum's exports could cross-subsidise its Eskom sales. But in 2012, coal prices started a downward spiral on the back of a slowdown in demand from India and China, halving over the next three years.[5]

At the same time, the cost of production at Optimum began to increase and soon outstripped what Eskom was paying. The mine was also steadily racking up penalties for supplying coal that didn't meet the original contractual specifications, which according to Eskom sources were particularly onerous.

Glencore began to panic. In 2013 it calculated Optimum would lose R881 million that year if it continued to supply Eskom at 1993 prices. Chief executive Clinton Ephron invoked a so-called hardship clause in the contract, threatening to shut the mine down if Eskom couldn't offer a better deal.

Negotiations began in 2014, with Nedbank appointed to conduct a cost analysis. By the end of the year, a workable solution was found. Optimum would be paid a 'break-even' price of R420 a ton, with an annual inflation-linked increase, and Eskom agreed to reduce its penalty. In addition, the contract would be extended by five years, until 2023, at a price that covered the cost of production plus an agreed on profit margin.[6]

The deal was approved in March 2015, subject to ratification by the board tender committee that met on 15 April, two days before Brian Molefe arrived at Eskom. But the committee wasn't willing to make the call and referred the matter to a full board meeting, which was held on 23 April.[7]

This left Optimum's fate in the hands of a board stacked with directors connected to a greater or lesser extent to Essa or the Guptas. The meeting was chaired by Ben Ngubane, who'd partnered with Salim Essa in a failed oil deal in the Central African Republic that was linked to the Guptas. In attendance were Mark Pamensky, a director in Gupta company Oakbay Resources and Energy; Kuben Moodley's wife, Viroshini Naidoo; Gupta deployee Chwayita Mabude; and Nazia Carrim, who is married to Essa's cousin. Also present were Romeo Kumalo, who had once started a company with Essa, although it never traded, and Zethembe Khoza, who was later accused of being a runner for the Guptas, although he denied it.

Pamensky was particularly conflicted. He had joined the board of Gupta mining company Oakbay Resources and Energy in September 2014 and two months later joined the Eskom board where he was appointed chairperson of the finance and investment committee. At the time, he was the chief operations officer of telecoms company Blue Label, where he'd got to know Kuben Moodley when Moodley, a friend of Essa's, worked at Telkom. In her 2016 report on state capture, Public Protector Thuli Madonsela found that Pamensky 'would have or could have access to privileged or sensitive information' about various Eskom contracts, including those involving the Guptas, by virtue of his position on the Eskom board.[8]

An Eskom executive who attended board subcommittee meetings told me it only became clear much later, after Madonsela's report had been released and the Gupta emails had been leaked to the media, that the membership of key committees must have been carefully orchestrated to further the business interests of the Guptas and their associates. The two committees that played a central role in influencing the allocation of mega contracts were both stacked with directors linked in some way to Essa or the Guptas. Zethembe Khoza, Mark Pamensky, Brian Molefe and later Anoj Singh sat on the finance and investment committee; and Khoza, Chwayita Mabude, Viroshini Naidoo and Nazia Carrim sat on the board tender committee. It was nicely sewn up.

Pamensky later denied he was conflicted. He described his conflicts as 'perceived, not real', by pointing out that Oakbay Resources and Energy had nothing to do with Tegeta, the Gupta company vying for Eskom coal supply contracts at the time.[9]

But leaked emails and other documents supplied by whistleblowers suggest that Pamensky was at the heart of the action. The emails show that he discussed Oakbay's plans for doing coal deals with Eskom with Atul Gupta, that he was directly involved in helping the Guptas buy Optimum from Glencore, and that he shared information on disposing of Eskom's unused real estate worth R10 billion with Gupta-linked Trillian.

When Pamensky attended the board meeting on 23 April that would decide Optimum's fate, he'd already been briefed by senior managers at Eskom about how the utility went about procuring coal without disclosing to them that he was also batting for the other team.

'I was furious when I found out,' one of the managers who'd spent hours explaining the intricacies of Eskom's coal procurement strategies to Pamensky told me. 'He knew all Eskom's secrets.'

At this juncture, the Eskom board could have prevented one of the greatest swindles in South African mining history by approving a deal with Optimum that the utility's negotiation team and executive procurement committee had finessed over two years and believed was a workable solution for both parties. Instead, the board decided to defer the decision to Brian Molefe.

On 18 May, exactly one month after Molefe arrived at Eskom, he met with Optimum's chief executive, Clinton Ephron. Theirs was not an amicable discussion. Molefe refused point-blank to entertain Optimum's offer and informed Ephron that Eskom would continue to enforce the 1993 deal.[10]

Four days later, Optimum wrote to Molefe to say the company was spending R100 million a month to keep the mine going. It had received R1 billion from its shareholders since October 2014 to stay afloat and had exhausted its R2.5-billion bank overdraft. Unless Eskom revised its position, Optimum would be forced into business rescue.[11]

Molefe wrote back on 10 June, informing Optimum that he wouldn't budge. This prompted Glencore chief executive Ivan Glasenberg to fly in from Switzerland for a last-ditch attempt at persuading Molefe to change his mind. The meeting ended acrimoniously, with Molefe apparently accusing Glasenberg of trying to use 'old South Africa tactics' to bully him into submission.[12]

Glasenberg hasn't commented publicly about the incident, but Molefe later depicted the encounter as a David and Goliath battle that he had won. 'He said to me: "I will stop the supply of coal to Hendrina and you will have more load shedding." I said, "bring it on",' Molefe told *The New Age*. 'I don't think anybody has spoken to him in that way. But I did. And the rest, as they say, is history.'[13]

On 30 June, after Glasenberg's disastrous intervention, Optimum's chief executive Clinton Ephron sent Molefe his final offer: he asked to be paid R300 a ton until 2018, which was R120 below cost, increasing to R570 a ton from 2018 to 2023.[14]

Molefe rejected the offer out of hand. One of his officials pointed out this was a win-win solution because the alternative was losing Hendrina's dedicated coal supply, which would result in load shedding.

Molefe snapped that he would truck in coal from other mines to build up a stockpile.

'It was absolutely stupid because the stockyard at Hendrina is too small,' the official told me. 'But Brian wouldn't listen. He was like that. He always had to show that he knew better than everyone else, even when he didn't.'

The next day, Glencore received an offer from audit firm KPMG on behalf of anonymous clients who wanted to buy Optimum. It later transpired that the clients were none other than the Guptas.

* * *

While Molefe was bullying Optimum into submission, a team of investigators from law firm Dentons were engaged in a 'fact-finding mission' to unearth the root causes of the malaise at Eskom.

It was an unenviable task, made worse by the uncooperative behaviour from the utility that had hired it. The Dentons investigators soon found that obstacles had been strewn in their path every step of the way. First they were denied access to emails and told that they could only peruse documents at the Eskom premises during office hours. Then they were prevented from interviewing key former and current executives, including those on suspension, and for the first five weeks they were even denied access to Eskom's power stations.[15]

The time allocated for the investigation was cut short dramatically too. Dentons was initially contracted for three months, although the Eskom board initially envisaged that the investigation could last for a year. But shortly after Dentons presented a preliminary report to the board on 25 June, public enterprises minister Lynne Brown ordered that the investigation be shut down and Dentons be paid its R20-million fee in full.[16] It delivered its final report on 15 July. By then the investigators had been at work for just forty days.

Dentons issued a lengthy disclaimer in the preamble to its report, describing it as 'a snapshot of the investigation at the midpoint of the investigation period' supplied to Eskom prior to completion 'at the specific request of Eskom'.[17]

'Why bother with a probe when you're afraid of what it might reveal?' asked *Financial Mail* deputy editor Sikonathi Mantshantsha.[18]

Mantshantsha had spent two years relentlessly hounding Eskom to release the report into failings at a state utility that taxpayers had just spent R83 billion bailing out, but Eskom chairperson Ben Ngubane insisted that it was 'not for public consumption'. In February 2017, Eskom finally partly relented, announcing that the report would be released to parties that had requested it in terms of the Promotion of Access to Information Act. By then, Mantshantsha had already obtained a copy, which the *Financial Mail* promptly published.[19]

Even though the Dentons investigation had been abandoned midway through at the express instruction of Lynne Brown, it did provide a devastating 'snapshot' of looting at Eskom.

The report found that corruption, often fostered by bad planning, was a major driver of cost overruns and delays at Medupi and Kusile and contributed to driving up Eskom's massive coal bill, with executives and senior managers accused of diverting business to themselves or their relatives, or taking bribes from suppliers. Spending over R1 billion a month on diesel to feed the emergency power plants during the height of load shedding provided further opportunities for Eskom officials to use family members to cash in on contracts.[20]

Dentons investigators said they had received alarming accounts of senior executives 'seeking opportunities ostensibly for the benefit of themselves at the expense of Eskom' by 'making deals with suppliers outside of the formal procurement process, and/or turning a blind eye to expensive contract breaches'. Rather than trying to obtain goods and services at the cheapest possible price, many of Eskom's managers in charge of the utility's R140-billion annual procurement budget devoted their energy to 'leveraging Eskom's considerable buying power for self-interest', the report said.[21]

Eskom officials I've spoken to said that the Dentons investigation had provided Brown and President Jacob Zuma with the ideal opportunity to fix Eskom if they had really been serious about rooting out corruption. 'Dentons had a team of good forensic people,' one told me. 'If they had been allowed to do a proper job they could have saved Eskom.'

Instead, Brown shut down the Dentons investigation before any of the allegations could be properly investigated. By then, three of the senior executives suspended in March had gone, without a single charge being brought against them. The fourth, Matshela Koko, returned to work four months later – exactly as he had predicted.

Koko would later make much of the fact that the Dentons investigation had found no evidence of wrongdoing against him. But this belies the fact that Dentons was specifically instructed not to investigate the suspended executives. The terms of reference and task order Dentons received 'never contemplated the investigation as being one that was directed specifically at the conduct of the suspended executives' and did not 'require investigation of misconduct of any specific individuals', the report said. 'Accordingly, no recommendations are made in respect of action to be taken to deal with misconduct by any specific individuals.'[22]

But, the matter did not end there. Minutes of an Eskom board meeting in August reveal that an earlier draft of the report was presented to the board on 27 May. This draft 'had Koko's name all over the place', a senior source at Eskom who read it told me. 'I remember thinking that a lot of things suddenly fell into place. Tsotsi's name was also there', but for petty transgressions.

Two Eskom directors who had read this draft also told the *Financial Mail*'s Mantshantsha at the time that 'if that version is made public, Eskom would again be leaderless – as the culprits would surely face disciplinary action'.[23]

Eskom's own minutes confirm that after this draft was presented to the board, the company secretary was instructed to collect all copies 'of initial reports' and shred them 'in exchange for the receipt of the final Denton report'.[24]

It was a gigantic cover-up: Eskom had spent R20 million on an investigation whose findings it did not want to hear.

* * *

Molefe's next step was to rearrange the deck chairs on the *Titanic*.

While Koko was on suspension, the technology and commercial division he headed was split in two, with commercial – the 'glittering prize of Eskom' that controlled all tenders – henceforth reporting to the chief financial officer. This wasn't a demotion, though. In October 2015, Molefe added the generation division to Koko's portfolio, placing him in charge of all Eskom's power stations.

In the meantime, Eskom chairperson Ben Ngubane announced on 16 July that the chief financial officer at Transnet, Anoj Singh, would be seconded to Eskom. Ngubane, who'd seemingly already had one of his public statements vetted by the Guptas, enthused about Singh's achievements at Transnet, which had maintained a rating above investment grade while launching a R336-billion seven-year infrastructure programme, including the acquisition of 1064 locomotives. Ngubane highlighted accolades Singh had earned 'in recognition of his outstanding performance and leadership', including winning the public CFO award for two years running, in 2014 and 2015.[25]

Thanks to Molefe's portfolio reshuffle, Singh would be in charge of Eskom's R140-billion annual procurement budget too, including for coal.

Molefe brought along a few other interesting characters from Transnet too. One was Tebogo Rakau, who would head Eskom's newly created security division. The other was Joel George Martins, a former Umkhonto we Sizwe operative. Both had previously held the rank of brigadier general and liked to be addressed as 'general' at Eskom.[26]

Eskom staffers described Singh to me as highly intelligent, charming and likeable. 'He was always immaculately turned out and popular with the ladies,' said one. 'He used to be called "Mr Cool". He always dressed well. We were convinced he manicured his nails.'

It only emerged much later, when the full weight of incriminating evidence against him became impossible to spin, that Anoj Singh lay at the heart of the Transnet and Eskom looting machine.

* * *

When we last encountered Anoj Singh in March 2014, Brian Molefe had just announced the winners of the 1064 locomotives contract at Transnet. Singh, according to senior McKinsey partner David Fine's testimony under oath in Parliament, had been responsible for fancy new financial calculations 'based on funding costs, exchange rates and inflation' that had seen the price tag skyrocket from R38 billion to R54 billion.[27]

An investigation by amaBhungane later revealed that on 20 March, three days after Molefe announced that China South Rail had won the lion's share of the contract, the Guptas set up a shell company called Venus Limited in the United Arab Emirates.[28] Venus Limited was registered in Ras al-Khaimah, one of the UAE's seven emirates, which is also – perhaps not coincidentally – where a shell company called Accurate Investments is located. Accurate Investments owns 8 per cent of Gupta mining company Tegeta.

Ras al-Khaimah is situated near the eastern tip of the Arabian Peninsula. The emirate has several advantages for foreigners engaged in illicit dealings. Like all the UAE's free zones, offshore companies registered here don't pay tax, can be 100 per cent foreign owned, are allowed full repatriation of profits and capital, and can own properties. But unlike most free zones, in Ras al-Khaimah there is no need to hire an office or local employees. It also takes particular pride in offering the highest levels of 'privacy and confidentiality' with 'full nominee service to protect your privacy' and 'no requirement to file accounts or have audits conducted'. This, together with 'easy access to banks in Dubai, Hong Kong, Singapore, Malta, Andorra or Latvia', makes it a money-laundering haven.[29]

On 21 April 2014, one month after China South Rail signed an R18-billion contract to supply Transnet with 359 locomotives, the UAE scrap-metal dealer JJ Trading started making large cash payments to the Guptas, followed by transfers to one of the Guptas' Bank of Baroda accounts in the UAE. Within a month JJ Trading had paid the Guptas about R590 million, documents from the Gupta leaks cited by amaBhungane show.[30]

You may recall from a previous chapter that JJ Trading was one of two Gupta-linked companies in the UAE that had received R1.4 billion in suspected kickbacks between December 2012 and January 2015 from China South Rail after it won locomotive contracts from Transnet worth more than R25 billion. The Gupta leaks show that most of the alleged kickbacks were subsequently funnelled to Gupta bank accounts in the UAE, India and Hong Kong to fund the family's lavish lifestyle.

On 30 April 2014, barely a week after China South Rail's money started flowing to the Guptas via their scrap-metal dealers in the UAE, Anoj Singh flew there himself, the Gupta leaks show. In Dubai he was hosted by the Guptas at the Oberoi Hotel, where he was joined by Tony Gupta and Salim Essa. The next day, Venus Limited was reportedly transferred into Singh's name.[31]

AmaBhungane was unable to establish if the Guptas paid any money into Venus Limited's accounts. But evidence that Singh received cash payments and other gratuities from the family suggests that they may have. For example, an internal Gupta spreadsheet records almost R600 000 in cash was paid to a 'Mr A Singh' on 29 August 2014, when the Transnet chief financial officer was in Dubai. An equivalent payment was made to a company believed to be 'for Anoj Singh's benefit'. Singh, who has steadfastly denied ever receiving a bribe from anyone and claims there's nothing untoward about his relationship with the Guptas, has declined to explain these payments.[32]

In the time between Transnet awarding the 359 locomotives contract to China South Rail in March 2014 and Singh's secondment to Eskom in August 2015, the Guptas hosted Singh in Dubai at least five times, where he often stayed in the same hotel as Tony Gupta, sometimes with Essa, the Gupta leaks show.

AmaBhungane reported that on one occasion in February 2015 the Guptas picked up the tab for the Transnet official's girlfriend too, whom the Guptas employed at their computer company Sahara, paying her top dollar for a nondescript job and loaning her R400 000 towards buying a new house.

This particular trip to Dubai, where Singh was joined by Essa and Tony Gupta, was significant because it was reportedly extended for three days to coincide with a stay-over at the Oberoi by a senior executive of China South Rail. Tony Gupta, Essa and the China South Rail executive then took a chartered flight together to India. The Gupta leaks show that an email from the Chinese executive was circulated among Gupta associates a few days later. Attached to it was the spreadsheet that detailed the suspected kickbacks China South Rail had already paid for its Transnet locomotive deals.[33] The spreadsheet stipulates that the 'advisory fees' due, totalling R5.3 billion, would be broken down as follows: R537 million for the first contract for 95 locomotives, R924 million for second for 100 locomotives and R3.8 billion for third for 359 locomotives. It records that a total of R1.4 billion had already been paid to JJ Trading and Century General Trading – R200 million for the first contract and R1.2 billion for the second and third contracts.[34]

Soon afterwards, on 18 May 2015, Salim Essa signed a new agreement between his company Tequesta, registered in Hong Kong, and China South Rail. The agreement states that 'advisory fees' of R706.8 million for the 'Project 359' locomotives contract had already been paid to JJ Trading, and that a further R3.1 billion remained due to Tequesta.[35]

The Organised Crime and Corruption Reporting Project (OCCRP), a transnational investigative journalism platform, reported that it had obtained banking records showing that by the end of 2015 China South Rail had paid Essa over R1.3 billion. Of this, R570 million was reportedly paid to Tequesta and R750 million to another company he'd set up in Hong Kong, Regiments Asia. 'The millions then went through more than three dozen shell companies around the world, mostly using HSBC accounts in Hong Kong and other locations, but also employing other banks in London, Johannesburg, Dubai, and the US,' OCCRP reported.[36]

In its analysis of the transactions, amaBhungane concluded that 'the amounts alone elevate the fees beyond consultancy to where only one explanation is possible: that these are the proceeds of corruption'.[37]

The Gupta leaks show that in June 2015, Singh went on his last trip to Dubai as Transnet's finance director. As usual, he was hosted by the Guptas at the Oberoi, along with Tony Gupta and Ronica Ragavan, who later became chief executive of the Guptas' holding company, Oakbay Investments. Dubai was rapidly becoming the new Saxonwold.

Six weeks later, Singh became the second-most powerful executive at South Africa's biggest parastatal. As chief financial officer in charge of procurement at Eskom, Singh was ideally placed to advance the Guptas' business interests at the power utility. It didn't take long before he got the opportunity to lend them a helping hand in the lucrative coal procurement sector they'd been eyeing for years. But first a few established coal players who'd cornered the market had to be forced out of the game.

12

Engineered Emergency

Early in 2015, an Eskom manager walked into a boardroom full of senior officials with a two-page presentation headed 'A failure to adequately spend on CAPEX now will result in an operational calamity.'

The first page contained a graph that projected Eskom's coal costs over the next eight years. There were two lines. The first showed what the utility would spend on coal if it allocated the full amount of R27 billion needed to recapitalise its tied mines – that is, mines situated close to power stations that are dedicated to supplying Eskom with cheap coal through 'cost-plus' or long-term supply agreements. Recapitalisation would involve anything from sinking new shafts to reach higher-grade coal deposits to refurbishing draglines, the gigantic crane-like machines that scoop up earth at open-cast mines. The second line on the graph represented coal spend, with no capital allocated to Eskom's tied mines.

From 2016, the lines begin to diverge dramatically as production plummets at the run-down tied mines near Eskom's power plants, forcing the utility to truck in coal at a much higher price. By 2023, the projected difference in coal costs as a result of failing to invest in the tied mines is R90 billion.

'It means that if Eskom had spent R27 billion investing in the cost-plus mines in 2015, we would have saved R90 billion,' the manager told me.

The problem is that tied mines have become a political football. Because the original contracts were signed thirty or forty years ago, Eskom's new top brass could claim the investments would subsidise the operations of traditionally white-owned companies such as Anglo American. This is true, but it ignores several salient facts.

Firstly, these mines supply Eskom with its cheapest coal by far, which means investing in them now will benefit all electricity consumers in the future. Besides, Eskom is contractually obliged to pay for capital costs.

Secondly, it is false to claim that only white monopoly capital benefits from this arrangement, because there has been significant progress in black empowerment at tied mines.

A good example is Exxaro. The company was formed in 2006 through a merger of the coal division of Kumba, a company owned by Anglo American, and Eyesizwe Coal. The merger created the largest black-owned mining firm in South Africa, which supplies coal for a third of Eskom's power generation.[1]

One of Exxaro's mines, Matla colliery, is tied to Eskom's Matla power station 130 kilometres east of Johannesburg. As with all cost-plus mines, Eskom was contractually bound to cover Exxaro's capital and operating costs. The cost of coal was calculated as the actual cost of production plus an inflation-linked management fee and a relatively low return on investment. In return, the mine provided Matla power station with a guaranteed supply of cheap coal that it wasn't permitted to sell anywhere else, including on the then lucrative export market.

Matla's three mines hold 250 million tons of coal reserves, which means it could be a significant secure source of cheap energy for decades to come. Since 2004, Matla repeatedly tried to convince Eskom to spend R1.8 billion on sinking a new shaft on one of the mines because the existing shaft had become unsafe, a cost Eskom would have to cover in terms of its coal supply agreement (CSA), but to no avail.

Exxaro later discovered that when the Eskom board finally approved the investment, public enterprises minister Lynne Brown blocked it. In a letter she wrote to Eskom in April 2017, she said she'd declined the request because she failed to see how 'the objective of the democratic government' would 'find expression in these arrangements' that predated 1994.

She said that Eskom must first demonstrate how it would 'use this opportunity' to further the 'socio-economic transformation imperatives of Government, given the evolution of policy since 1994'.[2]

Exxaro's chief executive Mxolisi Mgojo was gobsmacked. 'The Minister's stance is most surprising in circumstances where the CSA has been amended and affirmed on numerous occasions after 1994 and where

Exxaro is one of the largest and foremost black-empowered mining companies in South Africa,' he said. 'In any event, there are no such conditions provided for in our CSA with Eskom.'[3]

As a result, Exxaro was forced to close the shaft and reduce the amount of coal it supplied to Matla power station from 10 million to 7.5 million tons a year, leaving the door open to other suppliers. Mgojo calculated that the power plant was forced to make up the shortfall with 400 truckloads of coal a day, 'with the concomitant traffic congestion, damage to the road and risk to other road users, when this coal could otherwise be delivered by conveyor belt directly from the Matla mine'.

Eskom's failure to meet its contractual obligation to invest R1.8 billion at Matla colliery came at a great cost to the utility and its customers. Mgojo estimates that Eskom has paid R5 billion more than it needed to in just two years by trucking in coal 'at exorbitant prices', when it could secure cheap coal from Matla for another twenty years simply by investing R1.8 billion in the shaft. It made no logical, commercial or even political sense. Exxaro was justifiably convinced that a hidden agenda lay behind Eskom's actions.[4]

The hidden hand became abundantly clear to Exxaro when it was subjected to the same modus operandi with another of its tied mines, Arnot.

Since the 1970s, Arnot colliery south-east of Middelburg has been contracted to supply Arnot power station next door with four million tons of coal a year from its underground and open-cast sections. If it produced more coal than contracted, it charged a premium; if it fell short, it paid a penalty. As with other tied mines, coal was delivered by conveyor belt, keeping transport costs low, and Eskom was contractually responsible for capital and operating costs. In addition to this, Eskom's coal supply agreement with Exxaro specified that the utility was obliged to buy six portions of land known collectively as Mooifontein to allow the mine's open-cast operation to expand as underground mining became too expensive. But Eskom repeatedly delayed buying Mooifontein while refusing to fund other urgently needed capital costs despite being contractually obligated to do so. This forced Exxaro to reduce coal supplies from 4 million tons to 1.8 million tons, dramatically pushing up the cost per ton to over R1 000.

'Had Exxaro been able to mine the land as intended, it would have significantly reduced the cost per ton of coal supplied to Eskom,' Mgojo pointed out.[5]

Exxaro's forty-year contract at Arnot was set to expire at the end of 2015. When Brian Molefe arrived in April, the mine was at an advanced stage of negotiating a new deal with Eskom that would allow it to deliver cheaper coal to Arnot until the end of the power station's life in 2023 by opening up Mooifontein. But in September 2015, Eskom inexplicably announced that Exxaro's contract would not be extended.

Exxaro was stunned. The Arnot mine still had ample reserves, about seventy million tons, and was situated right next to Arnot power station. No mine was better placed to supply Eskom with cheap coal.

Despite being Eskom's biggest coal supplier, repeated attempts by Exxaro executives to meet with Molefe to resolve the deadlock were rebuffed.

In December 2015, Exxaro's Arnot contract came to an end and the company was forced to close the mine that had supplied the power plant since 1975. In one fell swoop, over 1500 jobs were lost.

Molefe employed the same tactic with Mafube, another mine twenty-five kilometres from Arnot that Exxaro jointly owns with Anglo American. Mafube delivers coal to Arnot power station on a long conveyor belt for a fixed price of R132 a ton. This makes it the cheapest coal in the country.

By 2015, a dispute had arisen between Eskom and Mafube over the contract termination date. Eskom contended it ran until 2023, while Mafube believed it expired in December 2015. In July 2015, Mafube offered to extend its contract by three years – until 2018, when one of its reserves would be depleted. For months it received no reply. Then, in November 2015, Mafube was informed that Eskom no longer wanted its coal.[6]

Looking back at these experiences, Mgojo said that they raised several uncomfortable questions.

'Why was the Mafube CSA terminated despite the mine delivering the cheapest supplies of coal in Mpumalanga to Eskom?' he asked. 'Why did Eskom avoid paying R1.8 billion for the mine shaft at Matla for so long, opting instead to procure coal for over R5 billion and thereby posing safety risks, traffic congestion and damage to the roads in respect of a mine that was not designed for stockpiling? Why did Eskom summarily terminate negotiations on the extension of Arnot's CSA? Why was Eskom unconcerned about the premature termination of the Arnot CSA despite the fact that Eskom was aware that it would lead to the loss of 1 500 jobs and an emergency with respect to the coal supply for the Arnot power station?'

He concluded that Eskom had 'unlawfully pushed Exxaro out of the coal supply space and contracted with a third party/ies at a considerably higher cost to the fiscus'. These 'third parties' included the Guptas.

Mgojo laid the blame squarely on Brian Molefe, whose arrival had precipitated a marked deterioration in the relationship between Exxaro and Eskom.

'Eskom's agreements with Exxaro were in certain instances not adhered to or, where they were being finalised, were frustrated,' he pointed out. 'Despite this, and the fact that Exxaro is the biggest supplier of coal to Eskom, Mr Molefe refused to meet with Exxaro throughout his tenure at Eskom.'[7]

Molefe clearly had other priorities.

* * *

Eskom's shoddy treatment of Exxaro was in stark contrast to the way the utility bent over backwards for the Guptas.

You may recall that in March 2015, after holding out for two years, Eskom officials had caved in to pressure from above to approve a cushy ten-year deal worth almost R4 billion for Brakfontein mine, operated by Gupta-owned Tegeta, to supply Majuba power station with substandard coal at R270 a ton – far more than it was worth.

An investigation by National Treasury later revealed that Eskom had broken its own rules by allowing Brakfontein to start supplying Majuba before its coal had passed a combustion test. When the results arrived two days after the contract was signed, they confirmed what numerous tests of Brakfontein's coal had shown in the past: it was decidedly below par.[8]

Despite this, Brakfontein was told to start supplying coal to Majuba soon afterwards. The Dentons report later revealed that Eskom was paying

Tegeta more than any other supplier to Majuba, despite it delivering the lowest-quality coal.[9]

It wasn't long before the Brakfontein coal started failing quality tests. By August 2015, Eskom could no longer pretend the problem didn't exist, and on 31 August Matshela Koko wrote to Tegeta, informing the company that its contract had been suspended because half its coal had been rejected.[10]

Then Koko performed a remarkable sleight of hand. He'd sent samples to the South African Bureau of Standards (SABS), which came back with results that apparently exonerated Brakfontein. Based on these inconsistencies, he suspended the two labs and four Eskom officials, including chief coal scientist Mark van der Riet and his lab manager Charlotte Ramavhona, who'd blown the whistle on Brakfontein's coal.

Days later, Tegeta chief executive Ravindra Nath wrote a letter to Koko that also painted a rosy picture of Brakfontein's coal. He claimed that his 'independent in-house lab at the mine site' had tested over 150 samples and found all of them to be compliant. 'In the light of the facts mentioned above, we request you to kindly expedite the procedure at your end so that the suspension may be revoked at the earliest.'[11]

The next day, with Van der Riet's troublesome team out of the way, Koko lifted the suspension.

Subsequent Treasury investigations suggest that Koko's SABS test may have been manipulated, possibly with his connivance, although he denies this. Another SABS test performed less than a fortnight later, on 17 September, found the coal non-compliant.[12] This was followed a month later by a damning technical memo from an official at Eskom's research division, Chris van Alphen. He concluded that Brakfontein's results were even worse than before, despite the change of test labs, and that 'the coal technically should have been rejected'.[13]

None of this made any difference to Eskom, which not only kept paying the Guptas top dollar to supply Majuba with defective coal but sought permission from Treasury the following year to ramp up deliveries and almost double the contract value to R7 billion. Treasury politely declined, informing Eskom that payments already made to Tegeta for Brakfontein's coal should be deemed irregular expenditure.[14]

Despite these findings supporting the concerns they'd raised about Brakfontein's coal, whistleblowers Van der Riet and Ramavhona remained on suspension for more than two years.

* * *

While the Guptas were struggling with Brakfontein, their gaze fell upon a far more attractive prospect: Optimum Coal Holdings. The company owned Optimum colliery close to Middelburg, as well as the nearby Koornfontein mine that supplied Komati power station, and a stake in Richards Bay Coal Terminal with an eight-million-ton annual export allocation.

It was the beginning of an epic battle between Swiss commodities giant Glencore and the Gupta family, who were swiftly inveigling their way into the highest echelons of power in South Africa. Going head to head with the world's largest commodity trader was not an insignificant undertaking, but the Guptas were fast making the right friends in high places. By the time they'd set their sights on Optimum, the family was on the verge of hand-picking South Africa's minister of mineral resources and, for a brief spell, the country's finance minister.

It's hard to picture a more improbable hero in the battle against state capture than Glencore, but in the topsy-turvy world of South African politics, that's how the game played out.

In 2012, Danish film director Christoffer Guldbrandsen made a documentary about Glencore called *Stealing Africa*, which details accusations of grand-scale tax evasion in Zambia. The film opens in Rüschlikon, a tiny village on the outskirts of Zurich. This is where Johannesburg-born coal trader and Glencore chief executive Ivan Glasenberg lives. Glencore's public listing in 2011 turned Glasenberg into one of Europe's richest men overnight, his stake in the company suddenly worth around $10 billion. The next day, Rüschlikon's mayor received a call from the canton tax office asking him to prepare to receive a payment of $400 million, a result of Glasenberg's windfall. This is close to what Glencore's Mopani copper mine paid in taxes and royalties to the Zambian government in over a decade.[15]

Over the years, Glencore and its predecessor, Marc Rich & Co, have been implicated in sanctions-busting in Iran, Iraq and apartheid South Africa and, more recently, in corruption scandals in the DRC and tax evasion in Australia.[16]

The Guptas made their play for Optimum on 1 July 2015, one day after Brian Molefe rejected Glencore's final offer designed to save the mine from going under. The Guptas wanted to buy all Optimum's assets, including Koornfontein and the Richards Bay export terminal share, for just R2 billion. This was clearly a fraction of what it was worth. Commodities giant Vitol later offered to pay R3.6 billion for the Richards Bay terminal stake alone.[17]

The shakedown began two weeks later. On 16 July Eskom sent Glencore a letter of demand. The utility wanted immediate payment of R2.2 billion in penalties for delivery of faulty coal since 2012. Up until then, reduction of the penalty had been a central plank in Glencore's negotiating position. By the time Molefe arrived, Eskom and Glencore had reached a compromise that included a substantial reduction in penalties.

'Glencore are no angels, and [Optimum chief executive] Clinton Ephron is not a pushover by any means. He was disputing every point,' one of the Eskom negotiators told me. 'But we would never have been able to enforce the full penalty.' The original contract, he pointed out, contained particularly onerous requirements that other mines weren't subjected to. The penalty would have gobbled up about 90 per cent of what Eskom had paid Optimum for its coal. Eskom was effectively asking Optimum to deliver its coal for free. There were also unresolved disputes over the accuracy of the coal-sampling process. 'The penalty would have been reduced during arbitration anyway,' he concluded.

Now it was Glencore's turn to play its hand. Optimum began to retrench workers, and on Friday 31 July the board resolved to place the company in business rescue. The mineral resources department responded by briefly suspending Optimum's mining licence on the Monday, complaining of 'inhumane' retrenchments, but reinstated it on Friday.[18]

Ngoako Ramatlhodi, the mineral resources minister at the time, later admitted publicly that Molefe and Eskom chairperson Ben Ngubane had visited him a few weeks later demanding that he suspend all of Glencore's mining licences in South Africa until Optimum had paid the R2.2-billion penalty. Ramatlhodi refused. Three weeks later, on 23 September, he was replaced by Mosebenzi Zwane, a colourful character from the Free State who would play a decisive role in the Gupta heist of Optimum coal mine.[19]

Zwane chose Kuben Moodley, the husband of Eskom board member Viroshini Naidoo, as 'special advisor'. Moodley later described his job as helping 'Mr Zwane in his dealings with white monopoly capital, both in South Africa and abroad, in light of my experience in the corporate financial sector'.[20]

* * *

Mosebenzi Joseph Zwane hails from the small rural town of Vrede in the Free State, where he returned to work as a teacher in 1989 after obtaining his diploma. The following year he joined the ANC, entering politics full-time a decade later. In 2009 he joined premier Ace Magashule's provincial government, where his portfolios included agriculture and economic development.

In 2012 he launched the province's 'Zero Hunger' strategy. The idea was to integrate a number of government programmes. These included reforms to redress historical racial imbalances in land holdings, repair farm infrastructure, provide better logistics and access to markets for black farmers, ramp up technical training for black smallholders, and boost food-processing businesses. The strategy was supposed to lead to increased food production, and more jobs and income in economically depressed rural areas. Instead, it became another licence to loot.

Zwane's flagship project was a mega dairy in his home town, Vrede. The provincial minister appeared to take an unusual interest in the scheme. Affidavits filed in an *ex parte* application brought by the Asset Forfeiture Unit allege he personally chose the location, even though a more suitable venue closer to larger urban centres had been suggested. Ten days after his department contracted a company to run the project, Zwane allegedly contacted the finance MEC to expedite the first R30-million payment on the same day even though there were no funds available. Free State Treasury official Anna Fourie was forced to rush back to the office from a staff function to attend to the payment request.[21]

It turned out that the company that was awarded the contract, Estina, was based in Sandton and run by an IT salesman at the Guptas' Sahara Computers who had never spent a day on a farm.

Flight and hotel records contained in the Gupta leaks later showed that the Guptas had financed trips that Zwane had taken to India and Dubai while serving in Magashule's cabinet.

By the time Estina was liquidated in 2017, it had received government grants totalling R250 million. Investigations by National Treasury and the Asset Forfeiture Unit allege that most of this money had been siphoned off to a constellation of Gupta-linked entities that had no business dealings or relationships with the dairy project. Prosecutors believe R169.5 million was paid to a Gupta-controlled shell company in the UAE called Gateway Limited, R10 million paid directly to Atul Gupta and R6 million to Westdawn Investments, the company that owned the Guptas' luxury Bombardier jet. Some of the money was allegedly used to pay for the lavish Sun City wedding in 2013 of the Gupta brothers' niece, Vega Gupta.[22]

The Gupta leaks later revealed that on 31 July 2015, the same day that Optimum coal mine went into business rescue, Zwane sent his CV to Tony Gupta. Less than two months later, President Zuma fired mineral resources minister Ngoako Ramatlhodi and replaced him with Zwane, suggesting that he'd been hand-picked by the Guptas. Now it was payback time.

* * *

In the middle of Eskom and Glencore's game of chicken, Brian Molefe suddenly took a close interest in the Gupta family.

Phone records cited in Public Protector Thuli Madonsela's report show that on 2 August, two days after Optimum went into business rescue, Molefe called Ajay Gupta. As the Guptas' negotiations to buy Optimum with Eskom's help gathered pace over the next eight months, Molefe made no fewer than forty-four phone calls to Ajay Gupta, who called him fourteen times during that period. Molefe was also in contact with Tony Gupta and Gupta executives Ronica Ragavan and Nazeem Howa, the phone records show.[23]

Madonsela's analysis of Molefe's phone records also place him in the vicinity of the Gupta compound in Saxonwold nineteen times from 5 August until 17 November, which coincided with the most intense period of the Optimum shakedown.[24] In his written submission to the parliamentary inquiry, Molefe pointed out Madonsela had failed to take into account that several calls were made or received around the same time, and that the records therefore reflected only five trips to or through the area. However, this does not alter the fact that Molefe's phone records place him in Saxonwold several times during critical milestones of the Optimum deal.[25]

Leaked emails later revealed that the Guptas were kept in the loop about unfolding developments at Optimum via email in real time.

For example, on 7 August business rescue practitioner Piers Marsden emailed a letter to Brian Molefe asking for an urgent meeting to discuss the mine's coal supply agreement with Eskom. Matshela Koko was among those Marsden copied in on the mail. On the same day, Gupta executive Ashu Chawla received a copy of Marsden's letter from someone called 'Business Man'. 'Sir please note ... license suspension has been lifted. They confirm their business rescue practitioner has given permission and therefore they will resume mining tomorrow,' Business Man informed Chawla.

Emails sent and received by Business Man appear numerous times in the Gupta leaks. In June 2015, Business Man, using the email address infoportal1@zoho.com, wrote to Duduzane Zuma:

please find attached my C.V and supporting documents
regards
Richard

The CV of the head of the Free State's Economic Development Department, Richard Seleke, was attached to the email. Among the references he lists is Mosebenzi Zwane, who was the Free State MEC for economic development at the time. Six months later, Lynne Brown appointed Seleke director-general of public enterprises, the department with jurisdiction over Transnet and Eskom.

The incident has led many to conclude that Business Man was in fact Seleke, although he has denied this. During Suzanne Daniels' disciplinary hearing, which ended in July 2018 with her dismissal, Eskom concluded that based on information contained in Matshela Koko's emails downloaded from the company server it was likely that Business Man was Salim Essa. Daniels was found guilty of forwarding Eskom documents to the email address knowing it belonged to Essa, although she claimed she had been told it was Seleke's.[26] However, the Organisation Undoing Tax Abuse said that based on its analysis of the leaked emails, it believed Seleke, Essa and other Gupta associates could have used the address as an information portal, as the name suggests.

Emails contained in the Gupta leaks show that several confidential Eskom documents were sent to Business Man from Koko's private Yahoo account. These documents were then forwarded to another anonymous user who goes by the name of 'Western' using the email address wdrsa1@gmail.com, and then on to Chawla. The leaked emails show that wdrsa1@gmail.com was used by Tony Gupta.

What became clear from the Gupta leaks is that every move made by Marsden and fellow business rescue practitioner Peter van den Steen was immediately relayed to the Guptas by their Eskom moles.

* * *

Shortly after his appointment on 4 August as Optimum's business rescue practitioner, Piers Marsden began playing hardball. He informed Eskom that Optimum would suspend supplies until an agreement was reached on a viable long-term coal price. He offered to revert to Ephron's R300-a-ton offer. This would at least allow the mine to keep supplying coal to Hendrina without making a loss and save the jobs of its 1500 employees and contractors.

Eskom refused. The best Molefe could offer was to suspend the penalty for sixty days if Optimum supplied the coal at the old price during that period. In September, Marsden agreed to go along with this stopgap measure on the understanding that it would afford everyone a breather to negotiate a fair deal. But Molefe refused to entertain any further discussion and told Marsden to settle the R2.2-billion fine 'in full without any delay'.[27]

The Guptas began to up the pressure on Optimum to sell. Marsden initially rebuffed their approaches, but after several entreaties he agreed to meet with Oakbay executives at the end of September to discuss their offer, which was for the coal mine only. Molefe and Ajay Gupta were in constant contact throughout this period.[28]

Barely a week after the September meeting, however, Marsden informed Oakbay that the deal was off. He had received a better offer from Pembani, the investment company that had bought Cyril Ramaphosa's business interests after he became deputy president in 2014.

It didn't take long for this deal to fall through too. A source close to the negotiations later told *Rapport* that Pembani had walked away because Molefe refused to sign a coal contract with the company.[29]

Two weeks later, Marsden went back to Oakbay to say he was willing to sell to the Guptas after all. He made it clear that only Optimum colliery was for sale. Glencore expressly wanted to exclude Koornfontein mine and the Richards Bay terminal from the deal.[30]

At this point, Matshela Koko took over as the point man in the Optimum negotiations. Eskom's power generation division had just been added to his portfolio, putting him in charge of ensuring the smooth running of all Eskom's power stations. It was now his responsibility to see to it that Hendrina received a steady supply of coal, including from Optimum. Any supply disruptions heightened the risk of load shedding, for which Koko would be blamed.

When Marsden sent Eskom another letter threatening to liquidate the company and cut Hendrina's fuel supply if a viable penalty and coal price agreement couldn't be reached, Koko went ballistic. 'Eskom is appalled at the blatant disregard Optimum displays for the impact that threats of liquidation has on the precarious balance of energy security and commercial viability,' Koko wrote in an email to Marsden and fellow business practitioner Peter van den Steen. 'Glencore surely cannot be perceived to be acting in the national interest when it threatens to cut off the fuel supply of a key strategic asset.'[31]

Koko threatened to 'seek intervention from such institutions as the

Department of Mineral Resources', which by then was headed by Zwane. 'It may also be an appropriate time for Eskom to review the engagement with Glencore from a portfolio perspective,' he warned. He signed off by proposing a round-table discussion with Oakbay, which Marsden had informed him was interested in buying the mine.[32]

Koko's high-minded outrage is completely undermined by what happened next. The Gupta leaks reveal that late that night two emails were sent from his private Yahoo account to Business Man, who forwarded them to Western – the account used by Tony Gupta. Western in turn forwarded Koko's emails to Ashu Chawla.[33] The first email sent from Koko's Yahoo account contains internal correspondence concerning a dispute between Eskom and a small coal supplier, Just Coal. It instructed Business Man to 'Please give the Boss'. Business Man duly forwarded it to the address used by Tony Gupta.

The second email had a sensitive legal opinion attached about the Optimum deal, addressed to Koko. Eskom had sought legal advice on whether it could go to court to enforce Optimum's onerous contract and remove Marsden and Van den Steen as business rescue practitioners. He was advised that there were no legal grounds for this and was urged instead to make Marsden a counter offer, as Hendrina was fast running out of coal.[34]

The leaks show that the Guptas got their hands on a draft of Koko's threatening letter to Marsden and Van den Steen on the same day that he sent it to the business rescue practitioners. Metadata shows that Daniels was the last person to work on the draft that landed up with Tony Gupta. Koko could simply have forwarded a draft to the Guptas that Daniels had worked on, but the incident raises the possibility that Daniels may have sent it to the family or their associates herself. Daniels has repeatedly denied deliberately sending any Eskom documents to members of the Gupta network and said she took instructions from executives, including Koko, when drafting letters.[35]

* * *

The Gupta leaks reveal that around this time, Eskom board member Mark Pamensky was dispensing advice to the Guptas on how they should handle negotiations going forward. 'As I'm at the tail end of the main acquisition of Optimum Coal, please ensure that a condition precedent is that the R2-billion claim from Eskom is withdrawn or it becomes the seller's problem,' he wrote to Atul Gupta on 22 November. 'I'm happy to get involved to assist with this acquisition. If you need me in India or Dubai to discuss, I'll meet you there.'

Pamensky's emails and Koko's threats to invoke the mining minister's wrath coincided with another important event. On 20 November 2015, almost a third of the shares in Tegeta, which had until then been controlled by the Gupta family and their employees, were transferred to Mabengela Investments, a company part-owned by Duduzane Zuma. Henceforth, Glencore would be negotiating with the president's son too.[36]

* * *

The round-table discussion was held on Tuesday 24 November at Megawatt Park. Koko, who had apparently been feeding inside information to the Guptas all along, chaired the meeting. It wasn't long before he dropped a bombshell: Eskom would only support the deal if Glencore agreed to throw the profitable Koornfontein mine and Richards Bay terminal into the pot.

You can almost picture Koko as Tony Soprano informing some small-time enterprise he was shaking down: 'The price just went up.'

Koko demanded an answer by the weekend.[37]

Neither Ephron nor Glencore chief executive Ivan Glasenberg has ever gone public about what happened next, although testimony at the parliamentary inquiry and internal Eskom correspondence provides some clues. Marsden told Parliament that Koko's ultimatum sparked off hurried discussions with Tegeta.[38]

No doubt emboldened by their newfound negotiating power at Eskom and the leverage they could exert through their hand-picked mining minister, Mosebenzi Zwane, the Guptas made a verbal offer of R1 billion for the whole shebang. Clinton Ephron must have felt insulted. Optimum's coal terminal alone was worth at least R3.6 billion; its Koornfontein mine had a profitable contract to supply Komati power station; and the holding company owed a consortium of banks worth R2.7 billion, with its assets held as security. There was no way they would agree to a write-off of that magnitude.

Marsden said that on Thursday 26 November, he met with the banks and put the latest R1 billion offer from the Guptas on the table. Predictably, they rejected it.[39]

The events that followed, recorded in official documents and leaked emails, strongly suggest Zwane stepped in to save the day for the Guptas.

The following day, 27 November, his office reportedly sent an email to the South African embassy in Switzerland, informing it that Zwane would undertake a three-day visit to Zurich. His itinerary reportedly showed that he was scheduled to hold three meetings with Glasenberg over three days, from 30 November to 2 December, at The Dolder Grand hotel.[40]

While Zwane was setting these plans in motion, Glencore was having second thoughts about selling Optimum to the Guptas. Marsden told Parliament that by the end of November or 'perhaps on the 1st of December', Glencore had made the decision to bail out the ailing coal mine after all.[41]

A meeting was hastily convened at Megawatt Park. Koko told Parliament that Marsden and either Ephron or Glencore's head of business development in South Africa, Shaun Blankfield, came to convey the message to him. Koko recorded further details of the meeting in a letter he sent soon afterwards to the director-general of mineral resources, Thibedi Ramontja. Koko was told Glencore would honour its miserly R150-a-ton contract 'with no amendments' until it expired at the end of 2018, and fund the losses. Its R2.2-billion penalty would be referred to arbitration. This meant Optimum mine could be taken out of business rescue and 1500 jobs would be saved.[42]

Marsden said that shortly after this meeting he met with Optimum's lenders 'to let them know this fortuitous piece of news'.[43]

This wasn't good news for the Guptas, however, who were once again about to see Optimum slip from their grasp. But by then their pet mining minister, Zwane, had already arrived in Switzerland after a short stopover in Dubai. Travel records cited in Public Protector Thuli Madonsela's report on state capture show that Zwane left Johannesburg for Dubai on Sunday 29 November and boarded an Emirates flight from Dubai bound for Zurich the following day. Madonsela said she had 'received information from an independent source' that during his stay in Zurich, Zwane had met with Glasenberg at The Dolder Grand hotel in the presence of Salim Essa and Tony Gupta. The *Sunday Times* later reported that it had obtained documents showing Essa and Tony Gupta stayed at The Dolder Grand at the same time.[44]

Flight records contained in the Gupta leaks show that on 2 December, after concluding his business with Glasenberg in Zurich, Zwane boarded the Guptas' infamous Bombardier jet and flew to India. Tony Gupta and Salim Essa were among the seven passengers on board.

According to Marsden, Glencore's decision to take Optimum out of business rescue, thus effectively scuppering the Gupta deal, was taken toward the end of November or, at the latest, on 1 December – in other words, either just before or after Zwane arrived at the Dolder on Monday. Shortly after he left on Wednesday, the deal to sell Optimum was on again. Two days later, on Friday 4 December, Marsden received Tegeta's offer of R2.15 billion for Optimum, which Glencore accepted. Zwane's visit had changed the game again.

Two months later, Zwane conceded publicly that he'd met Glasenberg in Zurich to discuss the Optimum deal, but claimed the purpose of his intervention had been to 'save jobs'.[45]

It turned out that this response had been scripted by the Guptas. Shortly before Zwane went public for the first time about the Zurich meeting, Gupta executive Nazeem Howa sent an email to Tony Gupta asking for help in drafting a question-and-answer template for the minister.

'Perhaps I can sit with someone his side to help me polish and add to the answers,' Howa suggested.

The document they were working on contained detailed responses to a list of fourteen questions they expected the media to ask Zwane after information about his trip to Zurich began to circulate. As a former journalist, Howa would know exactly the type of questions members of the Fourth Estate were likely to throw at the minister.

Howa's questions included gems such as 'What about the rumours of your being captured by the Guptas and [that] your appointment was made for you to do their bidding?' and 'Many would say your appointment was payback by the Guptas for the support you gave them around Vrede', to which he was instructed to reply: 'The Guptas have never been a part of the Vrede dairy project.'[46]

As to discussing the sale of Optimum with Glasenberg, Zwane was instructed to point out that he was 'happy to report that we saved 3 000 jobs due to that meeting'. He was to describe selling the mine to the Guptas in glowing terms. 'I certainly believe the purchase of Optimum by a black-owned consortium of which the Guptas form part is a major step forward towards broadening the ownership structures in our industry.'

In his answers drafted by Howa, Zwane was told to stress that the specific purpose of meeting Glasenberg was to save the mine from going under because 'Optimum was in business rescue and there was a very real danger of the deal not proceeding'.[47]

The evidence outlined above casts serious doubt on Zwane's explanation. I think it's far more likely that the Guptas dispatched him to salvage the deal after the banks refused to play ball. Glasenberg probably told him Glencore had decided to fund the mine out of business rescue. In all likelihood, Zwane then persuaded Glasenberg to sell it to the Guptas after all, not at the rock-bottom price they'd asked for, but still at a substantial discount.

I can't imagine that Glasenberg would have agreed to part with his South African coal complex on unfavourable terms without getting anything in return. One theory is that Zwane offered to cut him in on a lucrative oil deal. Shortly after Zwane's visit to Zurich, the Strategic Fuel Fund secretly sold off almost all of South Africa's strategic oil reserves, a total of ten million barrels, at a rock-bottom price. Glencore was one of three lucky companies invited to take part in the closed tender. Oil prices have almost doubled since then, which means Glencore stood to make a substantial profit. This could have been the company's payback for the Guptas' Optimum discount, with South African taxpayers picking up the tab. Glencore has never commented on the issue.

* * *

Two days after Zwane boarded the Gupta jet bound for India with Salim Essa and Tony Gupta, Piers Marsden wrote back to Koko to say that negotiations with Oakbay would continue. The game was on again.[48]

Koko immediately sprang into action. On Sunday 6 December, he dashed off a letter to mineral resources director-general Thibedi Ramontja.

Koko's letter was mostly devoted to painting a lurid picture of the risks posed by Glencore's continued ownership of Optimum. The company's 'intermittent veiled threats of liquidation' and 'erratic display of business stability' were not in the national interest and compromised security of fuel supply to three major power stations: Arnot, Komati and Hendrina. Exxaro's contract to supply Arnot would expire within weeks and the utility had not yet found a replacement supplier. But Koko pointed out to Ramontja that Optimum happened to produce the type and quantity of coal suitable for Arnot. 'Therefore, Optimum becomes a highly sought after source for Arnot as well,' he remarked. He urged Ramontja's department to intervene in this emergency by 'leveraging the necessary key authorities' to ensure security of supply for the Eskom power stations.[49]

Ramontja's response, sent on Monday 7 December, is an astonishing document. He pledges to fast-track the transfer of Glencore's mining right to Oakbay and smooth the deal's passage through the Competition Commission, which regulates anti-competitive behaviour. He then suggests that the Guptas should be rewarded for 'honouring the current contract up to 2018' – which Glencore had offered to do just days earlier – 'and for driving transformation'. In return, Oakbay should receive a prepayment of one year's coal supply. He justified these extraordinary measures as a way to guarantee coal supply from 'all of these critical mines, thereby averting any national crisis that we as South Africa can ill afford'.[50]

In essence, Ramontja was committing his department to bend over backwards for the Guptas, offering them way more than Koko had asked for. In my view, the only conclusion to be drawn is that he had been fully briefed by Zwane about what was expected of him. This view is strengthened by Koko's remark in his submission to Parliament that Ramontja's 'department was, clearly, abreast of ongoing developments, and of the identity of the potential buyer'.[51]

A week later, Ramontja stunned mining analysts by quitting 'for personal reasons'.[52]

Koko lost no time in getting the ball rolling. The day after he received Ramontja's response, he drew up a board submission and circulated it among Eskom's directors. It asked for board approval to pay the Guptas a total of R1.68 billion in advance for future coal deliveries from two mines they didn't own yet – R825 million from Optimum and R855 million from Koornfontein. In effect, Koko was asking Eskom to bankroll the Gupta purchase of both mines.

The submission, which was signed off by Koko and Anoj Singh, was largely a cut-and-paste of Koko's letter to Ramontja, with the mining DG's response attached for further justification. It concluded with the dire warning that Optimum's shutdown 'could potentially result in thousands of job losses and add to the negative publicity surrounding Eskom', despite the fact that Glencore had offered to honour the contract for another year at a loss.[53]

These events at Eskom took place against the backdrop of huge political upheavals that shook the country to its core. In October, the Guptas allegedly offered deputy finance minister Mcebisi Jonas a R600-million bribe if he would take the job of finance minister to promote their business interests. The Guptas wanted to replace the respected incumbent Nhlanhla Nene. He was proving a thorn in their side, especially in his opposition to a nuclear power deal the family would benefit from, and the habit his officials had of being sticklers for public finance rules. When Jonas declined, the Guptas opted for small-town mayor Des van Rooyen, who had visited Saxonwold several times shortly before his appointment. He was later dubbed 'Weekend Special' and 'Two-Minute Noodle' after lasting only four days as finance minister when Zuma's reshuffle caused a national uproar and sent the financial markets tumbling.

On the morning of Wednesday 9 December – just twelve hours before Zuma's shock announcement that he was firing Nene – Eskom's board duly rubber-stamped Koko's Optimum plan.

The Guptas, who appeared to have been kept in the loop every step of the way by Koko, clearly believed their prepayment was in the bag. The Gupta leaks show that just after 2 p.m. that afternoon, Tegeta chief executive Ravindra Nath sent Koko a letter, blind-copying Tony Gupta, thanking the Eskom executive for their meeting to discuss the deal. 'We humbly request you to kindly send us a written confirmation regarding the payment for supply of coal amounting to R1.68 billion,' he said, providing the details of his attorney Gert van der Merwe's bank account, where he expected the money to be deposited.

It must have been a particularly sweet victory for the Guptas, who could safely say they now controlled South Africa's mining ministry, its largest state enterprises, Eskom and Transnet, and – for a few days at least – held the keys to the national vault. With their hand-picked finance minister in place, they anticipated no opposition to their plan from Treasury.

The next day, 10 December, Glencore signed an agreement with Tegeta to sell Optimum colliery, Koornfontein mine and its stake in the Richards Bay terminal for R2.15 billion – probably only half of what it was worth but far better than the previous offer of R1 billion. For the sale to go through, Tegeta needed to meet a set of conditions by 31 March 2016: approval from the Competition Commission, Eskom and the mineral resources department, as well as a letter of comfort or guarantee showing that it had the money available.

That night, Mark Pamensky sent an effusive email to Atul Gupta: 'Congratulations (Mazeltov) on a brilliant and well thought out, planned and strategised acquisition of the Optimum group of companies,' he said. 'Well done and I'm proud of you all.'[54] He appeared completely oblivious to the blatant conflict of interest of dispensing advice to the Guptas about the deal as a board member of Oakbay while sitting on the board of Eskom.

Then Eskom's treasury division threw a spanner in the works. Treasury manager Caroline Henry pointed out that it was safer for Eskom to issue a guarantee for the payment through a commercial bank so that it could only be used once key conditions were met – most notably, that the Guptas actually owned the mine. In other words, Eskom wouldn't be financing the purchase price.

This wasn't quite what the Guptas and their Eskom deployees had in mind. 'They wanted the whole amount to be paid to Tegeta as prospective buyer of Optimum,' an official involved in the transaction told me. Although the strings-attached guarantee meant that the bank couldn't disburse the cash, it would still come in handy.

The official said that Singh and Koko placed everyone involved under intense pressure to ensure that the guarantee was issued urgently, although both claimed they'd done things by the book. Because it exceeded R1.5 billion, ministerial approval should have been sought, but it wasn't. The next day, Eskom deposited R1.68 billion on call at Absa. Even though this breached Eskom's own policy to limit the concentration of funds across banks, it was personally approved by Anoj Singh. On the same day, Absa issued a guarantee to pay the Guptas R1.68 billion on demand into their Bank of India account. It too was signed off by Singh.

The Guptas didn't have the money in their account, but they did have the next best thing: a guarantee from Absa saying that they were good for R1.68 billion. A week later, the Bank of Baroda issued a letter of comfort to Optimum's business rescue practitioners for R2.15 billion, even though almost no funds had arrived by then.[55]

Two days before Christmas in 2015, Eskom declared a coal emergency at Arnot power station. Tegeta was perfectly poised to step into the breach. Soon, champagne corks would be popping in Saxonwold and Emirates Hills.

13

Trillian's Billions

Tetris is a game invented by a Soviet software engineer named Alexey Pajitnov who worked at a state computer lab in Moscow during the Cold War. It was based on an ancient Roman puzzle played with wooden blocks called pentominoes. Pajitnov pictured the blocks falling from above, with players guiding them into place. In 1985, he turned his imaginings into a hugely popular video game.[1]

Brian Molefe likes to tell the story of how Tetris inspired the creation of a power plant maintenance tool that helped end load shedding. When Molefe asked two young Eskom engineers, Christo Murray and Lyle Timm, to explain the intricacies of maintenance planning, they described juggling shifting blocks of time when planned outages would be suitable at dozens of plants with minimal disruption to the power grid. Molefe thought it sounded like Tetris, and the idea stuck. He encouraged Murray and Timm to create a visual-planning tool that represented maintenance schedules for all of Eskom's plants in one dynamic multicoloured chart.[2]

Eskom's 'Tetris model' had its origins in the Top Consultants programme launched by McKinsey in 2013. The global consultancy had been hired to provide field training in consulting skills to Eskom engineers to reduce the utility's R1-billion annual consultants bill. Within two years, a total of thirty full-time Eskom employees had graduated from the McKinsey class and were providing helpful consulting services across different work streams. Among them were Murray and Timm, who with McKinsey's help had developed the Tetris tool.

In 2015, McKinsey submitted a proposal to ramp up its programme to create a fully fledged consulting unit at Eskom that would focus on risk management, including of the power crisis. The ambitious plan was submitted jointly with Regiments Capital. It included providing Eskom with advisory services on how to achieve substantial cost savings in coal supply, procurement and claims lodged by contractors at Medupi and Kusile.[3]

In a pattern that had become an all too familiar justification for looting, Eskom's energy crisis would be used as an excuse to break Treasury rules on public spending and pay astronomical fees to McKinsey, with up to half the proceeds going straight into the pockets of the Guptas and their associates, including Salim Essa.

In a previous chapter I described how Essa had allegedly used his connections to ensure Regiments displaced consulting firm Letsema as McKinsey's empowerment partner of choice at a number of parastatals. From Transnet alone, Regiments earned fees of up to R485 million during the tenure of Brian Molefe and Anoj Singh. Half appeared to have been diverted to Essa and some to his golfing partner Kuben Moodley, even though neither of them performed any discernible services for the logistics parastatal.

As we've seen, Singh had been hosted by the Guptas on at least five occasions in Dubai during this time, often staying in the same hotel as Tony Gupta and Essa, and had probably received cash payments from the family too. Singh later admitted that he had met Essa 'on two or three occasions' when he was 'seeking business opportunities' at Transnet. He also conceded that he was well acquainted with McKinsey partner Vikas Sagar and Regiments co-founder Eric Wood from his time at Transnet. He described Wood as a 'trusted business advisor'. Sagar was McKinsey's original point man with Regiments and enjoyed a close relationship with Salim Essa.[4]

When Brian Dames was in charge at Eskom, Essa had tried to get the parastatal to sign up Regiments to work on coal contracts for a R500-million fee. Regiments had been rebuffed. Now, with Brian Molefe in charge and Singh soon to be seconded, Regiments' prospects at Eskom looked decidedly rosier.

* * *

In June 2015, Mosilo Mothepu received a phone call that would change her life. She recounted the incident in her testimony in Parliament. It was her former boss at Regiments, Eric Wood. Mothepu had joined the fledgling firm in 2007 as a debt capital markets specialist, working closely with its three founding directors: Wood, Litha Nyhonyha and Niven Pillay. In 2010, she'd left to expand her horizons. Now Wood wanted her back.

'We've submitted a big proposal with McKinsey to work on Eskom,' he told her. 'I want you to lead the team.'

When Mothepu returned to Regiments, she couldn't believe her eyes. She'd joined a company with eight employees. When she left in 2010 there were fifty. Now there were 270 consultants. Their clients included Transnet, Denel and SA Express.

'I asked the chief financial officer, wow, what's happening? He said no, it's a new model; we have these guys called business development partners,' she later recounted.[5]

The company's new rainmakers were Salim Essa and Kuben Moodley. 'Salim knew the executives at Denel, Transnet and Eskom,' she said. His message to them was simple. 'He told them if they don't open the door, they're out. Suddenly Regiments was flying.'

In Mothepu's telling, by the time she arrived, McKinsey and Regiments had already worked out the finer details of the Eskom deal. She told Parliament that Eskom had been identified as 'the next cash cow' after Transnet.[6] As the main contractor, McKinsey would be paid 70 per cent of the fees, with Regiments receiving the rest. However, part of the proposal was to advise Eskom on how to optimise its balance sheet and 'unlock' cash. For this work, Regiments would be paid 95 per cent of the fees and McKinsey 5 per cent.

With the money taps about to open, other companies in the Gupta orbit began circling for their share of the spoils. One of these was Cutting Edge Commerce, a company majority owned by the Guptas that specialised in providing software to improve procurement processes.

The Gupta leaks later revealed that as early as June 2015 the company was discussing how it could profit from the project, expecting to make about R20 million every quarter as a Regiments subcontractor. Cutting Edge was also implicated in funnelling money it earned from Transnet to Homix, the suspected Gupta money-laundering front in Mayfair linked to Essa.[7]

McKinsey's mega deal at Eskom gathered momentum after Brian Molefe took over in April 2015.

On 18 May, a memo was submitted to the executive procurement committee justifying why Eskom should be allowed to deviate from Treasury rules and award the contract to Regiments and McKinsey without it going out to tender. The memo claimed that McKinsey was the only company capable of doing the job, which was patently false given the number of international consultancies with local partners operating in South Africa.[8]

The submission was requested by Prish Govender, the group capital official at Eskom soon to become the project leader on the deal, and supported inter alia by Edwin Mabelane, the executive standing in for Matshela Koko who would become chief procurement officer after Koko returned from suspension. In June, the submission was prepared for the board tender committee. It claimed that the contract wouldn't cost Eskom a cent because McKinsey would only receive a percentage of savings achieved, undertaking the work at its own risk with no guarantee of payment. In reality, this pricing model allowed consultants to earn literally billions of rands as a cut of savings that might never materialise.[9] For McKinsey there was to be no risk at all: Eskom promised to pay the firm hefty 'down payments' and reimburse its expenses.[10]

In July 2015, a round-robin resolution was circulated to members of the board tender committee for a mandate to negotiate an 'at risk' three-year contract with McKinsey without it going out to tender. It was duly signed off by Zethembe Khoza, Viroshini Naidoo, Chwayita Mabude and Nazia Carrim – all of whom, as we have seen, were linked in one way or another to the Guptas or their right-hand man, Essa.[11]

Mothepu told Parliament that when Anoj Singh arrived at Eskom in August, he immediately put McKinsey and Regiments to work, clearly confident that the necessary paperwork could be rubber-stamped down the line. Even though not a single contract had been drawn up yet, let alone signed, the team of consultants was issued with contractor access cards and allocated a boardroom at Megawatt Park.

Mothepu described the relationship between Regiments and its offshoot Trillian as 'improper' from the start. Singh was 'very close to Eric [Wood] from the Transnet days,' she said. Semi-clandestine meetings were held with Singh at hotels throughout the city rather than at Megawatt

Park 'to discuss the proposal and also to assist him with his first hundred days and an action plan'. At these meetings, Singh helped the consultants refine the proposals they would submit – a privilege other consultants vying for Eskom business could only dream of. 'He would give us information on a memory stick so that McKinsey and Regiments would have inside information that other people would not have,' said Mothepu.[12]

Singh and Koko allegedly also took the opportunity to add a few line items close to their hearts to the task list. One was managing a R6-billion insurance claim for a boiler at Duvha power station that had exploded in 2014, putting extra strain on the power grid. Another was a proposal for online vending of prepaid electricity.

Eskom's legal division immediately raised red flags about the McKinsey proposal. In August, officials were warned that McKinsey should be charging fixed fees at an hourly rate and that any deviation from this pricing model needed consent from the president and National Treasury. There was no justification for failing to go out to tender.

Aziz Laher, a public finance specialist at Eskom, relayed these warnings, inter alia, to the two officials in charge of the project: Prish Govender and chief procurement officer Edwin Mabelane. Laher warned them that without Treasury approval the entire contract value would be deemed irregular expenditure, regardless of savings achieved.[13]

Undeterred, Koko and Singh switched to Plan B. In September, they asked the board to approve a much smaller contract with McKinsey and Regiments for 'ad-hoc support on urgent finance and strategy work'. Once again they claimed that urgency obviated the need for a tender. Three weeks later, Eskom signed a R100-million six-month consulting contract with McKinsey, with R30 million earmarked for Regiments. It was enough to keep them busy while waiting for the main event.[14]

* * *

No doubt delighted by Regiments' ever-burgeoning parastatal order book, the Guptas moved in to secure a stake in the company.

Eric Wood told me through a company statement that in 2014 Salim Essa joined the three Regiments founders at one of their weekly strategy meetings at Tortellino D'Oro restaurant in Oaklands, Johannesburg. Wood said he was delegated to provide the Guptas with the company information they needed to table a formal offer. Internal documents show that the Guptas were prepared to pay R200 million for a 50 per cent stake in the company.[15]

Litha Nyhonyha and Niven Pillay dispute this. They claim that Wood was trying to sell their company to the Guptas behind their backs and that they only came to hear of the offer when he took Pillay to meet Tony Gupta in Saxonwold in April 2015. At that meeting, Tony Gupta offered to make Pillay a 'dollar billionaire' if he sold the family a controlling stake in the firm and cut Nyhonyha out of the picture. When Pillay refused, Regiments' government contracts began to dry up.[16]

Whichever version is true, the meeting marked the beginning of a breakdown in the Regiments founders' relationship. Three months later, after several acrimonious meetings, they decided to part company. Wood took half of the Regiments staff, including Mosilo Mothepu, with him.

As we've seen from Mothepu's testimony, Wood and Essa had no intention of giving up their lucrative partnership with McKinsey though, especially since their ambitious pitch to Eskom was about to bear fruit. But if they wanted to offer Eskom financial advice, they urgently needed a company registered with the Financial Services Board, which is where Trillian came in. Pretty soon all the lucrative contracts Regiments was getting from Transnet, and the deals it was hatching with Eskom, would flow Trillian's way.

* * *

Trillian Asset Management was a boutique financial advisory firm owned by four investment professionals: Daniel Roy, Jan Faure, and brothers Rowan and Ben Swartz. They'd named it after the 'beautiful, charming, devastatingly intelligent' astrophysicist Tricia 'Trillian' McMillan in Douglas Adams' cult sci-fi novel *The Hitchhiker's Guide to the Galaxy*.

Trillian was 'ticking along but it never shot the lights out', one fund manager familiar with the company's history told me. 'It was floundering, really.' In 2014, the company generated revenues of R2.5 million and posted a small loss. The following year, earnings increased to R2.7 million. By the end of 2014 the Swartz brothers told their partners that they wanted out.

Roy and Faure thought public sector work was the key to improving the company's financial fortunes, but parastatals would only do business with companies that were empowered, forcing them to start casting about for a black partner. Fortuitously, one of Roy's former partners, Stanley Shane, happened to know someone who wanted to buy a financial advisory company: Salim Essa.

The whole arrangement was disturbingly cosy. Shane ran his own capital-raising firm called Integrated Capital Management. Like Eric Wood, Shane's partners Clive Angel and Marc Chipkin had both previously worked for Investec. Shane occupied an influential position on the board of Transnet, having taken over from Essa's former friend and business partner Iqbal Sharma as head of the parastatal's acquisitions and disposals committee in December 2014. Shane and Angel were both co-directors, along with Essa, of another financial advisory firm, Antares Capital.

In August 2015, Daniel Roy called Trillian co-founder Rowan Swartz. 'Stan Shane has introduced me to a buyer but I'm not at liberty to disclose who the buyer is,' he told him. Swartz found this a little odd so he obtained a legal opinion. He was told that he wasn't breaking the law by selling his company to an anonymous buyer, provided anything material or untoward was disclosed. The Swartzes decided it was time to part ways with the 'beautiful, charming' little company for a modest sum.

Roy told me he was impressed when he met Essa for the first time. Essa sketched his vision of creating a top-notch financial services firm that would attract South Africa's best talent and clients. 'It was the holy grail,' he told me. 'Here was a BEE guy who's got cash and connections and doesn't want to be involved in operational matters. In hindsight it was too good to be true.'

Although the Guptas had become embroiled in several scandals by then, Essa was still a relatively low-key figure in the state capture rogue's gallery. 'When I met Salim and did a due diligence there was very little about him in the public domain,' said Roy. 'I had no idea he had anything to do with the Gupta family. All I knew was the one thing we were seriously lacking was a BEE partner.'

Whistleblower documents, company filings, information from my sources and testimony in Parliament suggest Shane and his partners at Integrated Capital put the whole thing together. In the convoluted shareholding structure they devised, which confusingly retained the company's original name for one of its subsidiaries, Essa's stake was kept well hidden. On 1 September 2015 they registered a shell company that bought the Swartz brothers' 50 per cent stake in Trillian Asset Management. The company was renamed Trillian Capital Partners (TCP) and five subsidiaries were created, including one that took the original name Trillian Asset Management. Essa became the majority shareholder of TCP, with a 60 per cent stake, followed by Wood with 25 per cent. In company brochures, Essa's share was simply referred to as Trillian Holdings. Roy and Faure's share was diluted to 3 per cent. The remaining 12 per cent was held by a mysterious entity called Aeriom Nominees on behalf of a mysterious group of shareholders Wood described as 'employees'.

In November, Clive Angel started recruiting staff for Trillian. Among them was Bianca Goodson, a young economic analyst at mining house Anglo American. She related her harrowing experiences at Trillian to Parliament and in a statement she made available on the Platform for the Protection of Whistleblowers in Africa. 'We've already secured public sector work,' Angel explained in Goodson's account. 'We're going to become the leading South African black empowerment management company. I'm looking for black South African leaders for this venture.'[17]

Goodson jumped at the chance and was appointed chief executive of Trillian's management consulting division. In her telling, she was informed she would report to Angel and that he in turn took his instructions from Essa, who was an additional signatory on her employment contract and took part in her final interview. 'He's the boss,' Angel told her. She said if she encountered any difficulties in working with McKinsey, she would go to Essa, who would resolve the issue with Sagar.[18]

Angel disputes Goodson's account that he played an operational role at Trillian and says he provided 'primarily establishment and startup services'. However, Goodson's statement contains evidence that suggests Angel played a more hands-on role than he's letting on, including in negotiations with McKinsey together with Essa. Goodson's statement contains screen grabs of two meetings in her electronic diary to discuss Eskom work streams attended by Essa, Eric Wood and the directors of Integrated Capital – Clive Angel, Stanley Shane and Marc Chipkin. She says in her statement that when she arrived for these meetings, McKinsey partner Vikas Sagar 'was attending'. On one occasion, she arrived early to find Essa, Shane, Angel, Chipkin and Sagar 'discussing the work at Eskom and Transnet'.[19]

Goodson said she met Essa regularly at Trillian's offices. Sometimes he would arrange for her to meet Eskom officials at Melrose Arch – including Matshela Koko.

She soon became uncomfortable with Angel's instructions and the way the company operated. For example, she related how she was asked to open Trillian's primary bank account with Absa, but wasn't given access to statements or financial flows. In her telling, when she confronted Angel, she was told the company's finances were managed centrally. 'Your job is to help draw up PowerPoint presentations and follow instructions,' he said.[20]

Another source of disquiet was her interaction with a company called eGateway. Trillian had farmed out almost half its power generation work at Eskom to eGateway, which was based in Dubai. This had left McKinsey decidedly uncomfortable. Trillian was its black empowerment partner at Eskom, but the work was being done by consultants who were 'either Indian or Emirati, not South African', said Goodson.[21]

In Goodson's account, when she objected, Angel told her that 'our boss [Essa] has found them and we are working with them'. Trillian ignored McKinsey's objections too. This became a major source of tension between the firms.

Whenever Goodson raised these issues with Angel, his stock response was: 'All businesses operated in this way – how do you think Investec or Anglo became so successful?'[22]

* * *

Given his senior position on a parastatal board, Stanley Shane's actions in the Regiments and Trillian saga deserve closer scrutiny.

I obtained two revealing memos prepared for Transnet by Werksmans Attorneys. They examined the legality of Regiments ceding its rights to Transnet payments to Trillian after Eric Wood split from his partners and took half their staff and state contracts with him. The memos show that in March 2015 the acquisitions and disposals committee at Transnet that Shane chaired had authorised that a lucrative tender for freight rail advisory services be open to Regiments only. Shane's committee later approved ceding this contract to Trillian after Essa became its majority shareholder.[23]

When I put it to Shane that his role through Integrated Capital in forming Trillian and allegedly helping the company do business with Transnet and Eskom while he chaired the Transnet board committee represented a conflict of interest, he – like Angel – sought to downplay his role at Trillian. He confirmed that he'd introduced Essa to Daniel Roy but claimed he'd played 'no direct role' in the transaction and that 'the parties concluded the deal themselves'. Shane also insisted that Integrated Capital 'performed no services for Trillian' and disputed whistleblower testimony that the company had been paid R700 000 a month to help Trillian. In an emailed response to my questions he said Trillian had 'contracted with a company operated by Angel and Chipkin to provide services (primarily establishment and startup services) for Trillian. This is the only context in which they would have represented the company.'

However, as outlined above, Bianca Goodson has provided evidence suggesting Shane took part in Trillian's discussion with McKinsey about work for Eskom. On at least one occasion this included liaising with representatives from Gupta-linked subcontractors. She also said Shane was 'operationally involved in management decisions', was a 'recurring invitee' to all Trillian management and executive committee meetings, and was included in the distribution of minutes from these meetings.[24]

Internal email correspondence I obtained also attests to Shane's involvement in Trillian's operations. Shane is copied in on an email from Chipkin, who uses a Trillian email address, that discusses a letter to be written to Vikas Sagar, the McKinsey partner who was later suspended and quit over his role in the scandal over suspect payments from Eskom to Trillian totalling R600 million. Another email is copied to Shane's Trillian Capital Partners' email address, stanley.shane@tcp.co.za.

A source familiar with the deal that led to Essa becoming a majority shareholder told me that Shane and his fellow Integrated Capital directors were the intended owners of at least some of the 12 per cent stake of Trillian held by Aeriom Nominees. This was supported by Goodson's statement, Mothepu's testimony to Parliament as well as Daniel Roy, who was involved in setting up the deal. 'There was a discussion with Stan [Shane] and Salim about [Shane] being remunerated for setting up the company,' Roy told me. Granting Shane shares in Trillian was 'one of the options on the table'. In the end, the alleged plan to cede the shares to Shane and other Integrated Capital members never came to fruition. In 2017, the shares were transferred from Aeriom Nominees to Trillian Nominees, again for the benefit of 'staff', according to Wood.

When I asked Angel and Shane if they were ever party to or aware of discussions to grant them or Integrated Capital any shares in Trillian, they dodged the question. In a cut-and-paste response, they said that the company 'has never owned and does not own any shares' in Trillian Capital Partners 'or any Trillian related companies'. Shane resigned from Transnet in 2017.

* * *

Just three months after Essa and Wood bought Trillian, the company hit paydirt. On 4 December 2015, an amount of R93.5 million landed in its bank account for advisory work at Transnet on a R12-billion loan for the locomotive deal – not bad for a company that until then had never earned more than R3 million a year.[25]

* * *

In September 2015, while Salim Essa, Eric Wood and Stanley Shane were putting together the Trillian group, Mark Pamensky dashed off his last email to the Guptas as chief operating officer of telecoms company Blue Label.

'Please find attached for information purposes, including Eskom's new procurement methods for coal,' said Pamensky, who at the time served on the boards of Eskom and Oakbay. He advised Atul Gupta that Oakbay should 'do a deal with Eskom' on mines tied to power stations. 'I have some good thoughts on these assets that can be a win-win for Eskom, the mine owners, and ourselves,' he wrote.[26]

Pamensky resigned as a director of Blue Label at the end of the month to start his own company, MarkPam Consulting. It wasn't long before he showed up at the door of Trillian, which would later contribute to the purchase price of one of the tied mines, Optimum colliery (see Chapter 14).

Bianca Goodson and Mosilo Mothepu said that when they met Pamensky at Melrose Arch, he was introduced to them as the chief executive of Trillian's property division. Pamensky was working with Michail Shapiro, an energetic young property mogul whose Fuel Property Group had developed a fancy ownership vehicle for monetising unused real estate belonging to state entities.

Shapiro's idea, which he'd refined over many years, was to create a ring-fenced fund that would buy properties from state entities at market value and develop them, with the returns flowing back to the parastatals. In fact, he'd pitched the model to Eric Wood, Niven Pillay and Litha Nyhonyha at Regiments a decade earlier, followed by several municipalities. He hadn't found any takers yet – until Wood partnered with Essa, the man with a magic knack for opening doors.

Transnet gave Trillian access to its entire portfolio, an enormous pile of documents listing 60 000 properties, for Shapiro to analyse. His team travelled the length and breadth of the country, visiting ports and provincial offices, eventually whittling the list down to 350 non-core properties worth about R10 billion.

Trillian's proposal to Transnet submitted by Eric Wood envisaged being paid a 2 per cent 'fund management fee' and a 20 per cent cut 'of the uplift created'. Trillian would take on some of the financial risk in the start-up phase in return for 'participating with our clients in the value realised'.[27] It sounded suspiciously like McKinsey's 'at risk' contract with Eskom. Had the plan succeeded, it would have turned Trillian's shareholders into billionaires once the properties were developed and sold. In the end, Transnet cancelled the project 'due to internal legal processes' after it had paid Trillian R41 million for the proposal.

As chairperson of Eskom's investment and finance committee, Pamensky was ideally placed to make use of privileged information to replicate the scheme at the power utility. In an email that was sent to Trillian executives, Pamensky pointed out that Eskom was under pressure to sell non-core properties to improve its balance sheet and that Treasury would withhold R5 billion of R10 billion in promised funding until it had done so. 'I have been reviewing from a high level the Eskom real estate department and the value of these properties,' he said, adding that Trillian would submit a plan to Eskom similar to its proposal to Transnet.[28]

Correspondence between Pamensky and Eskom employees leaves one in no doubt that he was using his privileged position to his own advantage and that of the Guptas, who wanted to ramp up their coal deliveries to Eskom. 'Hi Kulsum,' he wrote to an Eskom employee on 24 December. 'Please can you forward me the following documents urgently, per all the attachments in this mail: 1. Primary energy strategy; 2. The disposal of residential properties as mentioned.'

The Eskom property scheme flopped too, apparently because a senior official preferred to commission a real estate company to analyse its portfolio. Trillian quietly dropped its plans for a property division and Pamensky was 'seen less frequently in the office', as Bianca Goodson, who often used to share a smoke with him in the company courtyard, put it.[29]

As with his dealings involving Optimum mine at Eskom that favoured the Guptas, Pamensky tried to downplay these actions as 'a perceived rather than real conflict' when law firm Thomson Wilks was asked to investigate them. Its legal opinion, sent to the Eskom board in April 2016, accused Pamensky of being 'intellectually dishonest' in his conflict-of-interest declaration and recommended his removal from the board. Instead, the opinion was later watered down, allegedly under pressure from the board, allowing him to stay on as a director. He finally quit in November 2016 in the aftermath of Thuli Madonsela's report on state capture.

Bianca Goodson, for one, said that she was shocked to learn that Pamensky served on the Eskom board. 'We had one board member from Transnet on the one side and another board member from Eskom and he was a CEO of our properties division that was looking after Transnet's property portfolio,' she said. 'It was a bit weird.'[30]

* * *

Among the first jobs that Mosilo Mothepu's team of consultants was assigned to at Eskom was the Duvha insurance claim that Matshela Koko and Anoj Singh had allegedly slipped onto their to-do list.

In Mothepu's telling, in December Singh arranged for her and Eric Wood to meet Marsh, the insurance broker handling the claim. After two meetings it became clear there wasn't much for them to do any more, as Marsh had already submitted a detailed proposal to Eskom.

'I would say we did very little work on that because they were finalising the options,' Mothepu explained. 'So we wrote a report essentially advising Mr Anoj Singh which option to take.'[31]

For Wood, however, it became an opportunity to drum up extra work. In January 2016, Trillian formed part of a proposal put together by Chinese firm Hubei Hongyuan Power Engineering (Hypec) for rebuilding the Duvha boiler. In its R6-billion offer, Hypec said its 'local BEE partner' Trillian would meet 'the other statutory requirement and compliance of Black Empowerment rules of South Africa'.[32]

'It surprised me a little bit because we knew nothing about boilers,' said Mothepu.

Wood later told me that Trillian would do the 'financial structuring' for the deal. Given how the Regiments partnership with McKinsey operated at Transnet and Eskom, with Essa allegedly being paid a substantial cut just to open doors, I think it's fair to assume that Trillian, now majority owned by Essa, would play a similar role as Hypec's partner.

In the end, Trillian did not submit a proposal with Hypec, because the tender was cancelled. But the story did not end there. After the tender reopened, Trillian provided Eskom with a last-minute 'risk assessment' of the bids that favoured another Chinese firm, Dongfang. Days later, Eskom awarded the tender to Dongfang even though its price was R1 billion more expensive than rival bids. The contract was signed by Prish Govender, the same official who had originally motivated and led the McKinsey–Trillian consulting project at Eskom.

* * *

In October 2015, Prish Govender's team drew up a summary of its negotiations with McKinsey on the three-year mega contract to create a 'world class management consulting unit' at Eskom.

It was a blueprint to loot. Govender ignored the grave reservations expressed by Eskom's legal division and decided that McKinsey would be paid using the 'at risk' pricing model after all. This meant that McKinsey would be paid a percentage of potentially unlimited savings rather than fixed fees.

McKinsey's 'risk' was reduced to almost nothing because Eskom agreed to pay the company R475 million up front 'in lieu of project set-up costs'. Theoretically, McKinsey could be asked to reimburse Eskom if no savings were achieved. But the odds of that happening were slim to none given the uncomfortably close and in some cases improper relationship several Eskom executives enjoyed with McKinsey and its black empowerment partners. An independent review of the contract later revealed that the methodology agreed to by Eskom and McKinsey on how to calculate savings was heavily weighted in McKinsey's favour.

Aware that the McKinsey contract was a bomb waiting to explode, Eskom's legal division put up a valiant fight to stop it. It lodged a strong objection to McKinsey partner Alexander Weiss's opinion that the fees were 'completely in compliance' with Treasury rules and sought an external legal opinion on the contract. Eskom's assurance and forensics department also red-flagged the R475-million upfront payment to McKinsey, stressed that Treasury approval for the contract must be sought and warned that it overlapped with work already being done at Eskom.[33]

On 4 December, senior counsel Paul Kennedy delivered his verdict. His conclusion was unequivocal. The 'at risk' pricing model was in breach of a Treasury instruction 'having the force of law' that stipulated consultants must be paid fixed hourly rates set by the public administration department. The contract was essentially illegal and had to be renegotiated.[34]

Eskom ignored Kennedy's advice and signed up McKinsey anyway.

* * *

At 8.36 a.m. on Thursday 17 December, McKinsey senior partner Vikas Sagar sent an email to Eric Wood and Clive Angel. Sagar also copied in another senior partner at McKinsey, Alexander Weiss.

'Hello Clive and Eric,' Sagar wrote. 'Please find attached the documents for our discussion at 13h00 today at the McKinsey offices.'

Follow-up correspondence between Weiss, Angel, Wood and Sagar suggest that at 1 p.m. the four men sat down as planned to discuss the two documents at McKinsey's Johannesburg offices.

The first, headed 'McKinsey–Trillian partnership principles for the Eskom turnaround', was a template for how the two firms would work together based on robust discussions in previous weeks. It's clear from the document that McKinsey had objected to Trillian's subcontractors but had lost that battle. 'McKinsey commits to dealing with Trillian's sub-contractors with respect and an open mind,' the document records. 'This will include eGateway and Cutting Edge.'

In other words, McKinsey had committed itself from the start to sharing the Eskom spoils with Cutting Edge – a company majority owned by the Guptas – and eGateway, an opaque consultancy in Dubai linked to Salim Essa.

The second document under discussion that day was a spreadsheet that specified how the two firms would divide up the loot. In four years the consultants expected to earn R3 billion for their advice to Eskom on power generation, R1.6 billion on procurement, R2 billion on financing, R1.7 billion on coal and diesel contracting, and another R300 million on nuclear. Together with a few other bits and bobs, McKinsey and Trillian calculated that Eskom would pay them a grand total of R9.4 billion over four years. This excluded what they expected to earn for work on Kusile and Medupi, which would be negotiated after the contract was signed.

We need to pause here for a moment to take stock of these numbers: that's R9.4 billion *for advice*, to be split roughly fifty-fifty. Trillian, which had never made more than R3 million in one year until Salim Essa and Eric Wood bought the firm, suddenly stood to earn R4.4 billion in the next four years from one contract, and McKinsey, R5 billion.

For McKinsey and its newfound South African friends, 2016 was shaping up to be a great year. In January, the global consultancy delivered a presentation to a leadership meeting, describing the Eskom deal as 'the firm's biggest @Risk contract'. A total of 193 consultants were seconded to the utility from around the globe, including senior leadership and a team of twenty coal-mining experts from Poland. The rest hailed from Western Europe, the Middle East, Asia Pacific, Africa and North America.[35]

However, the presentation warned that the project's size and 'exorbitant fees' could cause damage to the company's reputation if leaked to the media. It also flagged its partnership with Trillian as a reputational risk trigger. To mitigate blowback, McKinsey would 'closely monitor public perception of our partner and in detail document contractual obligations and interactions'. This is an indicator – at odds with McKinsey's later pronouncements – that it was well aware of Trillian's dubious credentials. But like other consultancies vying for Eskom's business, McKinsey was willing to turn a blind eye as long as Trillian raked in billions for the partnership.

* * *

It soon became clear to McKinsey that Trillian wasn't bringing much to the table.

For a start, Trillian's management consulting division initially consisted of just two people: its chief executive Bianca Goodson and her chief operating officer Ben Burnand.

'McKinsey wanted to hit the ground running, they wanted to start the work, they already had teams going to Majuba power station,' Goodson explained. 'And here's Trillian coming to say: "We want to be part of it, we want to develop our people as well."'

In Goodson's telling, a recurring sticking point was Trillian's insistence on farming out most of its work to its own subcontractors. Goodson found herself caught in the middle. She said Clive Angel had told her she'd be building a 'proudly South African' consultancy that would eventually rival McKinsey. Goodson said that when she questioned why Trillian was subcontracting foreign consultants, Angel told her that Essa had 'an interest in those companies'.[36]

Goodson's testimony in Parliament and notes she kept from meetings show that matters came to a head during acrimonious meetings between McKinsey and Trillian's leadership at the end of January 2016. McKinsey made it clear that it regarded Trillian and its motley crew of Gupta-linked subcontractors as so much unwanted baggage, intent on extracting large fees from Eskom without doing any work. When Goodson complained that McKinsey didn't appear interested in the supplier development component of their partnership, McKinsey senior partner Lorenz Jüngling snapped: 'Just take your 30 per cent and go.'[37]

When Goodson subsequently took the matter up with Salim Essa, he turned to her and smiled: 'Bianca, don't worry. It's sorted.'[38]

In Goodson's account, the next morning, Vikas Sagar phoned her to apologise and shortly afterwards he wrote a letter to Eskom project leader Prish Govender asking the utility to pay Trillian directly. Eskom later used this letter to justify disbursing R600 million in consulting fees to Trillian for just six months' work, even though it did not have a contract with Eskom or McKinsey. McKinsey, which did have a contract with Eskom – albeit an illegal one, as it was never approved by the National Treasury – was paid R1 billion. Not quite the R5 billion it had been expecting, but not bad after a few months on the job.

About a week after Trillian's fallout with McKinsey, Anoj Singh entered the fray. Goodson described attending a project-steering committee meeting that he chaired, at which he lambasted McKinsey for failing to involve Trillian in its work programme or provide structured support and skills transfer.

It's probable that Essa and Singh were already considering replacing uppity McKinsey with Oliver Wyman, another international consulting firm waiting in the wings. Goodson's statement describes how by then Trillian executives had wined and dined directors from Oliver Wyman's Dubai branch, introducing them to Des van Rooyen, the 'Weekend Special' finance minister who was now in charge of local government and could open doors to lucrative municipal consulting contracts; Transnet chief financial officer Garry Pita, who had helpfully signed off on several suspect Trillian and Regiments invoices totalling R74 million; and Anoj Singh at Eskom. Goodson, who attended some of the meetings, including the one with the minister, said that the Oliver Wyman directors were so impressed with Trillian's ability to secure government work that they planned to open an office in Johannesburg. One of the Oliver Wyman directors, Bernhard Hartmann, told Goodson during a smoke break that he'd come to South Africa after being introduced to Salim Essa in Dubai.

Shortly after Singh read McKinsey the riot act, he sent the company a letter urgently asking for a full account of how it intended to develop the skills of its black empowerment partner. This letter most likely expedited a due diligence of Trillian by McKinsey's global risk committee.[39] On 10 March 2016, after working closely with Trillian and its subcontractors for several months at Eskom and for much longer at Transnet with the firm's previous incarnation, Regiments, McKinsey finally wrote to Eric Wood demanding an explanation of the company's ownership structure and its dealings with Hubei Hongyuan and eGateway. McKinsey also sought explicit assurances that none of Trillian's employees and shareholders or any of its subcontractors held interests that could conflict with their work at Eskom. At the end of March, after Wood failed to provide satisfactory answers, McKinsey informed Eskom that it had cut ties with Trillian. Two months later, with Salim Essa no longer in the mix, Eskom cancelled McKinsey's contract.

When she testified before a parliamentary inquiry into state capture almost two years later, Goodson summed up Trillian's business model as a vehicle created solely for rent-seeking. 'Trillian secured work through Essa's relationships and the work was passed over to internationally recognised companies,' she explained. Trillian, which then acted as the supplier development partner of choice, was an entity created simply to skim off 50 per cent of the revenues 'for not really doing much work'.[40]

* * *

In November 2017, McKinsey senior partner David Fine stood up in Parliament to defend his firm from being pilloried for being party to the Gupta looting spree.

With his hand on his heart, he made several concessions: the Eskom contract was too large and its uncapped fees were too big; McKinsey should never have worked with Trillian before completing its due diligence, which was done too late, and without a contract; Vikas Sagar had no right to ask that Trillian be paid directly by Eskom; and Lorenz Jüngling's purported remarks were 'completely against our values and beliefs about supplier development'.

Two law firms McKinsey had hired to investigate had found no evidence of illegality, bribery or corruption. Sagar and Jüngling quit the consultancy, another partner – believed to be Alexander Weiss – was 'sanctioned', and several consultants who'd worked on the contract were 'disciplined'.

The firm also offered to pay back the R1 billion in fees earned because it 'does not want to benefit from an invalid contract'. But Fine stressed that accountability lay with Eskom because it had assured McKinsey that the contract had Treasury's blessing.

Fine did not, however, admit that McKinsey had knowingly gone into business with the Guptas or any of their associates. 'Had we known that Trillian was owned by Mr Essa, we would not have worked with them,' he declared.[41]

This may be so for Fine and his risk committee, but it does not hold true for the firm's South African office. Vikas Sagar, after all, attended at least two documented meetings at the Trillian offices with Salim Essa to discuss the firm's work at Transnet and Eskom.

One took place at 12.30 p.m. on Thursday 10 December, in the presence of Althaf Emmamally and Santosh Choubey, directors of Gupta-owned software company Cutting Edge. Also in attendance were Eric Wood, Clive Angel, Marc Chipkin and Transnet director Stanley Shane. Essa and Sagar were both at another Trillian meeting held an hour later to discuss power generation work at Eskom, this time without Emmamally and Choubey.[42]

One week later, Wood and Angel drove up the road from Melrose Arch to McKinsey's office in Sandton, where they sat down with Sagar and Alexander Weiss to divide up the Eskom spoils. Call me a cynic, but the notion that neither Weiss nor any of the other senior McKinsey consultants who'd worked with Wood at Regiments since 2013 had any idea of Essa's involvement simply beggars belief.

Another important question to ask is: was McKinsey's intervention really needed?

Fine insists the firm is proud of its achievements at Eskom 'in its hour of need'. Load shedding was over thanks in no small part to McKinsey's Tetris maintenance-planning tool and its intervention at Majuba, one of Eskom's largest plants, where power availability had increased from

63 per cent to 84 per cent. Diesel costs of about R1 billion a month had been slashed in half in six months and then halved again in another year, and overall earnings before tax were steadily increasing. The Top Consultants programme, which had set the ball rolling, had trained fifty young Eskom engineers to become skilled internal troubleshooting consultants.

Critics of this glowing picture point out many of these initiatives were under way already. Several studies on achieving cost savings in coal procurement and transport had been done, detailed maintenance plans were already in place and Eskom's treasury, an area where Trillian was most active, was widely regarded as highly competent and effective. As for reducing diesel costs, you don't need a consultant to tell you that using diesel to generate electricity is akin to burning money.

Moreover, while improved coal deliveries and overdue plant maintenance certainly played a role in ending load shedding, it was also largely thanks to a sluggish economy that led to electricity demand slumping to 2007 levels.

While its expertise remains unquestioned, McKinsey has earned the reputation of painting a dire picture of impending doom to top decision-makers, including cabinet ministers, and then offering its services as a panacea. 'They wanted to create a perception of incompetence to create the need for their own business,' was how one former senior Eskom staffer described the practice, echoing a widely held view at the utility.

For many, the real bugbear is McKinsey's 'at risk' pricing model, with uncapped fees based on dubious methodologies to calculate savings. 'Some of these will only be realised years down the line, if ever. Others would have happened anyway,' the Eskom manager pointed out. 'Why would you pay for theoretical savings?'

In December 2016, Eskom commissioned Oliver Wyman and Marsh (which doubles as a risk management company and insurance brokerage) to peer-review the McKinsey contract and assess whether Eskom had received value for money. The conclusion, in short, was that it hadn't.

The review raised serious questions about how the savings on which McKinsey and Trillian's fees were based were calculated. In some instances one-off savings were treated as recurring; in others it wasn't clear whether an idea had originated with Eskom or the consultants. The report cited delayed spending being treated as a saving, and the use of cheaper materials – water pipes at Majuba, for example – that resulted in short-term savings but an increase in long-term costs. There were cases of double-charging, setting baselines that would exaggerate impacts achieved, inflating savings, and payments for expected or deferred savings rather than actual savings. Coal contract negotiations were charged at double the market rate.

The report warned that 100 per cent at-risk projects of this size were 'very unusual', complaining that negotiations on payments and impacts were conducted in secret and not backed by supporting documents.[43]

Oliver Wyman and Marsh submitted a preliminary report to Prish Govender in December 2016. By then, R800 million had already been paid to McKinsey and Trillian for the cancelled contract. The report should have served as a salutary warning that something was seriously amiss. Instead, it appears to have spurred Govender and Edwin Mabelane into action to process outstanding payments without delay. Five days later, on 13 December, the board approved Mabelane's recommendation that McKinsey should be paid another R850 million and Trillian another R134 million. Wood was informed at once and Trillian was paid before Christmas.

A day after Eskom authorised the payments, Oliver Wyman and Marsh presented Eskom with their final report. It recommended a legal review before making any more payments, pointing out that there was no contractual basis for paying Trillian any money at all. But by then it was too late.

* * *

The final straw for Bianca Goodson came, by her account, when she was asked to open a company account with the Bank of Baroda, then immediately sign over all transactional rights to Marc Chipkin. When she asked what the account was for, she was told it was 'to facilitate work with eGateway', the shadowy Dubai consultancy linked to Salim Essa. Goodson baulked, insisting on being a co-signatory.

As she was driving home that afternoon in March 2016, it hit her: she'd been used. She was the chief executive of a company whose bank accounts she didn't control. Any amount of money could be sloshing around without her knowledge. Now she was being asked to open another account she couldn't access, this time with a foreign bank. She quit the next morning.

A subsequent investigation for the Reserve Bank found that four days after Goodson resigned, Trillian paid R65 million into the Bank of Baroda account that the Guptas used to pay for Optimum coal mine. She got out just in time.

To her everlasting regret, Mosilo Mothepu held out for a little longer. In March, just as Trillian's relationship with McKinsey was imploding, she was promoted to chief executive of Trillian's financial advisory division. Trillian failed McKinsey's global risk review at the end of the month and Mothepu became increasingly worried that her team was still working at Megawatt Park without a contract. In her telling, she warned Eric Wood that the company was in contravention of the Public Finance Management Act, as well as breaking other laws.

'We have to stop working for Eskom now,' she told him.

Wood brushed her off. 'Don't worry about it,' he said. 'I'll talk to Anoj Singh. Anoj will sort it out.'[44]

For his part, Wood has always insisted there was nothing untoward in Trillian's dealings with Eskom, and that his firm has only billed for work done that was duly authorised.

Mothepu said that soon afterwards, Edwin Mabelane – Eskom's chief procurement officer – called her to say that he needed Trillian's BEE certificate to process a R30.6-million payment. 'I was quite surprised because, well, there was no contract between Eskom and Trillian, and Trillian and McKinsey,' she said.

Mothepu told Parliament that in May, Wood and Essa began negotiating in earnest for Oliver Wyman to take over from McKinsey, no doubt seeking to replicate the business model Goodson had described – partnering with an international firm to skim off half its earnings 'for not much work'. Mothepu resigned soon afterwards.

A few months later, a statement that Mothepu had made to Public

Protector Thuli Madonsela was leaked to the media. This prompted Wood to lay a criminal complaint against her for stealing company documents. For months, Mothepu was harassed by police investigators, one of whom confessed that he was under political pressure to expedite the case, scaring off prospective employers. In April 2018, following a sea change in government, prosecutors finally decided that there was no evidence to support the charges against Mothepu, allowing her to start rebuilding her life.[45]

14

Show Me the Money

On 16 December 2015, less than a week after the Guptas clinched the Optimum deal and just three days after Eskom's board approved paying fees to Gupta-linked consultancy Trillian for an illegal contract that would later total R600 million, Anoj Singh touched down at Dubai International Airport.

Singh must have felt right at home when he rolled up to the five-star Oberoi hotel in a chauffeur-driven BMW 7 Series. The Gupta leaks show that arms deal fixer Fana Hlongwane, deputy public works minister Ayanda Dlodlo, and Gift and Thato Magashule, the sons of Free State premier Ace Magashule, arrived on the same day. Singh was joined later at the Oberoi by Ashu Chawla, the chief executive of the Gupta family's Sahara Computers, and Des van Rooyen, the Guptas' 'weekend special' finance minister, who could still prove useful at opening doors to municipal contracts in his new post as local government minister. Atul, Ajay and Tony Gupta were also in town, as was Duduzane Zuma, who was staying less than three kilometres away in the luxury R18-million apartment he'd bought at the Burj Khalifa that month with help from the Guptas. Salim Essa, who also owns an apartment in the Burj, had arrived in Dubai on 5 December.[1]

Singh spent eight nights at the hotel, enjoying spa massages and room service. When he appeared before the parliamentary inquiry into public enterprises in 2018, Singh claimed that his 20 454 dirham bill was settled by an Emirati business associate. The Gupta leaks suggest that this is highly unlikely. His bill was made out to Sahara Computers and forwarded to Tony Gupta, who answered 'Ok'. The leaks show that this was one of at least five occasions on which the Guptas hosted Singh in Dubai – at a time when the family was receiving suspected kickbacks totalling

R5.3 billion from a locomotive deal at Transnet, where Singh headed the finance division. This, together with evidence that the family allegedly made cash payments to him in Dubai and set up a shell company for him in nearby Ras al-Khaimah, the most secretive of the UAE's seven emirates, in my view strongly suggests that Singh has a case of corruption to answer.

The stream of visitors to Dubai continued unabated.

At the end of December, the Guptas put up Kim Davids, the personal assistant of public enterprises minister Lynne Brown, at the Oberoi for a few nights. While Davids was staying at the hotel, Chawla arranged for a driver to take her to the Gupta residence in Emirates Hills.

Two days after Davids left, Daniel Mantsha, the chairperson of state arms manufacturer Denel, arrived at the Oberoi. As always, the Guptas picked up the tab and arranged for a ride to their villa at 7 a.m. the next morning. His visit to Emirates Hills coincided with Denel helping the Guptas muscle in on a dubious R100-billion arms deal with India.

While Mantsha was still in town, and barely a fortnight after Singh's departure, another key member of the Guptas' Eskom-capture cast touched down in Dubai. On 3 January 2016, Chawla received an email from the Oberoi confirming the arrival the following morning of one Matshela Koko. 'Sahara will pay the entire bill. Please do not ask any credit card guarantee from the guest at the time of check in,' Chawla emailed the reservations desk, before forwarding Koko's booking to Essa.

Koko later claimed – implausibly – that he happened to be passing through Dubai on his way home from a family holiday in Bali and, despite Chawla's emails, had paid for his stay at the Oberoi himself. He denied meeting any of the Guptas or their associates while in Dubai.

Koko and Singh would have us believe that their arrival at the Oberoi hotel in Dubai around the same time that half a dozen political luminaries were staying there while the Guptas, Essa and Duduzane Zuma were all in town was entirely coincidental. This stretches credulity too far. It's far more likely that Dubai had become the new Saxonwold, a place where shady deals could be plotted far from prying eyes during hushed meetings in hotel rooms and discreet dining booths, or in the secluded chambers of the Guptas' palatial mansion in the gated enclave of Emirates Hills.

Duduzane Zuma, who'd spent the Christmas holidays in South Africa, returned to Dubai shortly after Mantsha and Koko left, spending a week at his Burj Khalifa apartment in January. It's possible that this was when he and the Guptas drafted the letters to the rulers of Dubai and Abu Dhabi on behalf of Jacob Zuma. The letters, dated 16 January 2016, state that the president and his family had 'decided to make the UAE a second home' and had already bought a property in Emirates Hills – the same villa owned by the Guptas.

Two months later, President Zuma paid a working visit to the UAE to strengthen trade and investment ties between the two countries. Among his small entourage were state security minister David Mahlobo, a champion of Zuma's nuclear power plan that would benefit the Guptas, and home affairs minister Malusi Gigaba, who, as Lynne Brown's predecessor at public enterprises, had played a key role in stacking the boards of state-owned companies with Gupta associates.

It's tempting to conclude that Zuma's visit had more to do with advancing the Guptas' business interests than South Africa's, and that the seat of government had moved from the Union Buildings to Emirates Hills.

* * *

At this crucial juncture in the Gupta heist of Optimum, mineral resources minister Mosebenzi Zwane reportedly held a secret meeting in Dubai that would help unlock a sizeable chunk of the money the Guptas needed to buy the mine.

Flight records show that after Zwane met Ivan Glasenberg at the Dolder hotel in Zurich in early December 2015, he hopped aboard the Guptas' Bombardier jet with Salim Essa and Tony Gupta and flew to India for a few days to receive medical treatment at Medanta Medicity near New Delhi.

Incidentally, the Guptas had been in talks with Medanta co-founder Sunil Sachdeva about building a multibillion-dollar medical facility in Dubai with shareholders who were awarded lucrative mobile clinic tenders by the provincial health departments in the Free State and North West. In effect, public health care money for South Africa's rural poor was subsidising a world-class medical facility in Dubai for the mega rich.

After being treated at Medanta Medicity, Zwane flew back to Dubai. The Guptas booked him into the Oberoi hotel and picked up the 825 dirham (R2 700) tab for his chauffeur-driven ride to their mansion in Emirates Hills and then on to the airport, where he caught a commercial flight home on 7 December.

The *Mail & Guardian* reported that during this stopover in Dubai, Zwane met with executives from asset management firm Centaur. The company is registered in the offshore tax haven of Bermuda, with offices in the Burj Khalifa in Dubai. Soon after meeting Zwane, Centaur stumped up R885 million towards the purchase price of Optimum. It would only become apparent later how Centaur had managed to profit royally from this deal.[2]

* * *

Brian Molefe, Matshela Koko and Mosebenzi Zwane's shakedown of Optimum had been a complete success. Three days after Zwane touched down at O.R. Tambo Airport – and just three weeks after the president's son Duduzane Zuma had become a major shareholder of Tegeta – Glencore suddenly reversed its earlier opposition to the deal and signed over Optimum to the Guptas.

There was just one snag: even though Glasenberg had agreed to sell Optimum at a heavily discounted price of R2.15 billion, the Guptas still had to find the rest of the money to pay for it. It wasn't long before Koko, Singh and Molefe came to the rescue again.

* * *

On 23 December 2015, while Anoj Singh was still enjoying massages at the Oberoi, Eskom declared an emergency at Arnot power station that could easily have been averted if the utility had allowed Exxaro to keep supplying it with cheap coal.

Eskom's manufactured emergency set the scene for three very sweet deals for the Guptas that would net the family about R1 billion in three months.

The first was a contract in January 2016 to supply Arnot with 100 000 tons of coal for a month. The transaction took place entirely on paper. Despite Eskom's strict rule against using coal agents, Tegeta was allowed to buy the coal from Optimum at R370 a ton excluding VAT and sell it to Eskom for R440. The mine charged Tegeta another R60 a ton to deliver the coal to Arnot twenty-five kilometres away. Tegeta promptly charged Eskom R105 a ton for haulage. Eskom, which had just terminated an agreement with Exxaro–Anglo's Mafube colliery to supply Arnot at R132 a ton, was now buying coal from Tegeta for R545 a ton. In February, the scheme was replicated, this time for 500 000 tons of coal for two months. Eskom usually only paid coal suppliers thirty days after delivery; Tegeta was paid in just seven days. The Guptas had made a handsome profit in record time.

During the parliamentary inquiry, Exxaro's chief executive Mxolisi Mgojo made it clear that he felt Brian Molefe and Anoj Singh were deliberately snubbing his company in favour of Tegeta. 'Why were Exxaro's efforts to optimise Arnot mine and its escalating costs ignored, when a coal supply agreement with Tegeta was concluded with such haste?' he asked. 'Why does Mr Singh use the high cost of diesel to run the open-cycle gas turbines to justify the purchase of expensive coal from Tegeta when Eskom could simply have continued to procure coal under its coal supply agreement from the Arnot mine and Mafube mines at a lower cost?'[3]

One by one, all the conditions for the Optimum deal were being met – just in time for the 31 March deadline. In February and March, approvals were forthcoming from the Competition Commission and mineral resources department. The only outstanding issue was finding the funds. By then, relatively small payments from a dozen Gupta-related companies had begun to flow into a Bank of Baroda account that would be used to pay for the mine. A Reserve Bank investigation into the Bank of Baroda, expanding on evidence gathered by Thuli Madonsela, later revealed that inflows accelerated dramatically in March, when Tegeta funnelled over R400 million of Eskom's Arnot money into the account and Centaur contributed another R885 million. These investigations showed that Regiments had chipped in R40 million and Trillian a total of R235 million, money that had likely been siphoned off from fees earned from consulting work with McKinsey at Transnet and Eskom. According to the investigation reports, even Kuben Moodley, who was Mosebenzi

Zwane's 'white monopoly capital' advisor and whose wife Viroshini Naidoo sat on the Eskom board, threw in R10 million that was used as collateral for a loan to help fund the deal, although he continues to refute this. That still left the Guptas with a shortfall of R600 million – and time was rapidly running out.[4]

At this point, the phone lines between Brian Molefe and the Guptas began humming again. Records cited in Thuli Madonsela's report on state capture show that Molefe and Tony Gupta were on the phone to each other on 14 March. This was followed shortly afterwards by a flurry of phone calls to Molefe from Tegeta director Ronica Ragavan. She made eleven calls to Molefe from 23 March to 30 April, seven of them in just four days from 9 April, including one on Monday 11 April when Eskom convened an emergency board meeting to bail out the Guptas.[5]

On Friday 8 April, the situation became dire – Optimum's creditors approved its business rescue plan. This left the Guptas four working days to pay. If they didn't come up with the cash by Thursday 14 April, the deal was off.

First thing on Monday 11 April, business rescue practitioner Piers Marsden received a panicked call from Nazeem Howa, the chief executive of Gupta holding company Oakbay Investments. In Marsden's account, at a hastily convened meeting at 10 a.m., Howa informed him that the Guptas needed another R600 million to buy the mine. Howa asked Marsden to approach Optimum's consortium of creditors, led by First-Rand Bank, for a bridging loan. Marsden met the banks just after lunch. At 3 p.m. he called Howa to inform him that the banks wouldn't play ball.[6]

Suzanne Daniels told Parliament that less than five hours later, she was having dinner at home with her family when Zethembe Khoza, Eskom's board tender committee chairperson, called her.[7]

'I want you to arrange an urgent meeting tonight to discuss emergency coal supplies for Arnot,' he said. Daniels had been appointed company secretary towards the end of 2015; it was her job to convene board meetings.

She objected. She hadn't received any documentation, the committee was scheduled to meet two days later anyway, and the emergency had been declared three months earlier. 'It's 7:30 in the evening,' she protested. 'Can't this wait until Wednesday?'[8]

In her account, Khoza wouldn't take no for an answer, and shortly after

9 p.m. Eskom's tender committee held a telephonic board meeting that he chaired. The members who took part were Viroshini Naidoo, Chwayita Mabude and Nazia Carrim. Attached to the meeting note was a four-page submission signed on the same day by Matshela Koko, Edwin Mabelane and Eskom's head of fuel sourcing, Ayanda Nteta.

During the parliamentary inquiry into public enterprises, evidence leader Ntuthuzelo Vanara – citing phone records contained in Thuli Madonsela's report on state capture, which showed that Molefe was in contact with Tegeta executive Ronica Ragavan on the same day that the prepayment was authorised – suggested that Molefe may have induced Khoza to convene the late-night board meeting.[9]

The submission called for urgent approval to extend Tegeta's contract by five months and to pay the company up front to supply Arnot with another 1.25 million tons of coal. The total bill – R660 million including VAT – neatly covered the Guptas' shortfall in the purchase of Optimum.[10]

The move was so brazen that it even prompted board tender committee member Viroshini Naidoo to question why Tegeta was being favoured over other suppliers and if Eskom was receiving value for money. Despite her misgivings, the members present – including Naidoo – approved the prepayment. (Naidoo has consistently denied advancing the Guptas' interests.)

Two days later, on Wednesday 13 April, Eskom paid R660 million to Tegeta for future coal deliveries from a mine it didn't own. The next morning, the sellers received the full purchase price of R2.15 billion from the Bank of Baroda, and the Guptas and Duduzane Zuma became the proud proprietors of Glencore's Optimum coal complex.

* * *

On 12 June 2016, Piers Marsden settled down to watch the television show *Carte Blanche*. Presenter Devi Sankaree Govender was interviewing Matshela Koko. She asked him whether he had made the prepayment to the Guptas. At first he denied it. When confronted with a contract that committed Eskom to paying Tegeta R660 million for coal from Optimum, which he had signed a day before Glencore received its outstanding R600 million, Koko backtracked: 'Let's say I made a mistake.'

Then Nazeem Howa, the chief executive of Gupta holding company Oakbay Investments, said during an SABC interview that the money had been used to pay for equipment to increase production at Optimum. A jowly, balding and bespectacled Howa piously offered to 'set the record straight'. He claimed that Eskom had approached Tegeta to supply additional coal to avoid winter load shedding. 'We said to them we could do it on condition there was a prepayment so that we could fund additional development at the mine, and we used the funding to do that,' Howa said.

Marsden was stunned. Optimum was in business rescue, which meant that the business rescue practitioners controlled the mine. Marsden hadn't planned to spend over half a billion rand on new equipment. Moreover, the money was paid to Tegeta and not Optimum, the colliery that produced the coal but didn't yet belong to the Guptas. Lastly, Marsden found it highly suspicious that the irregular prepayment was done just after Howa had failed to secure almost the exact same amount from the banks and just before Glencore was paid. He decided to report the matter to the Hawks' anti-corruption desk.[11]

In 2017, following its investigation into billions of rands of obscure origin sloshing around in the Guptas' Bank of Baroda accounts shortly before the family paid for Optimum, the Reserve Bank fined the Indian bank's local branch R11 million for failing to report the payments as suspicious transactions or verifying the source of the funds. In 2018, the Bank of Baroda announced that it was pulling out of South Africa.

* * *

While the Guptas were buying up collieries with Eskom's money, Brian Molefe became a vocal opponent of renewable energy.

At a press briefing in May 2016, just one month after the Optimum deal went down, Molefe delivered a diatribe against renewables, saying Eskom was being forced to sign twenty-year power purchase agreements at a higher cost than its own generation for technologies that would be obsolete by the time they were transferred to Eskom. 'We will be like somebody who has an old phone, while everybody else has an iPhone,' he declared.

A solar power body immediately slated his remarks as 'ill-informed at best and misleading at worst'. It cited a recent study by the Council for Scientific and Industrial Research that found that renewables had resulted in diesel cost savings of R7.2 billion in eighteen months, while the cost of solar and wind power was steadily dwindling.

Greenpeace accused Molefe of spewing 'anti-renewable energy propaganda', urging the utility to 'join the energy of the future or be left behind struggling with an outdated, polluting and unreliable energy model that is taking South Africa nowhere slowly'.[12]

Molefe brushed aside the criticism and simply stopped signing new contracts. This caused investment to slow to a trickle. From 2011, over R170 billion had poured into clean energy; by 2017 new investments had virtually dried up, with only R50 million spent. By then over twenty projects that were ready to break ground were on hold, driving away new investors.[13]

At the same time, Molefe began to publicly promote nuclear energy, another sector where the Guptas and Duduzane Zuma held financial interests. A few months later, cabinet announced that Eskom would take over the nuclear build programme from the Department of Energy.

The future looked bright for anyone invested in coal and nuclear energy.

* * *

The Guptas didn't waste time extracting every penny they could out of the Optimum deal.

Ten days after they took ownership of Optimum, Tegeta director Ronica Ragavan mounted what appeared to be an attempted raid on the mine's R1.47-billion rehabilitation fund held in trust by Standard Bank. By law, mines are required to set aside ring-fenced funds in accounts controlled by independent trustees that can only be used for rehabilitation once a mine is at the end of its life.

On 24 April, law firm Werksmans Attorneys wrote a letter to Tegeta on behalf of the business rescue practitioners that said Ragavan had tried to access the mine's rehabilitation funds. Werksmans warned Tegeta that by law it had to ensure the trust held sufficient funds to rehabilitate the mine – using the money for any other purpose would be a criminal offence. Ragavan backed down – for the moment.[14]

Next, the Guptas tried to raid the R280-million rehabilitation fund of Koornfontein colliery, the other mine they'd bought as part of the Optimum package. In May 2016, Tegeta wrote to the mineral resources department to ask if it could use the money for concurrent rehabilitation, which is illegal. A day later the department granted approval.[15]

The Reserve Bank investigation found that a month later the Guptas transferred rehabilitation funds totalling R1.75 billion from Standard Bank to the Bank of Baroda. From there, the money was placed in fixed deposit accounts, earning an estimated R123 million a year in interest, which the Guptas allegedly pocketed.[16]

Information disclosed during legal proceedings in 2017 between the Bank of Baroda and various Gupta companies suggests the family used the mine rehabilitation money it placed in fixed deposits to raise further loans. The court filings contain a letter from the bank that shows the Guptas transferred R170 million from Koornfontein's rehabilitation trust into a fixed deposit account in June, and pledged this as security to raise a loan of R150 million.[17]

Brian Molefe then tried to help the Guptas squeeze another R1 billion from Arnot. In August, Molefe wrote to Treasury asking for permission to extend the Tegeta contract by another eight months to allow the Guptas to supply Arnot with another two million tons of coal without it going out to tender. The contract would be worth R885 million, plus another R220 million if the Guptas were allowed to charge their usual inflated haulage rates. Treasury's head of supply chain management compliance, Solly Tshitangano, politely declined the request.[18]

Molefe tried the same stunt with Brakfontein, the Gupta colliery whose substandard coal no one wanted. Over a year earlier, Brakfontein had clinched a suspect R3.8-billion deal with Eskom to supply coal to Majuba power station. Now Molefe asked Treasury if Brakfontein could supply Majuba with an additional 10.8 million tons of coal for an extra R2.9 billion. Tshitangano, ever a thorn in Molefe's side, demurred again. 'The National Treasury does not support extension of this contract until the question of quality of coal is cleared,' he wrote.[19]

The Guptas were more successful with Koornfontein colliery, which supplied the nearby Komati power station, south of Middelburg. When Glencore owned Koornfontein as part of the Optimum group, Eskom offered it only month-to-month contracts after its long-term supply agreement expired at the end of 2015. But no sooner had the Guptas taken ownership of Koornfontein as part of the Optimum deal than Eskom signed a seven-year agreement with Tegeta worth R7 billion, ignoring a Treasury instruction to test the market to determine whether other coal mines in the area could supply Komati with cheaper coal. The deal reportedly upped the value of the mine by R1 billion.[20]

Another piece of the puzzle only fell into place during court action from creditors after Optimum mine was placed in business rescue again in 2018. The court filings show that shortly after the Guptas took over Optimum colliery, a substantial portion of the coal they were contracted to supply to Hendrina at R150 a ton – a price that had almost bankrupted the mine – was exported at R1 075 a ton to Centaur.[21]

Centaur is the Bermuda-based asset management company that had advanced R885 million to the Guptas to buy Optimum after company representatives met Mosebenzi Zwane in Dubai. By November 2017, Optimum had sold 1.9 million tons of coal to Centaur for R2.3 billion. Half of Centaur's shares, it turns out, belong to Aakash Garg Jahajgarhia, the Indian-born businessman who married the Guptas' niece, Vega, at the infamous Sun City wedding in 2013. In effect, Centaur was a conduit for the Guptas to export coal at seven times the price Eskom was paying. Eskom took no action against the Guptas for failing to meet their quotas at Hendrina.

One of the questions that had exercised my mind greatly since I stood looking out at the Burj Khalifa from my hotel room in Dubai, wondering why on earth the Guptas would want to buy a mine that was losing Glencore R100 million a month, was finally answered. Thanks to the unflinching efforts of Eskom's top brass – in particular Molefe, Koko and Singh – the Guptas had turned loss-making Optimum Holdings into a major money-spinner. Under their watch, Koornfontein colliery scored a R7-billion Eskom supply deal that should have gone out to tender; Eskom allowed Optimum colliery to keep supplying Arnot twenty-five kilometres away at inflated coal and haulage prices; and most of its Hendrina quota was exported at seven times the Eskom price.

Even Optimum's R2.2-billion fine miraculously shrank to R577 million, with only R255 million still payable.

With connections like these, anything the Guptas touched turned to gold.

15

Things Fall Apart

Thuli Madonsela's letter landed on Brian Molefe's desk on 2 August 2016. She informed him that she was investigating allegations that President Jacob Zuma had allowed the Gupta family to wield improper influence to corruptly obtain state contracts, including with Eskom. She asked to be provided with Eskom's documents on Tegeta, including the Optimum deal and prepayment.

Molefe employed a trick that I've been subjected to many times over the years as an investigative journalist: he tried to drown Madonsela in paper. A month later, she received thirty-eight lever arch files, including twelve on Eskom's dealings with Treasury, ten on Optimum, six on Brakfontein and nine on Arnot.

Her team spent another month sifting through the pile of documents and receiving Eskom's responses to questions. On 4 October, Madonsela informed Eskom chair Ben Ngubane that an area of concern was the fact that Eskom began paying large sums to Tegeta, including the prepayment, after the president's son Duduzane Zuma became a shareholder, and she flagged serious conflicts of interest of board members with ties to the Gupta family. She warned that she was likely to make adverse findings against several board members, including Ngubane.

Eskom's response, delivered on 13 October, was by and large that Madonsela's conclusions were 'baseless and devoid of fact'.[1]

The following day, on 14 October, Madonsela finalised her bombshell report titled 'State of Capture', although legal action by Jacob Zuma, Mosebenzi Zwane and Des van Rooyen delayed its release until 2 November.

The report didn't pull any punches, laying bare in graphic detail how Eskom, and Molefe in particular, had strong-armed Glencore into selling Optimum for the benefit of the Guptas and Duduzane Zuma.

During her investigation, Madonsela subpoenaed Molefe's phone records. These showed that he was in constant contact with the Guptas and their executives in late 2015 and early 2016. He had spoken to Tony Gupta and Nazeem Howa, and he had called Ajay Gupta forty-four times. Ronica Ragavan had called him eleven times, including on the day when Eskom agreed to make the R660-million prepayment to the Guptas that saved the Optimum deal. Most tellingly, he had been in the vicinity of the Gupta residence several times during a critical time for the Optimum heist – from August to November 2015. There was nowhere for Molefe to hide.

* * *

The next morning, I attended a press conference at Megawatt Park.

Brian Molefe cast himself as a victim of attacks orchestrated by big mining houses that he had upset through his efforts to shake up coal procurement at Eskom. He claimed that instead of being thanked for saving South Africa from rolling blackouts, he was being vilified for being an unapologetic champion of transformation. He had heroically stood up to global commodities giant Glencore, whose chief executive Ivan Glasenberg had tried to blackmail him into doubling Optimum's coal price. 'He said if we stop supplying coal we will have more load shedding. I said to Mr Glasenberg: "If you are putting a gun to my head you must shoot." We did not agree to do it. That decision led to a domino effect of monumental proportions.'

Molefe became emotional when he accused Thuli Madonsela of failing to give him the opportunity to provide her with this explanation himself. To undermine the validity of her evidence of his visits to the Guptas, he claimed there was a shebeen in Saxonwold. 'I think it's two streets from the Gupta house,' he said. 'Now I will not admit or deny that I was going to the shebeen,' he added. 'Because my young wife is not aware that there is a shebeen there.' (By then he had divorced his wife Portia and was about to get married to a much younger woman, Arethur Moagi, at a celebrity wedding attended by Malusi Gigaba.) 'It made me think of another story that is actually more frightening,' Molefe continued, getting to the real point of his story: that he'd been unfairly tarred and feathered by Madonsela.

Molefe related how when he drove to work and back every day on the N1 motorway, he would pass the offramp to the strip club Teazers in Midrand. 'My cellphone records will reflect that I was near Teazers every day of the week, twice a day,' he said. '*Uncomfortably* close to Teazers. I'm not sure that is the spirit of our Constitution.' At that point, Molefe took out his handkerchief to wipe away a few tears.

And there it was: Molefe's sleight of hand. Suddenly, he was the victim and Madonsela the perpetrator. On another occasion, he expanded on this theme by accusing her of wanting to burn the Guptas at the stake like heretics on the basis of flimsy evidence grounded in rumour and denunciations. 'It is a dangerous culture. I have been to Limpopo, where people were burnt alive because people were saying they were witches,' he reportedly said.[2]

* * *

Thuli Madonsela laughed when I asked her about Brian Molefe's surreal swansong, saying that she wasn't fooled by his crocodile tears. 'He was a master of diversion today. By demonising the other he made himself look good by default. That was calculated. Even that dramatic exit when he looked emotional. It was a lovely movie moment. He put on a great show.'

Madonsela said that she'd given Molefe ample opportunity to explain his visits to Saxonwold and why he'd given the Gupta start-up company Tegeta a R660-million prepayment. Instead, he'd resorted to evasion and obfuscation. Molefe's phone records, together with Gupta driver and security guard John Maseko's meticulous note-taking of visitors to Saxonwold, were evidence enough to conclude that his dealings with the family were improper.

'When I asked him about his relationship with the Guptas he spoke about bars. He didn't mention one word about his relationship and visits to the Guptas and why he would visit them – or why he would phone Mr [Ajay] Gupta forty-four times.'

* * *

Despite the obvious absurdity of Brian Molefe's claims, newspaper editors immediately dispatched a posse of hapless reporters to track down the mythical 'Saxonwold shebeen'. Soon, Saxonwold's sleepy jacaranda-lined streets were besieged by scribes, one of whom described the shebeen 'as elusive as the Loch Ness Monster and Big Foot'. Twitter was soon ablaze with Saxonwold shebeen jokes. Poet Rustum Kozain joined the fray. 'Try our healthy Payola Granola. Only R600K, or our famous Billionaire's Bangers and Golden Eggs: R600K.'[3]

Of course, there is no shebeen in Saxonwold – as I'm sure Molefe well knows. I have no doubt the whole thing was a smokescreen; Molefe was a pickpocket engaging passers-by with small talk while an accomplice relieved them of their wallets.

After failing to simply own up to his visits to the Guptas, Molefe finally conceded to the parliamentary inquiry on public enterprises a year later that he 'never denied' meeting the family. 'I have known them for some time since they came into South Africa. They tried to do a deal at the Public Investment Corporation that never succeeded. I knew them from that time, but that does not mean that I have done anything wrong as far as they are concerned.'[4]

* * *

On 11 November, a week after his tearful press conference, Molefe resigned 'in the interests of good corporate governance'. He expected to ride off into the sunset – but not before milking Eskom for everything it was worth. A week later, Eskom's pension fund received a request to calculate a pension payout for Molefe as though he were retiring at the age of sixty-three, even though he was about to turn fifty. The fund worked out that he should be paid R25 million, adding another R5 million because his wife was almost twenty years younger than him. Even though Molefe had been a full-time employee at Eskom for just sixteen months, he would walk off with R30 million, a third of it in cash.[5]

Next to go was Mark Pamensky. On 8 November 2016, he wrote to Ben Ngubane offering to resign: cabinet had resolved that Eskom should drive the nuclear build programme and Pamensky sat on the board of

Oakbay Resources and Exploration, the owner of Shiva uranium mine, which was 'involved directly in the nuclear energy industry'. Pamensky finally agreed that he was conflicted. There was no mention of the damning 'observations' in Thuli Madonsela's report that as head of Eskom's investment and finance committee he could have accessed sensitive information to further the business interests of the Guptas – as indeed the Gupta leaks later confirmed he had.

A week later, Pamensky emailed Ngubane, asking Eskom to pay for guards at his home and to cover all his legal fees related to the state capture report. 'I still require security at my home for the next three to four months to ensure that my family is safe, based on all the negative publicity,' he wrote. Ngubane duly complied; Eskom covered his security costs for twelve months and paid his lawyers.[6]

In effect, taxpayers were footing the bill to protect the looters.

* * *

Shortly afterwards, Trillian chair Tokyo Sexwale asked Advocate Geoff Budlender to investigate the firm's relationship with the Guptas and allegations that it had sought to milk the state's coffers through its government connections and been paid for work not done and without contracts. One by one, the chickens were coming home to roost.

16

'A Brazen Thief'

Brian Molefe's departure set off a succession battle for the Eskom crown. The first man to inherit the throne was Matshela Koko, who was appointed interim chief executive in December 2016.

The new Eskom chief's wife, Mosima Koko, liked to do business with the utility.

In his declaration of interest for 2013 and 2014, Koko lists his wife's involvement with Basil Read, a construction company that had been awarded contracts worth billions of rands at Kusile and Medupi (a report submitted to Parliament later showed that Eskom had overspent on its Basil Read contracts by R1.8 billion). Koko subsequently asked his wife to relinquish her interest in Basil Read, as well as in two other construction firms doing business with Eskom – Group Five and Murray & Roberts.[1]

Mosima Koko must have grown rather weary of the way in which her husband's position was limiting her ability to do business with Eskom. Then she met Pragasen Pather who, it emerges from a subsequent investigation by law firm Cliffe Dekker Hofmeyr and auditors Nkonki, came up with a handy way of disguising her dealings with the power utility.

Pather's company Impulse International had scored some lucrative quantity surveying work at Medupi, where it had been accused of shady dealings while subcontracted to engineering firm Parsons Brinckerhoff Africa.

In 2015, Eskom's assurance and forensic department was asked to investigate complaints that Impulse was supplying fraudulent time sheets as well as submitting and being paid for invoices after its contract had expired. That investigation, according to sources at Eskom, 'just went into a black hole' (Pather, for his part, has denied any wrongdoing).[2]

Mosima Koko said she had met Pather at the end of 2014 or early 2015 and had introduced him to her husband. Koko told investigators their interaction was confined to discussing various community projects that Impulse International was involved in, including a mobile clinic in Diepsloot township outside Johannesburg.[3]

In October 2015, Koko signed off on a deviation order that allowed a lucrative contract in his own division to go Impulse's way without following a normal tender process. Impulse was hired to supply maintenance services to turbines at various power stations. The original contract for R66 million 'excluding VAT, accommodation, business travel and per diem' ran until June 2016. It was later extended by twelve months for another R29 million, bringing the total value to R95 million.[4]

In the meantime, Koko's wife had roped her twenty-six-year-old daughter from a previous marriage, Koketso Choma, into the deal. Mosima Koko told the investigators that in March 2016, as the Impulse contract her husband had set in motion got into full swing, she introduced her daughter to Pather. He appointed Choma to his company's board – according to Choma this took place at her mother's recommendation – and transferred 25 per cent of his company's shares to her, later increasing this to 35 per cent. Mosima Koko claimed she decided not to tell her husband about Choma's shareholding in Impulse because she had 'lost previous business opportunities as a result of his position within Eskom'.[5]

At the time, Choma was living with Koko and his wife, and was listed as a beneficiary of his medical aid scheme.[6]

From then on, business really started flowing Impulse's way. In little over the year that Koko's stepdaughter had been on board, Eskom had awarded the company another nine contracts worth R340 million. Eskom subcontractor ABB, an international engineering firm, awarded Impulse a further five contracts worth about R300 million. This brought the total value of contracts since Koko's stepdaughter got involved to R640 million, most of them awarded by bypassing tender processes. Choma clearly possessed the Midas touch.

* * *

In February 2017, public enterprises minister Lynne Brown went on an ANC field visit to Mpumalanga, home to almost all of Eskom's coal-fired power plants, including Kusile, and by far the most important province for the utility.

On 1 March, Brown presented Eskom chairperson Ben Ngubane with a handwritten note summarising issues of concern at the utility that were raised during her meetings in Mpumalanga. The note included an entry on Impulse International, remarking that the company was initially awarded a small contract under an emergency procurement order that was later 'modified' and kept growing. The note reads: 'Total R226 million within 24 months.'[7]

The next day, Abram Masango, the executive in charge of group capital at Eskom, handed Ngubane a document he had compiled that came to be known as the 'whistleblower's report'.

Masango and Koko were once close. 'We call each other "*maatjie*"... because we were neighbours in Mpumalanga,' Koko later told the parliamentary inquiry into public enterprises.[8] But Masango was reputedly also close to Mpumalanga premier David Mabuza. Initially a Jacob Zuma supporter, Mabuza would cannily switch sides later in 2017 – a move that would become a deciding factor in Cyril Ramaphosa's victory over Zuma's preferred successor, Nkosazana Dlamini-Zuma, at the ANC's elective conference in December. This placed Masango, another contender for the Eskom throne, in a political camp diametrically opposed to Koko, who was a Zuma man and in bed with the Guptas. (Masango denied he was affiliated to any political camp. An Eskom source who knows both men told me he came to be seen as a Mabuza man because he liaised closely with the premier's office when dealing with strikes at Kusile.)

Now that Masango and Koko were both vying for the Eskom crown, the former *maatjies* had become bitter enemies.

Masango's report paints a picture of Koko unilaterally removing contractors and senior Eskom managers from Kusile with whom he'd clashed and sidelining officials with 'a different political agenda to him'. This included Masango, whom Koko accused of lobbying Mabuza to get the top job at Eskom. Masango's report also accuses Koko of orchestrating the 'militarisation' of the utility by using Tebogo Rakau, a former army general whom Brian Molefe had brought from Transnet to head Eskom's security division, and former MK operative Joel George Martins to enforce his instructions.[9]

The report, together with Brown's handwritten note, prompted Ngubane to convene a board meeting at 6 p.m. on 2 March 2017 to discuss the allegations. The directors agreed that Koko should be suspended, and he was told to wait in his office.

What happened next is a matter of some dispute.

Khulani Qoma, who'd been hired as a reputation advisor to the board, told Parliament that he'd received a first-hand account of the events of 2 March from Zethembe Khoza.[10] In this version, just as Ngubane was about to suspend Koko, Khoza had snuck out to warn one of the Gupta brothers, who called Lynne Brown and asked her to halt the suspension. Brown then called Ngubane and ordered him not to proceed; Ngubane dutifully obeyed.

In his submission to Parliament, Qoma said 'Dr Ngubane has confirmed to me the key elements of Khoza's narrative and more particularly, that he indeed received a call from Minister Brown to not go ahead with the suspension.'[11]

The narrative is not uncontested: when asked about this incident during the inquiry, Khoza and Brown both denied it; Ngubane confirmed that Brown had called him during the board meeting, but he claimed their conversation 'was not about Koko, it was about Eskom business'.[12]

Either way – and for whatever reason – Koko managed to avoid suspension. A few days after the meeting, to Masango's surprise, Ngubane called him and Koko into his office and told the former friends to bury the hatchet. 'If you start a fight you must win it,' Koko snarled – a statement that Masango took to be a threat. After being followed in his car, having his photograph taken in a restaurant, and experiencing three suspicious muggings, Masango took to travelling with a team of bodyguards. He blames Ngubane for compromising his safety by distributing the 'whistleblower's report' to the board and telling Koko that Masango had authored it.[13]

The stakes were getting higher by the day – and more dangerous.

* * *

While this saga was unfolding, Brian Molefe was up to his own tricks.

In February 2017, he managed to get himself appointed as a member of Parliament. This sparked speculation that respected finance minister Pravin Gordhan was about to be axed to make way for Molefe. It was feared that this was the Guptas' second attempt at 'capturing' Treasury, after their 2015 bid to install Des van Rooyen had failed to get out of the starting blocks.

It came to light later that this had indeed been Jacob Zuma's plan all along. In December 2017, ANC deputy secretary-general Jessie Duarte said during an interview with the SABC that Zuma had 'brought the name of Brian Molefe' into a discussion about who should replace Gordhan as finance minister. 'He did say: Here's a young man who's put Eskom straight, why can't he assist us elsewhere?' Duarte said. But the rest of the top six ANC leaders shot down Zuma's proposal. 'We said no, we don't think that would be a useful change … of course there were very strong words used.'

Zuma fired Gordhan in a midnight cabinet reshuffle in March. But instead of replacing him with Molefe, Zuma appointed Malusi Gigaba, who as public enterprises minister had stacked the boards of state entities with Gupta associates.

Then, in April, the *Sunday Times* broke the story that Molefe was set to receive a R30-million early retirement pension payout, of which R7.7 million after deductions had already been deposited into his bank account. By then he'd bought a R17-million mansion in Pretoria, complete with its own gym and cigar lounge.

Three days after the story broke – and amid public outrage – Lynne Brown told a hastily convened Eskom board meeting that the payout must be reversed and the utility should negotiate a new severance package with Molefe. Brown criticised the board for failing to tell her about the payout and took full credit for blocking it. But subsequent events suggest she may have known about it all along and was only trying to placate the public. During later court proceedings, Molefe produced a letter Eskom had sent to Brown asking for her approval to boost his pension and waive early retirement penalties. Brown denied receiving the letter.

After scrambling around for a solution to the pension fiasco, Eskom returned to Brown with a recommendation that the simplest and cheapest option would be to reinstate Molefe and have him reimburse the utility the money he'd been paid. Brown supported the plan. On Friday 12 May she announced that Molefe would be returning to Eskom and Matshela Koko would be placed on 'special leave' to allow an investigation against him to take place.

When Molefe arrived back at Megawatt Park on Monday, ululating workers sang and danced happily, waving placards with the words: 'Welcome Back Papa Action.'[14]

Not everyone was happy with the turn of events. The ANC issued a statement describing the decision as 'tone deaf to the South African public's absolute exasperation and anger at what seems to be government's lacklustre and lackadaisical approach to dealing decisively with corruption – perceived or real'. The DA, EFF and trade union Solidarity also went to the High Court to challenge the legality of Molefe's reinstatement and R30-million payout.

Just two weeks later, after a meeting of the ANC's national executive committee, Brown told the board to fire Molefe.

Not one to give up, Molefe went to the Labour Court to challenge his dismissal. But the court decided that the High Court should first hear the application to decide if his reinstatement was lawful in the first place.

Broader political plays apparently also threatened to hold up the matter. Suzanne Daniels, who was by then head of legal at Eskom, later told Parliament she was approached by Salim Essa to have tea with Ajay Gupta, Duduzane Zuma and deputy public enterprises minister Ben Martins to discuss delaying Molefe's court case until after the ANC's elective conference in December. She said the Guptas believed that they stood a better chance of influencing the outcome of Molefe's case if Nkosazana Dlamini-Zuma rather than Cyril Ramaphosa was elected party president. (This account is also heavily disputed: Martins and Ajay Gupta produced evidence afterwards suggesting that they could not have attended the meeting and accused Daniels of fabricating the story. She stands by her claim.)

When he appeared before the parliamentary inquiry in November 2017, Molefe continued to play the victim. He insisted he was perfectly entitled to retire from Eskom at the age of fifty and be paid the pension of a sixty-three-year-old. He also claimed to have solved the power crises – though energy analysts pointed out that dwindling power demand had played a far bigger role in ending load shedding. And he said he'd saved Eskom from being blackmailed by Glencore, which was 'prepared to let South Africa suffer crippling power shortages to secure an increased price' for coal from Optimum mine.

Molefe denied that he'd demanded that mineral resources minister Ngoako Ramatlhodi suspend all of Glencore's mining licences until Optimum had paid a R2.2-billion penalty. He seemed startled when DA MP Natasha Mazzone asked him why Ramatlhodi would lie. 'He is very senior to me, a senior member of the ANC, I have never said he lied,' Molefe countered. 'Perhaps he made a mistake or maybe he had forgotten some of the facts.'[15] (At least Molefe ventured something of an answer at the parliamentary inquiry; he'd previously ignored my requests for an interview about Eskom's prepayment to Tegeta, his shakedown of Glencore and his relationship with the Guptas.)

In the end, Molefe's case was heard late in November 2017, shortly before Ramaphosa won the ANC presidency. In January 2018, the Pretoria High Court delivered a scathing judgment against him, declaring his R30-million pension unlawful and ordering him to pay back the money. 'What is most disturbing,' the judgment said, 'is the total lack of dignity and shame by people in leadership positions who abuse public funds with naked greed for their own benefit without a moment's consideration of the circumstances of fellow citizens who live in absolute squalor throughout the country with no basic services.'

But Molefe is doggedly determined to continue the fight. In May 2018, he approached the Supreme Court of Appeal to challenge the ruling. His hubris, it would seem, remains intact.

* * *

The first half of 2017 was not proving particularly auspicious for Eskom – or for Matshela Koko for that matter. At the end of March, the *Sunday Times* splashed Koko's largesse to his stepdaughter across the front page under the headline 'Billion rand babe'. The public outcry that followed finally prompted Eskom to take action, appointing law firm Cliffe Dekker Hofmeyr to investigate the matter, assisted by Nkonki.[16]

The Brian Molefe pension fiasco compounded the utility's problems. At the end of May 2017, Eskom's external auditors, SizweNtsalubaGobodo, flagged the contracts awarded to Koko's stepdaughter as well as Molefe's payout as serious irregularities and reported them to the Independent Regulatory Board for Auditors. Eskom had no choice but to act against Koko.

On 13 June, Cliffe Dekker Hofmeyr and Nkonki submitted their report to Eskom. It analysed Eskom payment and contract records as well as information and documents provided by Koko, his wife Mosima and her daughter Choma, and the chief executive of Impulse International, Pragasen Pather. The report detailed how Impulse's Eskom order book had grown substantially since Koko's stepdaughter became a shareholder.[17]

Koko told the investigators he was only informed of his stepdaughter's interest in Impulse in September 2016, and that when he became aware of it he instructed her to cut ties with the company. Instead, her shares were hidden in a trust. Koko said his wife only disclosed this to him in February 2017. After Koko expressed his displeasure, Choma was removed as a trustee and was henceforth 'only a beneficiary to the trust', and Koko submitted a declaration to Eskom that his stepdaughter's 35 per cent shareholding in Impulse represented a possible conflict of interest 'if the company does business with Eskom'. His declaration, dated 24 February 2017, was duly approved by Eskom chairperson Ben Ngubane.[18]

The report also noted that Impulse had paid R16 million to a company called Ukwakhiwa Investments, of which Choma was the sole director and shareholder. Ukwakhiwa was building a townhouse complex in Middelburg together with High Echelon Trading 94, a company that belongs to Koko's wife. Pather told investigators the money was 'an investment' in Ukwakhiwa paid via a loan account, without providing any supporting documentation.[19]

The implications were strikingly obvious: Koko's wife and stepdaughter had benefited financially from a company that had been awarded contracts worth over half a billion rand from Koko's division at Eskom.

Later, I was shown a payment analysis drawn up by financial investigators as part of an official probe into Koko and Eskom. It shows that Pather's payments to Ukwakhiwa were made from Impulse International's current account at Standard Bank that had received Eskom payments. The analysis shows that from September 2016 to February 2017 payments totalling R15.1 million were made from Impulse to Ukwakhiwa, and that R11.6 million was paid from there to Koko's wife's company High Echelon from November 2016 to August 2017. Koko himself made three payments totalling R285 000 to High Echelon in March 2016 – the same month Choma joined Impulse. From High Echelon, R2.5 million was paid into the townhouse development and R1.2 million to another of Mosima Koko's companies, Turnkey Finishings.

However, in what appears to be a breathtaking display of wilful blindness, Cliffe Dekker Hofmeyr and Nkonki decided to give Koko a free pass. When you read the report's conclusion, you can almost hear their spines creaking as they bend over backwards to exonerate him. The investigators accepted at face value Koko's claims that he didn't know about his stepdaughter's directorship and shareholding, and that once he found out he declared it to his employer. Nor did they interrogate the financial benefits Choma and her mother derived from Impulse's Eskom work.

'There is no evidence that supported and/or indicated that Mr Koko committed an act which undermined the internal control system of Eskom and no action in terms of section 51 of the PFMA was therefore required from the accounting authority relevant to the conflict of interest matter,' the report concluded. As far as Cliffe Dekker Hofmeyr and Nkonki were concerned, Koko was in the clear.[20]

Not everyone was prepared to swallow this. Suzanne Daniels warned the board that the report was a whitewash, and obtained a legal opinion from Advocate Azhar Bham.

Bham ripped Cliffe Dekker Hofmeyr and Nkonki's work to shreds. He said their report had provided no plausible explanation why Impulse should appoint twenty-six-year-old Choma to its board and give her shares potentially worth tens of millions of rands. It also failed to interrogate why Impulse had been awarded most of its Eskom contracts after

Koko's stepdaughter acquired an interest in the company, and why Koko had failed to confront Pather for not declaring it to Eskom. Bham found it 'troubling' that Koko's own declaration to Eskom was silent on 'the extent of Impulse International's contractual relationship with Eskom, its value' and that most of the contracts were awarded after Choma received shares. 'Nor is there any declaration that Impulse International was in fact doing business with Eskom,' said Bham. 'In other words, the declaration suggested that a conflict of interest could arise, without a full disclosure that a conflict of interest had already arisen.' He concluded that there were sufficient grounds to suspend Koko.[21]

Cliffe Dekker Hofmeyr and Nkonki hurriedly amended their report to incorporate Bham's opinion, issuing an updated version on 23 June 2017 that recommended Koko should be disciplined. However, the final paragraph repeated the rider: 'If there are proper answers and explanations from Mr Koko and any other witnesses he calls on his behalf, then the issue can properly be closed off and no further steps need be taken against Mr Koko.'[22]

A clue to Nkonki's eagerness to exonerate Koko came to light a year later when the audit firm's alleged ties to the Guptas were exposed. In March 2018, amaBhungane reported that Nkonki director Mitesh Patel held most of the firm's shares as a front for Gupta lieutenant Salim Essa, whose company Trillian had funded their purchase. In what resembles an attempt to replicate the McKinsey and Trillian 'at risk' looting model, Nkonki became a supplier development partner to international audit firm PwC. In February 2017, PwC reportedly signed an 'at risk' contract with Eskom that would allow Nkonki to earn up to R1.1 billion in two years, the profits presumably flowing to Gupta-linked entities. In the end, PwC opted instead for hourly rates and Nkonki was paid only R18 million.[23]

* * *

In mid-2017, as this drama was playing out, the *Sunday Times* and *City Press* published the first of a series of leaked emails that would unleash an avalanche of evidence that put the Guptas at the heart of a systemic programme of mass looting. Among the Eskom top brass implicated in the emails were its chairperson Ben Ngubane and finance chief Anoj Singh, their business dealings with the Guptas and their associates exposed in lurid detail. By then, Singh had also been implicated in the growing scandal surrounding R1.6 billion paid to McKinsey and Gupta-linked Trillian without a proper contract.

Ngubane quit two weeks later. Singh, however, decided to tough it out. At Eskom's annual results presentation on 19 July 2017, he tried to deflect persistent questions about his Gupta-sponsored massages in Dubai by claiming that he would submit a 'tell-all' document to the parliamentary inquiry.

But Eskom's lenders had had enough. Irregular expenditure under Molefe and Singh's stewardship had ballooned from R348 million to R3 billion. The Development Bank of Southern Africa threatened to recall a R15-billion loan unless the utility acted against its finance chief. The bank said Eskom had breached its loan covenants, which required the utility to maintain a clean audit. The recall risked triggering a run on Eskom's total debt of over R360 billion, most of it underwritten by the taxpayer. Corruption at Eskom was threatening to sink the entire economy.

A week later, Eskom placed Singh on special leave, ostensibly to look into the allegations against him without the risk of interference. But he was soon spotted sipping tea at the Hyatt hotel in Johannesburg with Joel George Martins, one of Koko's enforcers, and Prish Govender, leader of the McKinsey and Trillian project, suggesting that he was being kept in the loop every step of the way.[24]

As usual, public enterprises minister Lynne Brown made all the right soothing noises about wanting to calm investor nerves and embark on a transparent process to root out corruption and instil confidence, but her actions belied her words. After all, she had appointed Zethembe Khoza – the man accused of being a runner for the Guptas – as acting chairperson in Ngubane's place, and she stood accused of furthering the family's interests herself.

Khulani Qoma told Parliament that shortly after Khoza's appointment, he'd visited him at his home in Durban. Qoma was there to present his proposal for rebuilding public trust in Eskom – something that he thought would require the removal of Anoj Singh and Matshela Koko as a first step. Qoma said Khoza had told him that Brown would never support the plan, because she was 'captured and takes instructions from the G-brothers'.[25] (Khoza denied saying this.)

Once in charge at Eskom, Khoza is alleged to have immediately set about trying to sabotage the probe into Koko by shifting it from the legal division to human resources and relegating it to junior officials.[26] Koko was finally charged and suspended in August 2017 – five months after allegations of impropriety were first brought against him. The charges were based on the Impulse investigation and Abram Masango's 'whistle-blower's report'.

The whole process was shambolic from the start. The original charge sheet drawn up by the legal division was watered down from ten to six charges. Eskom's procurement division supplied a list of three candidates to lead evidence. Suzanne Daniels flagged one of them, an attorney named Sebetja Matsaung, as particularly unsuited to the job. 'His credentials cannot be compared to that of the other candidates,' she wrote in a memo to Khoza. 'He is too junior to chair the inquiry, and lacks the experience and expertise.'[27]

Khoza promptly endorsed his appointment.[28]

Matsaung, a portly, flamboyant character who likes to dress up in ANC regalia when attending soccer games, would end up exposing himself as being little more than a hired thug.

In the meantime, Eskom had appointed law firm Bowmans to look into the McKinsey and Trillian matter. In August, Bowmans delivered a damning report that confirmed several earlier legal opinions: the deal was unlawful and disciplinary action should be taken against all the key officials involved – including Singh, Koko, Govender, chief procurement officer Edwin Mabelane and senior procurement manager Charles Kalima. In September, Eskom's legal division drew up supplementary charges against the officials for their involvement in the Trillian and McKinsey payments and, in the case of Singh and Koko, the Optimum deal too.

Despite further alleged attempts by Khoza to derail the process, Singh was finally suspended at the end of September 2017 amid increasing public pressure, as were the other officials in early October.

* * *

Through all this, Lynne Brown continued her double game of purporting to root out corruption at Eskom but taking actions that had the opposite effect.

In September she started gunning for Suzanne Daniels. Eskom's head of legal had become a driving force in ensuring Matshela Koko was brought to book for the Impulse contracts. She had also taken a leading role in going after those responsible for the unlawful payments to Trillian and McKinsey. On 1 September, Daniels submitted a report on the Bowmans investigation to Brown. It was a devastating account of how Eskom officials had colluded in allowing the looting.

Brown immediately set out to discredit Daniels' report, issuing statements that alluded vaguely to lapses by the legal department.

On 2 October, Daniels was handed a suspension notice by the interim chief executive Johnny Dladla, who in June had replaced Brian Molefe, who had displaced Koko just weeks earlier. Dladla, said to be under pressure from the chairperson Zethembe Khoza, accused Daniels of wasting R66 000 on a team-building exercise.

Two days later, Daniels submitted letters of demand to Trillian and McKinsey, requiring them to return the R1.6 billion they'd earned from an unlawful contract and warning of possible criminal proceedings.

Perhaps realising how ludicrous the team-building charge must appear when billions of rands were being looted out the back door, Dladla apparently baulked and declined to go through with Daniels' suspension. He was summarily removed and replaced by Sean Maritz, another lacklustre long-serving functionary who was said to be close to Matshela Koko. Maritz promptly suspended Daniels.

Like Koko, Maritz had a chequered record at the utility. As head of IT he had previously been accused of deleting information from the Eskom computer servers that incriminated Koko, although he denied doing so. He had also received a written warning after hiring a friend from his church on a R100 000-a-month contract without declaring their relationship.[29]

Maritz's apparent penchant for following orders without question would land him in hot water. That, along with his signature on a questionable R400-million payment authorisation that had all the hallmarks of a kickback, would soon cost him his job too.

* * *

Matshela Koko's disciplinary hearing kicked off on Wednesday 18 October. By then the supplementary charges against him for his involvement in the Trillian, McKinsey and Optimum deals had mysteriously vanished.

The man Eskom chose to prosecute Koko, Sebetja Matsaung, appeared determined to torpedo his own case. Witnesses complained of being treated unprofessionally with last-minute scheduling. Some simply refused to appear before the hearing, which on one occasion led to proceedings being abandoned early. One witness, Annemari Krugel of Nkonki, was asked to testify about events of which she had no direct knowledge.

During the hearings, I obtained an email with a three-page document attached. The document showed that Koko had personally signed off on a deviation order that allowed his own division to award a lucrative contract to a company his stepdaughter was about to join without it going out to tender. 'It basically means he's choosing a supplier that would soon be owned by his stepdaughter to work in his own division,' the whistleblower who gave it to me said.

Koko declined to discuss the memo he'd signed and whether he deemed it a conflict of interest. 'I will only respond to evidence under oath at the hearing,' he told me. 'I can't testify to you – you are not the presiding officer.'

Instead, Koko came up with what, in my view, amounted to little more than a conjuring trick. For the first time since the investigation began six months earlier, he produced a second declaration of interest he said he'd handed to then chief executive Brian Molefe in September 2016 when he first found out about his stepdaughter's directorship and shareholding in Impulse. Questions were immediately raised about the authenticity of the document, which could not be found in Eskom's electronic records, even though company policy requires it to be filed there. The reports by Cliffe Dekker Hofmeyr and Nkonki both state that Koko first alerted Eskom about the 'possible conflict' in February 2017 and make no mention of an earlier declaration in September 2016. Sources told *TimesLIVE* the memo was 'fake' and had been 'manufactured after the fact', questioning why Koko had failed to mention it during interviews with the law firm and Nkonki.[30]

Two days into the proceedings, my colleague Sikonathi Mantshantsha and I wrote another story in *Business Day* that exposed Matsaung for owning shares in FBC and Associates, a company that was awarded a R500-million tender from Koko's power generation division at Eskom. The company was hired to provide scaffolding for maintenance work at fifteen power stations (the contract was later interdicted by a rival bidder and never went ahead). At the end of the day's proceedings, Matsaung got into an altercation with Mantshantsha, threatening to beat him up. He hurled a torrent of abuse at the *Financial Mail* deputy editor, offering to settle the matter outside, 'the African way'. The *Sunday Times*'s Mzilikazi wa Afrika had to step in to calm Matsaung down. Eskom fired its evidence leader the following day.

Unsurprisingly, these farcical hearings resulted in Koko being found not guilty of all charges in December 2017, and he was told to report for duty after the festive season. Koko was back in the saddle.

* * *

Like Abram Masango, Suzanne Daniels began to fear for her life. There were attempted break-ins at her home, she was followed and bullied on the road shortly before she was due to testify in Parliament, and she received threatening messages on her phone from an anonymous caller. 'If you know what's good for you, you'll keep quiet,' said one. Daniels began to take different routes home every day and beefed up security at her house, installing extra gates and cameras. The cameras recorded vehicles in the street outside; their occupants appeared to be keeping her under surveillance. She was clearly becoming a threat to the looters.

When Daniels appeared before the parliamentary inquiry in November 2017, she was asked about the R1.6 billion paid to McKinsey and Trillian.

'You know the material conditions under which [the] majority of this country live in,' evidence leader Advocate Ntuthuzelo Vanara said. 'There are people that struggle to make ends meet. When Eskom pays these amounts of money to companies that do not have contracts with them, where there was no procurement process, where we cannot verify the value add – what message are we sending to the poorest of the poor in this country?'

'There's only one way to describe this,' Daniels declared. 'This was brazen theft.'

'Do you identify the thieves?' Vanara asked.

'Yes, I do,' replied Daniels.

'Can you share with the committee who the thieves are?' Vanara asked her.

'The people implicated and who I identify as thieves – that's my view – are Matshela Koko, Anoj Singh, Edwin Mabelane, Prish Govender and Charles Kalima.'[31]

Govender was the contract manager who, with Mabelane, had led the project since 2015. Both were instrumental in allowing McKinsey and Trillian to be paid a percentage of savings, which allowed fees to balloon astronomically, despite repeated warnings that this payment model broke Treasury rules. Govender and Mabelane also authorised most of the payments, including a final settlement that was paid despite several legal opinions warning that the deal was unlawful. For his part, Kalima was accused of instructing a procurement official to load a payment of R134 million for Trillian without a contract or any supporting documents.[32] Govender, like Koko, was miraculously cleared by a subsequent investigation and reinstated, though he later quit.

Singh's fingerprints were all over the project after he moved to Eskom from Transnet in August 2015. He was accused by Trillian whistleblower Mosilo Mothepu of helping the consultants refine the proposals they would submit to Eskom and providing them with inside information on a memory stick. Singh was also instrumental in ensuring the consultants were paid R1.6 billion without a valid contract. This included signing off on a board submission in August 2016 to authorise an R800 million payment.

Koko left less of a paper trail than the others. Although he, together with Singh, had motivated for the smaller R100-million contract with McKinsey and Trillian, his signature did not appear on documents for the larger contract, which was initiated while he was on suspension. However, witnesses at the parliamentary inquiry placed him squarely in the Trillian nexus. Another Trillian whistleblower, Bianca Goodson, described Koko as a 'key stakeholder' of the project who had introduced her to the project leader, Mabelane, and was in close contact with Salim Essa.[33] Daniels and Abram Masango also told the inquiry that Koko had introduced them to Essa in 2015.

Koko put up a spirited defence when he appeared before Parliament in January 2018. He flatly denied taking Daniels and Masango to see Essa at Melrose Arch; he denied bankrupting Optimum so that the Guptas could buy it, claiming Eskom had simply ensured that Glencore complied with its agreement, which was to supply the utility with coal at R150 a ton; he glossed over the anomaly of prepaying the Guptas for coal from a mine they didn't own; and he stuck to the thoroughly discredited line that the advance payment was perfectly justified because it would ensure a secure supply of coal to Eskom and therefore prevent winter load shedding.

Despite evidence to the contrary in the Gupta leaks, Koko also denied emailing confidential Eskom documents to a person calling himself Business Man – emails that were subsequently forwarded to the Guptas. When pressed on this point by opposition MP Natasha Mazzone, he claimed he'd been hacked.[34]

When it came to his division dishing out lucrative contracts to his step-daughter's company, Koko selectively quoted from the first discredited report by Cliffe Dekker Hofmeyr and Nkonki, which had found no evidence that he'd committed an offence. He conveniently failed to mention the second report, which had incorporated Advocate Azhar Bham's scathing legal opinion that said he had a serious case to answer, choosing instead to highlight that he'd been cleared at his disciplinary hearing. When Natasha Mazzone pointed out the hearing was 'a sham', he suggested she take it on review.

Then Koko turned to Daniels. 'I find it extremely offensive for some-one to call me a thief, a brazen thief,' he said. He pointed out that on more than one occasion he'd refused to approve Eskom payments to Trillian because the utility did not have a contract with the consultancy. This included Trillian and McKinsey's final settlement, which was signed by Govender, Mabelane and Daniels. 'I declined to sign off on the document for the same reason as before – I could not authorise payment to an entity with whom Eskom had no contract,' Koko said. 'The long and the short of it is that Ms Daniels' attributing responsibility to me for Eskom's payments to Trillian is pure fabrication.'

Koko did, however, admit to travelling to Melrose Arch more than once to meet Essa to discuss the Trillian payments. The curious thing is that Koko really had no business to be discussing Trillian's dealings with Eskom at all. EFF MP Mzingisi Dlamini forced Koko to concede that the contract did not fall under his division. When Dlamini asked Koko what prompted him to leave his office and drive to Melrose Arch to meet Essa 'about a contract that is not yours', Koko replied: 'I'm interested in all the BEE partners of the big suppliers.'[35]

* * *

Matshela Koko did not last long under the new dispensation.

In January 2018, Cyril Ramaphosa announced the appointment of a new board at Eskom. One of its first instructions was 'to immediately remove all Eskom executives who are facing allegations of serious cor-ruption and other acts of impropriety, including Mr Matshela Koko and Mr Anoj Singh'.

Within days, Singh, Edwin Mabelane, Prish Govender and Charles Kalima resigned. But Koko dug in his heels. He had already written a letter to new board member Malegapuru Makgoba – who had told him Eskom's funders were demanding his head because he was perceived to be the face of corruption at Eskom – insisting that he would not be bullied into resigning.[36]

Next, newly installed chief executive Phakamani Hadebe summoned Koko to his office and issued an ultimatum: resign in twenty-four hours or be fired. The reason he gave was 'the concerns expressed by the lenders'. Instead of quitting, Koko went to court and won an interdict declaring Hadebe's ultimatum unlawful. The court said Koko's rights to fair labour practice had been infringed and he couldn't be forced out by a government directive or 'unhappy lenders' who 'unwaveringly see [Koko] as a face of corruption, even if he was cleared of the allegations of corruption'. If Eskom wanted to fire Koko, it would have to follow due process.

Eskom promptly laid new charges against Koko. This time he was accused of distributing confidential Eskom documents to the Gupta network; misleading parliament by claiming to be a bit player in the Trillian saga when he was in fact a central figure; being hosted by the Guptas at the Oberoi hotel in Dubai; and failing to prevent unlawful payments to McKinsey and Trillian.

In my view, there is no doubt that a properly constituted and run disciplinary hearing into these charges would have found Koko guilty and led to his dismissal. Perhaps sensing this, Koko elected not to face the music. Shortly after Koko submitted a not guilty plea denying all the allegations against him, he handed in a terse resignation letter. 'I hereby, with immediate effect, resign from my employment with Eskom,' he said. He did so 'without any admission of wrongdoing', claiming to have 'good defences against these charges'. Nevertheless, he'd decided that ending his twenty-two-year career at the utility was 'in my and my family's best interests at this time'.

Despite the crushing weight of evidence against him already in the public domain, and a Hawks investigation that will no doubt unearth more, he continues to protest his innocence, regularly railing at his detractors on Twitter.

17

Secrets and Lies

As Eskom imploded, public enterprises minister Lynne Brown's efforts at obfuscation became increasingly tortured and her claims that she was cleaning up the utility harder to swallow.

For nine months Eskom had tried to pretend that it wasn't doing business with Trillian. The *Sunday Times* got the ball rolling in October 2016 when it reported that the Gupta-linked consultancy was plundering a range of state entities, including Eskom.[1] After being 'inundated with media queries' about Trillian, Eskom issued a statement claiming it had no dealings with the company.[2]

In response to a follow-up question by DA MP Natasha Mazzone in December, Brown assured Parliament that Gupta-linked Trillian wasn't doing any work for Eskom and hadn't been paid a cent.

This was a blatant lie. By then, Eskom had already paid Trillian R234 million and was poised to pay the consultancy R134 million before Christmas, followed by another R154 million in February 2017. That would bring the total to R595 million including VAT.

Not everyone was happy to go along with the lie. As internal correspondence shows, Eskom staffers were becoming increasingly exasperated with the ducking and diving. 'Dear Khulu, what are you trying to hide?' one Eskom media official, Nwabisa Tyupu, wrote to national spokesperson Khulu Phasiwe, berating him for cutting and pasting the false denial in response to yet another media query. 'Let me make it very easy,' she continued. 'Has Eskom paid any amount to any company in the Trillian group (I can list them for you if you need this) at any time since June 2015?'[3] Despite Tyupu's entreaties, Eskom issued the same stock denial.

Then a bombshell dropped. In 2016, Trillian chairperson Tokyo Sexwale had commissioned respected advocate Geoff Budlender to probe alleged state capture at the consultancy. On 29 June 2017, Budlender released the results of that investigation. Among various damning findings, his report showed that despite consistently denying doing any business with Trillian, Eskom had paid it over a quarter of a billion rand without a contract (Budlender wasn't aware at the time that the actual figure was more than half a billion). The report placed the utility's finance chief Anoj Singh at the heart of the rot.

Seeking Eskom's response to the report for *Business Day*, I dashed off a few questions to Phasiwe, including one about Singh's central role in the whole debacle.

Shortly before 8 p.m. I gave Singh a ring. He told me to wait for Phasiwe's reply. The response that dropped five minutes later would henceforth be Eskom's stock media response to the report. It was obvious that Singh had written it to exonerate himself. It pointed out that the contract had been in the pipeline for months before the finance chief joined Eskom, that he'd cancelled it after initiating a review, and that international consultancy Oliver Wyman had given the payments a clean bill of health. There was no mention of the fact that Eskom had spent eight months flatly denying doing any business with Trillian.

I was stunned. Why on earth would Oliver Wyman stake its reputation on endorsing a deal that, if Budlender's report was anything to go by, was so obviously a scam? It didn't make any sense.

At its results presentation on 19 July 2017, Eskom did an about-turn and finally admitted that it had paid Trillian half a billion in consulting fees.

* * *

About a month later, out of the blue, an email from Suzanne Daniels landed in my inbox. It referred to Eskom's reply to my questions about the Budlender report, sent on 29 June.

Daniels said that Eskom had received 'a legal query from Oliver Wyman concerning a factually incorrect statement we issued'. In effect, she was admitting that Eskom had lied to me and other journalists when it claimed Oliver Wyman had declared the payments to Trillian and McKinsey above board. Oliver Wyman's report had not endorsed the payments at all. In fact, it had red-flagged them and recommended a legal review of the entire contracting process.

'Oliver Wyman is fully justified to be aggrieved by this occurrence,' Daniels wrote. 'We are in the process of remedying our relations.'

Daniels declined to tell me who had supplied the false information I'd been fed, but I subsequently obtained a paper trail that showed it had originated with Anoj Singh.

A few hours later I released a report on *BusinessLIVE* headlined 'Eskom lied to SA about R1.6bn payments to Gupta-linked Trillian', in which I quoted Daniels.

Shortly afterwards, according to a close associate of hers, Daniels received a text from Salim Essa on the messaging service Telegram that was set to self-destruct after a few minutes. 'You have turned against us,' it said.

She ignored the message, but more followed.

'You can go on sabbatical for six months – everything will be paid for.'

After a few more messages, she decided to block him. By then Daniels knew too much.

* * *

True to form, Lynne Brown would stick to her script throughout, telling the parliamentary inquiry that her actions were all aimed at fixing Eskom and solving the energy crises that could cripple the economy.

She took no responsibility for stacking Eskom's board with the Gupta associates who proceeded to facilitate wholesale looting at the utility, for Brian Molefe's R30-million pension payout, for appointing Matshela Koko as acting chief executive and then dragging her heels in taking action against him despite abundant evidence of his malfeasance, and for misleading South Africans about payments to Trillian. Instead, Brown gave the impression that her best efforts had been stymied by Eskom's executives and directors. 'I believe that Eskom deliberately lied to me about the Trillian matter,' she declared. 'It became clear that I had been manipulated into lying to parliament.'

In her submission to the parliamentary inquiry, Brown was adamant that she had 'never consulted with anyone on my executive functions. Not

Tony Gupta or Salim Essa or anyone else.' When pressed about Khulani Qoma's claim that she was 'captured and takes instructions from the G-brothers', she retorted frostily: 'If they have told you, you should ask them please.'

In February 2018, Public Protector Busisiwe Mkhwebane released her findings into a complaint laid by the DA's Natasha Mazzone against Brown for lying to Parliament. The report found that Brown should be sanctioned for 'inadvertently misleading parliament' and directed the president to take disciplinary action against her.

By then Jacob Zuma had been replaced as president by Cyril Ramaphosa. He immediately sacked Brown as part of a cabinet reshuffle, appointing Pravin Gordhan to take her place. Four days later, Brown resigned as a member of Parliament, her political legacy in tatters.

* * *

Suzanne Daniels appears to have some skeletons of her own in the cupboard.

In March 2018, the Commission for Conciliation, Mediation and Arbitration ruled that her suspension under the previous board was unfair and ordered her reinstatement. Eskom, however, had other ideas: it immediately served her with new, far more serious charges.

Daniels was accused of knowingly emailing confidential Eskom documents – including its coal agreements with Koornfontein colliery, which the Guptas would acquire through their purchase of Optimum – to Business Man, who Eskom officials believe is Salim Essa. She allegedly blind-copied Business Man's address to hide it from her colleagues, who were copied in on the emails. Another serious charge was telling the board that the proposal for a R1.68-billion prepayment to Tegeta had been verified independently, when this had actually been done by Regiments employees, including Eric Wood, who were in the process of establishing Trillian – a company that had a vested interest in the outcome. She was also accused of failing to provide the board with adequate legal advice on the final McKinsey and Trillian settlement of R460 million, which she had co-signed in February 2017 along with Prish Govender and Edwin

Mabelane in the absence of a valid contract and despite adverse external legal opinions.

Daniels had already answered some of these allegations in a supplementary statement she submitted to Parliament in April. In it, she acknowledged that her signature on the Trillian and McKinsey settlement was 'a severe lapse of judgment' but claimed she had signed under pressure from Prish Govender once the payments were already being processed. She also claimed that she was 'effectively bypassed' when she raised concerns about the legal validity of the contract.[4]

In June Daniels pled not guilty to all charges. In her plea explanation, she denied playing any role in getting Regiments to vet Tegeta's R1.68 billion prepayment. She said she'd had no contact with the advisory firm and had simply relied on information provided by Anoj Singh and Matshela Koko. As to being branded a Gupta mole, she denied knowingly forwarding Eskom correspondence to Essa, insisting she had merely been copied into a chain of emails that included the address of Business Man, who was 'publicly reported' to be public works director-general Richard Seleke.[5] During her disciplinary hearing, Daniels expanded on this theme, testifying that when she'd asked former Eskom chairperson Ben Ngubane who the email address belonged to, she was told it was Seleke's.

On 20 July 2018, advocate Nazeer Cassim, who chaired the hearing, found her guilty of all charges. He rejected Daniels' explanation for forwarding emails to Business Man, arguing that Seleke would be entitled to the Eskom emails anyway given his official position. Hence 'there would be no need for secrecy'. In his ruling, Cassim depicted Daniels as someone who had turned whistleblower to save her own skin, describing her disclosures as 'opportunistic' and 'selective'. As a competent lawyer she should have immediately recognised that the McKinsey and Trillian transactions were 'imbued with wrongdoing and illegality', and that the Optimum deal had 'all the hallmarks of corruption'. But rather than protecting Eskom's interests, she supported the utility's top brass in committing 'what is, in essence, a fraud on the fiscus' – then helped them cover their tracks.[6]

In a public response to the ruling issued shortly afterwards, Daniels said she planned to consult her legal team to decide on 'the recourse I shall be seeking against Eskom'. Cassim's findings displayed 'a very rudimentary understanding of the facts' and 'a severe lack of empathy for my situation'. She said she had taken 'a conscious decision as a South African citizen to play my role in the clean up of the company that I was employed at and I do not regret taking that decision for one moment. However, it dismays me that I am now being vilified, insulted, degraded and humiliated.'[7]

At the time of writing, it seemed likely that Daniels would seek a court review of the findings against her. Whatever the outcome of that process, hers will be a tarnished legacy. She occupied a privileged position close to the centre of power when large-scale looting at Eskom reached its apogee. For several years she was effectively chief of staff under Matshela Koko and Ben Ngubane, and she dealt closely with Brian Molefe and Anoj Singh. Before that, she specialised in advising executives on coal contracts. Someone so close to the rot for so long could not emerge untainted. But that is precisely what makes her such a valuable whistleblower. I suspect that at some point, when she realised that things had gone too far, she decided to spill the beans on her former confidants. As far as I know, no one has ever found any evidence that she benefited financially from actions that aided the Guptas or their associates. Unlike some of her senior colleagues, she was not a member of the Dubai club.

This does not make her an angel. But it does not diminish her contribution to exposing wrongdoing, nor does it devalue the quality of evidence she brought to the table, which is likely to be crucial in building criminal cases against the perpetrators. As a close associate of hers put it: 'You need someone who knows where the bodies are buried to nail the culprits. Without Suzanne Daniels, the corruption at Eskom would not be known to the extent that we know it today.' For that she deserves the credit she's due.

18

Tea Money

In 2014 a huge explosion ripped through Unit 3 of Duvha power station. One of the plant's six boilers was destroyed, taking 600 megawatts off the grid when the country was about to be plagued by rolling blackouts.

After reaching a settlement with its insurers, in August 2016 Eskom issued a request for proposals to replace the boiler, specifying it would whittle down the list of bidders for final negotiations to two contenders, and that price would be the determining factor. The insurance settlement stipulated that Eskom had to sign a binding contract with a supplier by the end of March 2017 or be liable for a penalty of R1.7 billion.

Six companies threw their hats in the ring before bids closed in November 2016. After a technical evaluation of the bids, only General Electric, Murray & Roberts, a Polish company called Rafako and Chinese firm Dongfang remained.

A month later, Eskom's group capital division recommended that negotiations should be confined to the two cheapest bidders – Murray & Roberts and General Electric. Dongfang wasn't even in the race. However, internal Eskom documents and a bid evaluation report by audit firm KPMG suggest that the utility bent over backwards to award the tender to Dongfang, despite being warned of a host of irregularities.

To begin with, board approval was obtained to allow negotiations to go ahead with up to four bidders, letting Dongfang in by the back door. Though it was back in the game, it still faced formidable hurdles. The first was cost: the Chinese company's quoted price of R6 billion was roughly double that of the other three bidders, which should have automatically knocked it out of the running. Dongfang also scored lowest by far of the three bidders in the safety, health and environment category because it failed to submit key documents. It was also short on local contractors.

Somehow Dongfang managed to shave off R2 billion from its quoted price during negotiations, but its quote remained R1 billion more expensive than the other bidders left in the race – Murray & Roberts and General Electric.

Then, in March 2017, just eight days before Eskom's deadline to sign the contract, Gupta-linked consultancy Trillian entered the fray.

According to whistleblower Mosilo Mothepu, Eskom's finance chief Anoj Singh had, back in 2015, arranged for Trillian executives to manage the insurance claim. By then most of the work had already been done, so Trillian took the opportunity to join a R6-billion pitch by Chinese engineering firm Hypec, although that proposal was never submitted, because the first tender issued in 2015 was cancelled.

Now Eskom asked Trillian to conduct a 'risk assessment' of the Duvha bids. In presenting its findings, Trillian relied on the argument – already rejected by KPMG's analysis – that Dongfang's quote was a less risky bet, despite being the most expensive by far, because the Chinese firm's costs were fixed, whereas its rivals allowed for cost escalations. Trillian then posited a worst-case scenario: if costs escalated at a rate of 45 per cent, which had been the case at Kusile power station, then General Electric's bid would rise to R4.5 billion and Murray & Roberts's to R4.9 billion.

Suddenly, Dongfang's bid came in cheapest, at R4 billion, and it won the contract. To sweeten the deal, Eskom sneaked in an inflated R600-million advance payment, which was R200 million more than what was agreed on during negotiations with the bidders. Eskom also secretly sought to pay Dongfang an R800-million 'contingency fee'. This would take Dongfang's price tag to R4.8 billion, demolishing Trillian's argument that the bid would work out cheapest if a worst-case cost-escalation scenario was applied to the rival bids.[1]

Abram Masango, Eskom's head of group capital, later told Parliament he had been removed from his post after he raised concerns about the deal. He said Eskom usually follows a strict evaluation process that results in two shortlisted companies being selected for the board to choose between. 'I was shocked when the board asked the team to negotiate with all the companies that presented tenders,' he said.[2] Masango said he also queried why Eskom was paying Dongfang a contingency fee for a fixed-price contract, and whether Dongfang met Eskom's BEE requirements.

With Masango asking too many awkward questions, Matshela Koko, who was the acting chief executive at the time, suddenly 'seconded' the group capital executive to his own office, ostensibly to help execute Eskom's corporate plan. Koko appointed Prish Govender, the official in charge of the McKinsey and Trillian consultancy project, in Masango's place. Five days later, Govender signed the Dongfang contract without complaint – raising the ire of the losing bidders, who accused Eskom of rigging the tender. (Murray & Roberts and General Electric later interdicted the implementation of the contract, pending the outcome of a legal review.)

The only reasonable inference to draw from Eskom's unseemly enthusiasm to award a contract to a company charging almost R2 billion more than its rivals is that someone, somewhere along the food chain, must have been promised a kickback. In China it's known as 'tea money'.

* * *

In March 2017, Eskom's finance chief Anoj Singh signed a term sheet with a Chinese company called Huarong Energy Africa for a R25-billion loan that the utility would use to refurbish power stations, build power lines and buy substations.

The document committed Eskom to paying Huarong what it described as a 'facility fee' of R400 million, to be paid when the loan agreement was signed, and a R100-million due diligence fee for each approved project worth more than R4 billion.

If Eskom were to pay the loan off early, it would still be liable for interest for the full term of the loan. Should the utility back out of the deal after signing, it would immediately become liable for a penalty of R50 million. The Chinese firm would also get to pre-approve contractors and make the final decision about which companies were selected, in effect giving Eskom no say over who was awarded contracts, despite footing the bill.

A strict confidentiality clause committed the signatories, Singh and

Huarong chairperson Jianbao Chen, to keeping the terms of the deal secret, including from the prying eyes of Treasury officials and external legal advisors.[3]

Unsurprisingly, officials at Eskom's legal compliance and treasury divisions smelled a rat and decided to dig deeper. Shortly before Singh signed the term sheet, they sought a legal opinion from international law firm White & Case.

The term sheet describes Chen's company as a subsidiary of China Huarong Asset Management, a large state-backed financial firm based in Beijing. But it turned out that Beijing had no idea what Chen was up to – his company, registered in Sandton as a special purpose vehicle with the sole purpose of financing Eskom capital projects, was not even listed on the 'parent' company's website.

White & Case raised several more red flags. The law firm took issue with the 'unusually high' levels of secrecy surrounding the deal and found its terms 'onerous on Eskom, and ambiguous at best as to what is being offered'. Furthermore, the punishing cancellation fee was 'highly unusual' and there was no evidence that Chen's firm would commit any of its own funds, suggesting the company was merely inserted as a middleman to charge a 'facility fee' without adding value, the legal opinion said. Interest rate calculations, a security deposit and an early prepayment clause were all described as unusual and detrimental to Eskom. The law firm advised Eskom to run a mile.

'Our strong advice is not to sign at this stage,' White & Case's Adrian Lawrence said in an email to Eskom treasurer Andre Pillay, with the firm's legal opinion attached.[4]

Singh ignored these warnings and went ahead and signed the term sheet anyway.

Subsequent correspondence between officials from Eskom's legal and treasury divisions shows that they had serious reservations about the R400-million 'facility fee'. One official told me this led them to suspect it might be a disguised kickback. The officials found it peculiar that Chen wanted the money to be paid into the Hong Kong HSBC bank account of an obscure offshore company registered in the British Virgin Islands called Ideva International Group. The Eskom officials and their lawyers could find no link between Ideva and Huarong in Beijing, which appeared to have no knowledge of the fee.

Gabriela Palacios, an official in Eskom's legal and compliance division, wrote to Pillay expressing her concern at 'the sudden appearance of a third party [Ideva], which Eskom is obliged to pay a facility fee'. Her email suggests that although Eskom was informed that Chen was the sole director and shareholder of Ideva, Palacios suspected he could be fronting for someone else. Eskom's legal advisors were supplied with British Virgin Island documents that did not disclose the identity of the owners of Ideva. 'The documentation provided, to be frank, does not look legit, in my humble opinion,' she wrote. 'It is imperative that a proper due diligence is performed on every single player in this transaction to ascertain who Eskom is contracting to.'[5]

Palacios said Eskom would face awkward questions from its auditors if Chen was paid R400 million simply as a facilitation fee with 'no further value attached to it'. She concluded that Eskom would be better off being in breach of a term sheet that lacked 'value and commercial sense to Eskom' than abiding by its 'questionable' terms.

Eskom treasury official Sincedile Shweni shared this view. She wrote that it was 'not convincing at all [that] this is the party to which the money must be paid'.[6]

Perhaps because he became aware that Eskom's own officials were against the deal, Chen's company sought political backing from public enterprises minister Lynne Brown. In August 2017 he sent her a letter inviting her to sign a cooperation agreement for the R25-billion loan facility during the BRICS summit to be held in China in September. Chen had the full backing of Eskom chairperson Zethembe Khoza. A few days later Khoza wrote to Brown too, informing the minister that Eskom had signed a 'binding term sheet' with Huarong Energy Africa for a 'fully funded solution to the value of $2 billion'. He attached a cooperation agreement between Eskom and Huarong's parent company, asking that it be signed in the presence of Brown, President Jacob Zuma and Chinese President Xi Jinping as part of the summit's official proceedings.

Brown's office confirmed that she had supported Khoza's request for

Eskom to sign the cooperation agreement on condition she was provided with the term sheet, which was not forthcoming. In the end, she did not attend the summit.

When I asked Huarong Energy Africa to explain its mysterious 'facility fee', the company told me it planned to issue a joint statement with Eskom. It was never heard from again.

Soon afterwards, the wheels came off at Eskom. At the end of September and early October 2017, half a dozen of Eskom's top executives and managers were suspended on corruption charges, including the Huarong deal's signatory, Anoj Singh. Eskom's treasury officials must have breathed a sigh of relief, believing that the R25-billion Huarong loan and its R400-million 'facility fee' would be quietly dropped now that the man championing the deal was no longer in the driving seat. As it turned out, they were wrong.

* * *

If I had to put one person at the heart of most of the major scandals at Transnet and Eskom in the last five years, it would have to be Anoj Singh.

As the chief financial officer at Transnet he had paid Regiments R485 million for advice that had led to the parastatal's locomotive deal going up by R16 billion. A sizeable portion of Regiments' fees were diverted offshore to Gupta-linked entities, and at least R5 billion of the final R54-billion price tag for the locomotives ended up being paid as kickbacks to the Guptas and their associates into bank accounts in Dubai and Hong Kong. At the same time, the family was wining and dining Singh in Dubai and setting up an offshore company for him in the most secretive of the seven emirates, Ras al-Khaimah.

Once at Eskom, Singh was accused of handing over a memory stick with inside information to Trillian executives, who were pitching for work at the utility that they hoped would net them R4.4 billion in four years, although they were only paid R600 million. Singh had also been instrumental in trying to secure a R1.68-billion prepayment for Gupta mining company Tegeta in December 2015 and approving a R660-million prepayment four months later that enabled the family to buy Optimum mine. He also signed off on what Eskom's own officials believed was a questionable R400-million 'facility fee' for a loan from China.

It would eventually be Eskom's lenders who forced the utility to act against Singh. When the utility posted R3 billion in irregular expenditure at its results presentation in July 2017, the Development Bank of Southern Africa threatened to call in its R15-billion loan unless Singh was suspended. This could have sparked a run on Eskom's other loans too, forcing the government to stump up the entire R220 billion it stood surety for. That's close to South Africa's entire borrowing requirement for a year. Such a move could in turn have sparked a run on government debt worth R2.7 trillion. Suddenly, there was a very real risk that the looting at Eskom could result in a national economic meltdown.[7]

A week later Singh was placed on special leave, and two months later, as public pressure intensified, he was finally suspended. In January 2018, two days after Cyril Ramaphosa appointed a new board at Eskom, Singh decided to call it a day and quit. He knew his time was up.

The next day he appeared before the parliamentary inquiry, but his much-anticipated tell-all dossier failed to materialise. Instead, he submitted reams of internal documents that sought to justify a multitude of sins, ranging from Tegeta's prepayments to Trillian's bloated fees. No mention was made of Venus Limited, the shell company that the Guptas had set up for him in the UAE, or of his Gupta-sponsored massages at the Oberoi hotel.

Singh's appearance before the inquiry consisted of a string of denials and bouts of amnesia.

ANC MP Namhla Nobanda asked him about Trillian whistleblower Mosilo Mothepu's allegation that he'd passed her and chief executive Eric Wood inside information to score deals. 'I categorically deny that,' he said.

When EFF MP Mzingisi Dlamini asked him about Eskom's prepayment to Tegeta coming in the nick of time for the Guptas to buy Optimum after banks had turned down their request for a loan hours earlier, Singh replied: 'I was not aware at the time.'

Asked about the agreement he signed committing Eskom to paying a suspect 'facility fee' of R400 million to Huarong Energy Africa, he said:

'I don't recall anyone raising the concerns contained in it prior to me signing the term sheet.'

When his Gupta-sponsored trips to Dubai were raised, he claimed they were paid for by a business associate. Confronted with evidence from leaked emails that the Guptas had picked up the tab, his response was to question their authenticity. He claimed to have 'no knowledge' of the Ras al-Khaimah shell company.

Asked if he'd ever met the Guptas during his stay-overs in Dubai, he replied: 'I think I have seen the Gupta brothers in passing in Dubai, but I have never had any formal meetings with them in Dubai.'

Evidence leader Advocate Ntuthuzelo Vanara asked incredulously if Singh was suggesting it was entirely coincidental that he had on several occasions stayed at the same hotel in Dubai as Gupta executives while the Guptas were in town. 'I think that is a possibility,' said Singh.

Eventually Pravin Gordhan, who was an ordinary MP at the time, lost his cool. 'Do you think we are little children that each time we ask you a question you say: "I don't remember, it's somebody else who did it"?' Gordhan said. 'We can't sit through this farce, because that's what this is.'

Gordhan recommended that Singh should be declared a delinquent director and barred from serving on the board of any company in South Africa.

* * *

Sean Maritz took over the hot seat at Eskom from Johnny Dladla in October 2017. Dladla himself had occupied it for just three months, having taken over after Brian Molefe's three-week stint in May. Maritz's first act, on the day of his appointment as acting chief executive, was to suspend Suzanne Daniels after she sent letters of demand to Trillian and McKinsey to return the R1.6 billion they'd earned from an unlawful contract.

Three weeks later, Maritz finalised the deal with Jianbao Chen's Huarong Energy Africa.

This included signing a 'fee letter' committing Eskom to pay Huarong 60 per cent of its 'facility fee', despite Eskom's legal advisors and the utility's own staff flagging it as an expense that would add no value to the utility.

The Chinese company promptly submitted an invoice for $21.8 million including VAT to be paid to Ideva International's Hong Kong account within three days, even though Eskom's policy is to pay invoices thirty days after submission. At the time, with a rapidly depreciating rand, this amounted to R306 million. The remaining R204 million was due soon after, taking the total value of the fee to R510 million.

Sources at Eskom told me that the utility's treasury officials held out on paying Huarong. By the time I obtained the paper trail for the 'facility fee' in January 2018, it had still not been paid, despite increasing pressure on officials to do so.

Around the same time, I sat down with a contact of mine to pore over two remarkable documents. Both were emails Maritz had sent to McKinsey on 16 January. On behalf of Eskom, Maritz said he withdrew the Bowmans letters of demand that Daniels had served on McKinsey and Trillian in October, which had said the payments made to the consultancies were unlawful and possibly criminal. Now Maritz said Eskom's board had finalised its own investigation into the payments and found no wrongdoing by Eskom executives, declaring that 'the payments are valid'.

The move came a day after the National Prosecuting Authority announced it had been granted *ex parte* preservation orders for R1.6 billion paid to Trillian and McKinsey. In court papers, the NPA's Asset Forfeiture Unit said that the payments amounted to the proceeds of crime, 'namely fraud, theft, corruption and money laundering' (the unit later conceded that its curator couldn't find Trillian's R600 million, which made it impossible to recover).

By then McKinsey had already offered to reimburse Eskom its portion of the fees, amounting to about R1 billion, saying it did not want to receive the proceeds of an unlawful contract. Despite declaring the payments valid, Maritz said he wanted the money back anyway, providing the banking details of Eskom's FNB account.

Cyril Ramaphosa appointed the new board at Eskom four days later. When the new board got to hear of Eskom's bizarre U-turn after I published a story about it in *Business Day*, Maritz's days were numbered. He was suspended the next day.

Maritz faced a string of accusations, ranging from nepotism and scrubbing Eskom's servers of incriminating evidence at Matshela Koko's behest to giving McKinsey and Trillian a free pass for unlawfully extracting R1.6 billion from the utility and signing off on a suspicious fee of R510-million for arranging a R25-billion loan. In March 2018, the disgraced executive quit before he was due to appear before a disciplinary hearing. It was an ignominious end to his twenty-eight-year career at Eskom.

19

On the Run

At 6.30 a.m. on 14 February 2018, the Hawks descended on the infamous Gupta compound in Saxonwold. They arrested three people, including Varun Gupta, a nephew of the Gupta brothers who was formerly chief executive of Oakbay Resources and Energy. The next morning he appeared in court alongside three other key Gupta executives – Ashu Chawla, Nazeem Howa and Ronica Ragavan – on charges of fraud and theft.

Ajay Gupta was wanted by the Hawks too, but he had skipped the country and was deemed a fugitive from the law. Salim Essa and Duduzane Zuma also went to ground, presumably in Dubai.

That night, Jacob Zuma resigned as president after being recalled by the ANC the day before.

Overnight, the looters' world was turned upside down.

* * *

Proceedings had actually kicked off a month earlier, on 16 January, when the Asset Forfeiture Unit announced it had obtained preservation orders against Trillian and McKinsey for Eskom fees totalling R1.6 billion.

This was part of a much bigger picture: the Asset Forfeiture Unit's head of operations Knorx Molelle said his unit had teamed up with the Specialised Commercial Crimes Unit, the Financial Intelligence Centre, the Hawks and Treasury to pursue seventeen cases related to state capture, hoping to recover R50 billion in ill-gotten gains. By law, the Asset Forfeiture Unit has the power to freeze assets that are deemed to be the proceeds of crime; these can be confiscated in the event of a successful prosecution. The unit began to wield this weapon with gusto.

Two days later, on 18 January, Molelle's team went after R250 million in government grants meant for the Estina dairy project in the Free State. The money had allegedly been siphoned off to a constellation of companies linked to the Guptas and their associates. The case may have been focused solely on the Estina matter rather than the more extensive looting at Transnet and Eskom, but it fuelled public expectation that the Guptas and their henchmen would soon be behind bars.

As it happened, this turned out to be somewhat premature.

In a legal to and fro, the Guptas fought back. In March, the family successfully challenged the order freezing assets related to the Estina case. Then, in April, the Asset Forfeiture Unit pounced again, obtaining another preservation order for the same assets. The items on its list provided a glimpse of the lavish lifestyle that the Guptas led thanks to years of looting South Africa's public enterprises. There were several Mercedes-Benzes and Land Rovers, a Porsche Cayenne, a Lamborghini Gallardo, a Bell helicopter, a Cessna jet and the Bombardier. Incidentally, although Ronica Ragavan was a kingpin in the Gupta empire, the only cars registered in her name were a modest Toyota Tazz and Ford Fiesta – not the type of vehicles one associates with an executive of a regular company, never mind one that stands accused of fleecing the taxpayer of billions. Properties seized included the Guptas' Saxonwold complex, houses in Roggebaai and Constantia in Cape Town and Umhlanga in Durban, and farms and plots in Mpumalanga, the North West, Free State and Gauteng.

* * *

As this drama unfolded, shockwaves from the Saxonwold raid were being felt around the world. In Ottawa, Canada's export credit agency was particularly concerned. Export Development Canada (EDC), a government agency that finances export deals for Canadian companies, had loaned the Guptas $41 million toward the purchase price of their Bombardier jet. Some of the Estina money had allegedly been channelled to Westdawn Investments, the company that owned the aircraft.

The day after the raid, EDC served papers on the Guptas and the Civil Aviation Authority in South Africa to ground the Bombardier. At the time, the Guptas still owed EDC $27 million.

EDC had already cancelled its loan agreement with the Guptas back in December 2017, citing reputational damage and several 'trigger defaults'. One of these was that maintenance company ExecuJet had cancelled its contract to service the Guptas' jet, also for fear of reputational damage. Other triggers included a late repayment for the jet, the delisting of Gupta company Oakbay Resources and Energy after its JSE sponsors and auditors jumped ship, and the preservation orders obtained by the Asset Forfeiture Unit – including for money belonging to Westdawn Investments.

Instead of returning the jet, the Guptas had switched off its public tracking device. 'The location of the aircraft is now completely unknown to the applicants,' EDC said in court papers. The agency said it feared the Guptas would use the jet to flee from justice or commit crimes, including transporting funds allegedly looted from state entities in South Africa.[1]

The 'disappearance' of the Gupta jet sparked a worldwide hunt by aviation enthusiasts for the whereabouts of the mysterious missing jet with the tail number ZS-OAK. After going off the grid, the aircraft was spotted flying to St Petersburg, Russia, before returning to Dubai. Then it was picked up flying to Delhi before returning to Dubai again shortly before Indian tax authorities raided Gupta offices in Delhi on 6 March 2018. The family's dealings in South Africa had raised flags in their native country. Indian tax authorities were suspicious that the Guptas were bringing 'illegal money' made elsewhere into the country.[2]

Soon afterwards, the High Court in Johannesburg ordered the Guptas to return their jet to South Africa and hand it over to EDC or face having it deregistered, which would effectively prohibit it from flying anywhere in the world. In April, ZS-OAK finally landed at Lanseria Airport outside Johannesburg. It was handed over to ExecuJet for safekeeping on behalf of EDC, pending the final outcome of legal proceedings in South Africa and the UK.

* * *

Throughout these tumultuous events there was no sign of Salim Essa, Duduzane Zuma or the Gupta brothers, including Atul, whose arrest warrant remained in place. It turns out he was holed up in Dubai, where he was spotted leaving a building by South African businessman Justin van Pletzen. Van Pletzen filmed himself confronting the fugitive. For his efforts he was arrested days later, apparently at Atul Gupta's behest, for violating Dubai's strict privacy laws.

From the safety of Dubai, the Guptas continued to protest their innocence, sticking to the line that they were victims of a politically motivated smear campaign. But they weren't prepared to return to South Africa to face the music. In a letter sent by their lawyers to the parliamentary inquiry in March, the Guptas said they were out of the country 'for business reasons' and declined to appear before the hearings. They described the inquiry as 'an exercise in political showboating' by parliamentarians intent on making political speeches and insulting witnesses, who were 'confronted with allegations, which amount to nothing but conjecture, speculation and biased conclusions without any underlying evidence'.

It was as though a mountain of evidence implicating them in wholesale looting had never been unearthed.

In May, the authorities suffered another setback when the courts again unfroze the Gupta assets in the Estina case. The High Court in Bloemfontein, where the case was heard, ruled that although the flow of Estina funds was suspicious, there was not enough evidence to prove that the frozen assets were the proceeds of crime. The state's case simply wasn't strong enough.

Prosecutors had now been dealt two blows by the Guptas – but they weren't about to give up. Instead, they took the fight to the family's Emirati safe haven. In June, the National Prosecuting Authority confirmed that it had obtained an order to go after R169 million in the UAE allegedly looted from the Estina dairy project.[3]

Apart from the Estina matter, there are also cases being built against the family and their associates for their dealings at Transnet and Eskom. Next in the law enforcement line of fire must surely be the R5.3-billion suspected kickback paid to an offshore company controlled by Salim Essa for a Transnet locomotive contract, and the Gupta shakedown of Glencore to buy Optimum coal mine, with a little help from their friends Brian Molefe, Matshela Koko and Anoj Singh at Eskom.

* * *

With the Guptas on the run, it soon became apparent that they had pillaged not only several state-owned entities but also their own companies. Many, including Optimum, were put into business rescue. In the process, it was found that while Optimum had made billions by exporting coal that was meant to be delivered to Eskom, the company's profits had been 'loaned' to other Gupta companies. Much of that money left the country instead of being reinvested in the mine. In the meantime, mine machinery was being stripped and trucks disappeared, while workers went unpaid. [4]

But by then the Guptas and their loot were long gone.

20

Garden of Hope

'Stephan, I've got a *big, big* story for you …' The call had come out of the blue, just like Calvin's had on that night in April 2016 in Dubai. Except this was eight years earlier – in 2008 – and the person on the other end of the line was Grace Silaule. She was about to tell me an extraordinary tale about a man named Phil Mohlahlane.

At the time, Silaule ran an AIDS support group called His Grace is Sufficient from her garage in Mamelodi township outside Pretoria. Her team of thirty-six volunteers raised funds to distribute food parcels to people like themselves who were living with AIDS, and they held educational workshops at clinics on how to deal with side effects of antiretroviral treatment and prevent infection.

Silaule was introduced to Mohlahlane, the acting chief executive of the Land Bank, through a relative of his who'd attended one of her counselling sessions. Mohlahlane told Silaule that the bank's Agri-BEE Fund could help her charity establish an agricultural project. All she had to do was bring him the support group's constitution and its registration certificate as a non-profit organisation.

'What about a business plan?' she asked.

'Don't worry about that. I'll do it myself.'

Silaule soon developed reservations about Mohlahlane. At first she went to see him with his relative to discuss the project. When she started visiting him at his home by herself, he would be curt to her, treating her as a hindrance rather than someone he wanted to help. Sometimes she would arrive to find he'd been drinking heavily, which made her feel afraid. 'The one time he said he will take me home. He got into his car with his bottle of whisky and carried on drinking,' she recalled. She never accepted a lift from him again. Silaule began to wonder why someone of his seniority involved himself with a small charity like hers.

The Agri-BEE Fund bought a sunflower and cattle ranch near the village of Settlers in Limpopo, where Silaule and her volunteers planned to establish a thriving vegetable farm. But the project never really took off, because the funds promised for establishment costs had failed to materialise. She became suspicious when she saw an article I'd written about how the Land Bank's R100-million Agri-BEE Fund was being plundered.

'I think they just used us,' she said. 'You must come and see what happened.'

Silaule's vision was to create a haven for AIDS orphans. 'I wanted a place where the children will feel safe and be able to go to school and live a healthy life on the farm, eating the vegetables that we grow here,' she explained. She called it Garden of Hope.

In less than a year, the place was falling apart. 'We don't have the money to pay workers' salaries or plant again,' she said, pointing to empty vegetable tunnels and struggling tomato bushes. 'Eskom has threatened to cut us off because we can't pay for our electricity, which means our cattle will die because we won't be able to pump water from the boreholes.'

The Agri-BEE Fund was supposed to support land-reform projects with micro-grants of up to R460 000 per beneficiary. Instead, it became a looting vehicle for Mohlahlane and his friends and relatives.

I obtained a paper trail that showed the Land Bank had allocated the Garden of Hope a whopping R12 million from the fund in 2007. This was meant to pay for the land, some start-up costs, including farm equipment, seed and fertiliser, and running costs until the project was on its feet. It turned out that the project only received R6.7 million. Of this, R6.4 million was spent on buying the farm, which Mohlahlane promptly transferred into the name of his sister-in-law, Jessica Mojanaga; only R300 000 was left for start-up costs. The rest of the R12 million Mohlahlane spent on a luxury home for himself, paying R2.7 million in cash, and on fancy cars and houses for his friends.

In July 2008, the Land Bank was transferred from the Department of Agriculture to Treasury. The man who took over the bank from Mohlahlane was Phakamani Hadebe. He immediately froze all payments from the Agri-BEE Fund and vigorously pursued criminal cases against Mohlahlane and his band of thieves. In January 2018, exactly ten years after Grace Silaule called me to relate how Phil Mohlahlane had squandered the Land Bank money meant for AIDS orphans, he was finally convicted of fraud and money laundering, with more cases pending.

* * *

I was reminded of Silaule's story when Hadebe was appointed acting chief executive of Eskom the day after Mohlahlane was convicted for looting the Land Bank.

Once again Hadebe, whose appointment was made permanent in May 2018, wasted no time in cleaning up a corruption-infested utility to stave off financial disaster.

First, he ordered mandatory lifestyle audits on Eskom's top fifteen executives, followed by about 400 managers. A key focus will be identifying conflicts of interest. So far, dozens of employees have been found to be doing business with Eskom and instructed to stop.

Meanwhile, six teams of investigators have been appointed to probe 239 corruption cases brought to Hadebe's attention by whistleblowers, the audit and risk committee is reviewing 160 contracts over R1 billion and more than 5 000 contracts under R1 billion, and a moratorium has been imposed on procuring goods from suspect suppliers – especially those implicated in state capture. Eleven criminal cases have been opened, five involving nine senior executives. In 2018 Eskom posted a staggering R19.6 billion in irregular expenditure, including from 'criminal conduct', while recording a R2.3-billion loss.[1]

By April 2018, the five most prominent executives or senior managers facing allegations of corruption or mismanagement, namely Anoj Singh, Matshela Koko, Prish Govender, Edwin Mabelane and Sean Maritz, had quit; another four executives remained on suspension, joined by Ayanda Nteta, the head of primary energy. The following month, chief procurement officer Jay Pillay was served a precautionary notice after being accused of providing preferential treatment to Tegeta, and the managers of Kendal, Matla and Hendrina power stations were suspended over coal shortages that raised the spectre of renewed power cuts. By July, ten implicated executives had left Eskom.

So far the impact of Hadebe's interventions has been impressive. In 2017, major financial institutions stopped loaning money to Eskom because of rampant corruption, and in February 2018 the utility was forced to take a thirty-day loan from the Public Investment Corporation just to pay for salaries and operational costs. But after the new board was appointed, Eskom managed to raise R43 billion in less than three months.

Suddenly, South Africa's renewable-energy sector gained a new lease on life. In April, the government signed agreements worth R56 billion with twenty-seven independent power companies to supply 2 300 megawatts of renewable energy to Eskom in the next five years. The programme had ground to a halt when Brian Molefe and Matshela Koko favoured coal and nuclear energy – two industries from which the Guptas stood to benefit handsomely – and refused to sign power purchase agreements with renewable-energy suppliers.

Finally, the country can look forward to a future increasingly powered by green energy rather than choking on coal dust and sulphur emissions.

* * *

Despite these spectacular early successes, Eskom's future looks anything but rosy.

The utility is drowning in debt thanks to its decision to build two mega power stations, and it is now paying R23 billion a year in interest on loans totalling R387 billion that are expected to increase to R600 billion in the next four years. Compounding the problem is that the demand for Eskom power is declining as the economy contracts. Consumers are also generating their own electricity rather than paying the utility's exorbitant tariffs, which have increased by more than 400 per cent in the past decade while services have deteriorated.

The solutions to these problems are all politically toxic.

One is enforcing municipal debt. For years, executives caved in to political pressure not to cut off defaulting municipalities, especially during election years. In March, Phakamani Hadebe told Parliament that municipalities owed Eskom over R13 billion with interest, which excludes R12 billion owed by Soweto alone.

Another sorely needed intervention is reducing Eskom's bloated workforce. Hadebe has imposed a freeze on hiring, signalling the start of slimming down the utility's staff complement of 48 000 – and a bruising battle with labour unions.

Ultimately, Eskom will have to face up to its blunders if it hopes to survive, let alone thrive.

It was a mistake to delay building new power plants while dramatically expanding domestic electrification during a time of steady economic growth. Even worse was the decision to build some of the world's largest coal-fired plants just as renewable energy was becoming affordable, then completely mismanaging the construction process. This allowed costs to skyrocket and corruption to flourish.

Lastly, the decision to not invest in collieries tied to power stations, which produce by far the cheapest coal, was turned into a vehicle of enrichment for the Guptas and the president's family. Carried out under the guise of transforming Eskom's R50-billion-a-year coal market dominated by traditionally white-owned companies, it opened the door to corruption so blatant it almost caused Eskom's creditors to pull the plug on the utility, coming close to dragging the entire economy down with it.

* * *

Now that the parliamentary hearings are over and a commission of inquiry into state capture is about to get under way, it's worth reminding ourselves who should feature prominently in the Eskom rogues' gallery, and why.

First on my list – for all his charm, intelligence and snappy dress sense – is Malusi Gigaba. He was instrumental in stacking the boards and executive committees of parastatals with Gupta cronies, including Brian Molefe. Without Gigaba, Molefe might have remained in the twilight zone of his civil service career after falling out of political favour. Instead,

Gigaba appointed him head of Transnet, which became a stepping stone for his takeover of the country's largest parastatal, Eskom.

Gigaba helped ensure the tender to replace Koeberg's generators went to Areva after Jacob Zuma signed a cooperation agreement with the French company during a visit to France, even though the utility's procurement committee had recommended awarding it to Westinghouse. Gigaba's team of advisors tried to bully Eskom executives into doing deals with the Guptas, and he replaced the board with directors he knew would do the president's bidding. These included Zola Tsotsi, who took orders directly from Jacob Zuma, and Collin Matjila, who at every opportunity tried to cut deals for the Guptas and their trusty proxy Salim Essa, who appears to be a grand-scale looter in his own right.

Brian Molefe occupies pride of place in the gallery. He launched Transnet's ambitious locomotive fleet-renewal programme based on questionable calculations of anticipated demand for freight rail. This would turn into South Africa's biggest corruption scandal since the arms deal, with billions in suspected kickbacks flowing to Gupta-linked companies in Dubai and Hong Kong. At Eskom, he squeezed Glencore's Optimum mine out of business so that it could be bought by the Guptas for a song; he then helped them pay for it by engineering coal emergencies, which allowed the family to extract billions from the power utility by charging inflated prices. In my view, his unceasing enthusiasm for spending R1 trillion on a fleet of nuclear power plants, even if it meant bankrupting the country, and his pig-headed refusal to sign green energy deals can only be understood as being aimed at serving the business interests of the Guptas rather than the country as a whole. Even his exit from Eskom turned into an undignified scramble for loot as he tried – unsuccessfully – to persuade several courts that he was entitled to a R30-million pension after sixteen months' service.

Anoj Singh, perhaps more than any character in this drama, was responsible for almost bringing down the whole house of cards. As chief financial officer at Transnet, he was instrumental in getting the parastatal to pay R16 billion more than it should have for its locomotives, with huge suspected kickbacks flowing to the Guptas (who hosted him lavishly in Dubai) and their associates. At Eskom he helped Gupta-linked consultancy Trillian unlawfully score work worth R4.4 billion, although in the end the company only managed to get R595 million out of the deal. He also approved prepayments to help the Guptas buy Optimum and signed off on a R400-million 'facility fee' that strongly resembled a kickback to raise a Chinese loan. It was Eskom's reluctance to act on the abundant evidence of corruption against Singh that almost led to the utility's lenders recalling their loans, putting the entire economy at risk.

Gigaba's successor, Lynne Brown, has the special distinction of being a prime enabler of looting by purging the Eskom board of competent members and filling it with no fewer than five directors with ties to the Guptas or their close associates, then feigning ignorance when these directors promptly did the family's bidding. Brown's claims that she was the innocent victim of greedy, mendacious executives rang increasingly hollow as the utility teetered on the brink of ruin under her watch.

Former Oakbay director Mark Pamensky joins the rogues' gallery for his actions while brazenly occupying the influential position of chair of Eskom's investment and finance committee while sitting on the board of a Gupta company. His blatant efforts at furthering the family's business interests while feathering his own nest included advising the Guptas on coal deals and how to bring down Optimum mine's R2.2-billion fine, and seeking to implement a multibillion-rand property scheme at Eskom that he'd pioneered at Transnet.

Matshela Koko takes the cake, with his bombastic insistence that he'd done nothing wrong. In reality, the division he headed awarded his stepdaughter's company contracts worth R680 million; he was placed at the heart of the Trillian nexus with Essa by several Eskom and Trillian executives; his private email was used to share confidential Eskom documents with the Guptas; and he played a pivotal role in allowing the family to milk the utility for everything it was worth with cushy prepayments and inflated coal contracts, while 'coincidentally' staying at the Oberoi in Dubai at the Guptas' expense at the same time the family, their executives and several politicians close to them happened to be in town.

Last but not least is Sean Maritz, the man who gave his church buddy a R100 000-a-month job, was accused of wiping incriminating evidence from the Eskom servers for Koko, and who signed off on a suspect

R400-million payment to a Chinese middleman for sourcing a R25-billion loan. His final act of infamy was to try to whitewash the unlawful deal that saw global consultancy McKinsey and its local partner Trillian pocket R1.6 billion without a proper contract.

The plunder of Eskom and other parastatals brought the economy to the brink of collapse. If anyone must carry the can for almost sinking South Africa, it's these guys. Without Gigaba, Molefe, Singh, Brown, Pamensky, Koko and Maritz, the looting game could never have been played to such devastating effect. That they are gone is small solace for taxpayers forced to foot the R50-billion bill. But for now, at least, the licence to loot has been revoked.

Notes

CHAPTER 1: ZUMA'S DUBAI BOLTHOLE

1. Floyd Shivambu, 'SA is under colonial administration', *Floyd's Views!*, 15 December 2015, available at: http://floydn.blogspot.co.za/2015/12/sa-is-under-colonial-administration-of.html.
2. Mzilikazi wa Afrika, 'Ajay "offered millions" to Jonas to "work with us"', *Sunday Times*, 23 October 2016.
3. Floyd Shivambu, 'Guptas have moved over R2bn out of SA', *Politicsweb*, 10 March 2016.
4. Department of International Relations and Co-operation, Media Statement, 28 March 2016.
5. Karabo Ngoepe, 'Zuma dropped off billions in Dubai, Malema claims', *News24*, 31 March 2016.
6. The Presidency, 'Zuma did not courier R6bn to Dubai for Guptas', Media Statement, 2 April 2016.
7. Uday Rana, 'Gupta family just caught in South Africa's political crossfire', *The Times of India*, 6 April 2016.
8. Oakbay Investments Annual Results, *RNS*, London Stock Exchange, 8 September 2016.
9. Erika Gibson and Ferial Haffajee, 'Why Guptas left SA', *City Press*, 10 April 2016.
10. Riccardo Orizio, *Talk of the Devil* (Vintage, 2004).
11. Katy Scott, 'It's official: Dubai has world's fastest police car – and it can go 253 mph', *CNN*, 27 March 2017.
12. The Presidency, Media Statement, 4 June 2017.
13. Democratic Alliance, 'DA challenges Zuma to take legal action against *Sunday Times* over Dubai mansion story', Press Statement, 4 June 2017.

CHAPTER 2: PRESIDENT FOR HIRE

1. Mpumelelo Mkhabela, 'Nzimande and Vavi: former allies reunited as Zuma outcasts', *City Press*, 20 October 2017.
2. The Scorpions, an elite crime-fighting unit comprising both investigators and prosecutors, had been set up by Thabo Mbeki to target organised crime

and high-profile corruption cases. The unit achieved a high conviction rate, but Jacob Zuma and his supporters accused Mbeki of using it to target him. It was shut down after Zuma ousted Mbeki as ANC president.

3. KPMG, 'Forensic Investigation, The State versus Jacob G Zuma and others', September 2006.

4. Van der Walt's report shows that Jacob Zuma attended meetings with Thales executives who were persuaded to cut Schabir Shaik in on the French company's contract with the South African navy. Shaik's company, Nkobi, obtained a stake in the South African firm African Defence Systems, which partnered with Thales to win the R2.6-billion combat suite contract. Nkobi's shares were funded with a loan from Thales, to be repaid with dividends. Van der Walt calculated that by the time Shaik was convicted in 2005, the value of Nkobi's shares and dividends totalled R33.8 million.

5. The Heath Special Investigating Unit headed by Judge Willem Heath was set up by Nelson Mandela in 1996 to investigate misuse of public money. After Heath resigned in 2001, it was renamed the Special Investigating Unit.

6. The court heard that Alain Thetard had given the note to his PA, Sue Delique, to type up. He instructed her to use the office's encrypted fax machine to send it to Yann de Jomaron, the company's Paris-based sales director for Africa. Schabir Shaik had proposed the bribe to Thetard, and Jacob Zuma had signalled his acceptance via a pre-arranged codeword. Soon after the meeting between Thetard and Zuma in 2000, Zuma began construction work worth R1.3 million at Nkandla, which was completed in March 2001. None of the contractors were paid directly by Zuma, but investigators found evidence that in February 2001 Thales had funnelled a R250 000 payment to Zuma through a consultancy agreement between Thales' Mauritian subsidiary and Shaik's company Nkobi, which deposited the money into a trust that footed the bill for Zuma's Nkandla renovations.

7. Media24, 'Kill for Zuma discussed', News24, 23 June 2008.

8. Former national director of public prosecutions Bulelani Ngcuka had provided the ammunition for this conspiracy theory five years earlier, in 2003, when he announced that he would be prosecuting Schabir Shaik for bribing Jacob Zuma to further his business interests, including with Thales. Ngcuka said there was a *prima facie* case of corruption against Zuma but that it wasn't winnable in court. Ngcuka's remarks allowed Zuma to play the victim and claim that he was being tried in the court of public opinion because the prosecution knew it had no case. The FBI-style raids on his home in 2005 following Shaik's conviction fuelled the fire. Recordings of phone intercepts that came to be known as the 'spy tapes' were seized on by Zuma's defence as further evidence that the case against him was politically motivated. The tapes

contained conversations between Ngcuka and the head of the Scorpions, Leonard McCarthy, about the timing of charging Zuma. Ngcuka had quit as head of the NPA in 2004 but remained a staunch Mbeki ally. Zuma's defence argued that the recordings proved that Ngcuka had conspired with McCarthy to delay serving Zuma's indictment until after the ANC's 2007 elective conference, supposedly to undermine his chances of winning. Charging Zuma before the conference would have bolstered the popular narrative that Mbeki was using the Scorpions to fight his political battles. The prosecution dismissed the spy tapes as irrelevant and wanted to press ahead with the case, but on 6 April 2009, barely a fortnight before the general elections that swept Zuma to power, acting NPA head Mokotedi Mpshe decided that, despite fierce opposition from his own prosecuting team, the suggestion of political interference was reason enough to drop the charges against Zuma. Subsequent court rulings strongly rejected Mpshe's argument.

9. Transcript of arbitration between Ajay Sooklal and Thales, March 2014.
10. Ajay Sooklal testified that the details surrounding the codeword were explained to him by Alain Thetard, the former Thales director and author of the encrypted fax. Sooklal and one of Zuma's lawyers, Kessie Naidu, had gone to meet Thetard in Mauritius in February 2006 to discuss the case. Thetard had suggested a walk on the beach, fearing that the hotel room was bugged. Thetard then spilled the beans on the Zuma bribe for the first time, telling Sooklal that Schabir Shaik had proposed the bribe at a meeting in September 1999. Thetard had pressed Shaik to obtain unambiguous confirmation from Zuma that he would shield Thales from prosecution and offer permanent support for its future business endeavours in South Africa. On 10 March 2000, Shaik called Thetard for an urgent meeting at his office in Durban. He told him that Zuma was ready to play ball. They would meet him at Zuma's official residence, King's House, the following day to seal the deal. Thetard told Shaik that if Zuma accepted the offer, he should use the codeword 'Eiffel Tower' when they met. Shaik and Thetard drove to King's House together. When they arrived, Shaik motioned to Thetard to remain in the car. He disappeared inside for a few minutes, then returned to fetch Thetard. When the French arms dealer walked into the room, Zuma greeted him with the words 'I see the Eiffel Tower lights are shining today.' Afterwards, Thetard jotted down notes from the meeting. These were turned into the notorious encrypted fax that led to Shaik's conviction.
11. Ajay Sooklal testified that Pierre Moynot had told him the cheque had been issued by a bank in Dubai from an account belonging to a 'friend of the Thales group who pays all our commissions abroad'. It was made payable to a trust registered in South Africa, nominated by ANC treasurer Mendi Msimang. When confronted with this information, ANC spokesperson Zizi Kodwa said

that the party had 'no record of such a donation', calling it hearsay. But Sooklal repeated the same allegation in an affidavit he filed in 2017 and has never been compelled to retract it.

12. Human Rights Watch, 'Equatorial Guinea, Events of 2016', 2016.

13. Daniel Bekele, 'Equatorial Guinea: Why Poverty Plagues a High-Income Nation', Human Rights Watch, 27 January 2017.

14. Jason Burke, 'French trial reveals vast wealth of Equatorial Guinean president's son', *Guardian*, 2 January 2017.

CHAPTER 3: THE DRC MOMENT

1. The Presidency, 'President Jacob Zuma concludes state visit to the United Kingdom', 5 March 2010.

2. Branko Brkic, 'ArcelorMittal SA vs Kumba: chickens coming home to roost', *Daily Maverick*, 2 March 2010.

3. Stuart Theobald, 'Political solution is likely in Kumba-Mittal debacle', *Business Day*, 24 August 2010.

4. Stuart Theobald, 'Hawks should dig out case against Guptas over Kumba', *Business Day*, 29 January 2018.

5. Tim Cohen, '"Close personal" links twist to ICT–Kumba standoff', *Business Day*, 12 May 2011.

6. City Press, 'Controversy dogs ICT founder', *News24*, 10 October 2010.

7. Sam Sole, 'The great iron ore heist', *Mail & Guardian*, 25 June 2010.

8. Mzilikazi wa Afrika and Kyle Cowan, 'Duduzane is my only child involved with money', *Sunday Times*, 18 June 2017.

9. Mail & Guardian staff reporters, 'Everything you wanted to know about the Sishen row', *Mail & Guardian*, 18 August 2011.

10. Sam Sole and Stefaans Brümmer, 'Guptas key to ArcelorMittal deal', *Mail & Guardian*, 20 August 2010.

11. Stefaans Brümmer, 'Zuma jnr heading for first billion', *amaBhungane*, 13 August 2010.

12. miningm[x] staff reporter, 'Tide turns on ArcelorMittal deal', *miningm[x]*, 4 October 2010.

CHAPTER 4: WHAT THE DRIVER SAW

1. Prega Govender, 'From Saharanpur to Saxonwold: The incredible journey of the Gupta family', *Sunday Times*, 27 February 2011.

2. Hlengiwe Nhlabathi, 'Punished for snubbing the Guptas', *City Press*, 9 October 2016.

3. Mzilikazi wa Afrika and Stephan Hofstatter, 'New details of visits to Guptas', *Sunday Times*, 6 November 2016.

4. S'thembiso Msomi, 'Born to lead? Absolutely, except ...', *Sunday Times*, 26 February 2017.
5. Donwald Pressly, 'Mbeki's rising star will take time to cool off', *Business Report*, 14 March 2010.
6. S'thembiso Msomi, 'Born to lead? Absolutely, except ...', *Sunday Times*, 26 February 2017.
7. Ibid.
8. Sikonathi Mantshantsha, 'PIC whips Barloworld into line', *Fin24*, 25 January 2007.
9. Ibid.
10. Mail & Guardian staff reporter, 'New dirt on Telkom deal', *Mail & Guardian*, 17 December 2004.
11. Duncan McLeod, 'Elephant exits Telkom', *TechCentral*, 2 July 2010.
12. miningm^x staff writer, 'Tide turns on ArcelorMittal deal', *miningm^x*, 4 October 2010.
13. Mondli Makhanya, 'The tragic fall of Brian Molefe', *City Press*, 13 November 2016.
14. Kingdom Mabuza, 'Guptas open books for scrutiny', *Sowetan*, 2 March 2011.
15. Sam Sole and Craig McKune, 'Going off the rails?', *Mail & Guardian*, 4 March 2011.
16. Ibid.
17. Brian Molefe, Memo to Transnet Board Acquisitions and Disposals Committee, 15 October 2013.

CHAPTER 5: TRAINS AND PLANES

1. Transnet Freight Rail, Investor Relations Report, 2017.
2. Bronwyn Gerretsen, 'Transnet rail services "on the brink of disaster"', *The Mercury*, 29 September 2010.
3. SAPA, 'Capital investment by Transnet critical', *IOL Business Report*, 25 March 2011.
4. Brian Molefe, Memo to Transnet Board Acquisitions and Disposals Committee, 15 October 2013.
5. Lucky Montana, Testimony before the Portfolio Committee on Public Enterprises Inquiry into Eskom, Transnet and Denel (hereafter referred to as the parliamentary inquiry into public enterprises), 30 January 2018.
6. Ibid.
7. Lucky Montana, Submission to parliamentary inquiry into public enterprises, 30 January 2018.
8. AmaBhungane, 'Meet the money launderers', *amaBhungane*, 19 January 2018.
9. Lucky Montana, Testimony before the parliamentary inquiry into public enterprises, 30 January 2018.

10. Lucky Montana, Submission to parliamentary inquiry into public enterprises, 30 January 2018.
11. Ibid.
12. Mzilikazi wa Afrika and Kyle Cowan, 'Duduzane is my only child involved with money', *Sunday Times*, 18 June 2017.
13. Stephan Hofstatter, 'Guptas could lose jet over unpaid bills', *Financial Mail*, 21 December 2017.
14. Ibid.
15. Ben Martins, Submission to parliamentary inquiry into public enterprises, 31 January 2018.
16. Mark MacKinnon, Geoffrey York and Nathan VanderKlippe, 'The price of success', *The Globe and Mail*, 30 December 2017.
17. Robert Goyer, 'We fly the Bombardier Global 6000', *Flying Magazine*, 22 April 2013.
18. Phillip de Wet, 'Mystery of the Zuma utility bill', *Mail & Guardian*, 25 October 2013.
19. Jonathan Faurie, 'BEE deal benefits steel company', *Engineering News*, 11 July 2008.

CHAPTER 6: SHARING THE SPOILS
1. David Fine, McKinsey statement to parliamentary inquiry into public enterprises, 11 November 2017.
2. AmaBhungane and Scorpio, '#GuptaLeaks: Meet the money launderers', *Daily Maverick*, 19 January 2018.
3. Minutes of Transnet board acquisitions and disposals committee, 21 August 2012.
4. The documents, which the author has accessed, are cited in Gabriele Steinhauser and Margot Patrick, 'HSBC accounts used for transactions linked to suspected South Africa kickbacks', *The Wall Street Journal*, 10 November 2017; Hindustan Times, amaBhungane, Scorpio and Finance Uncovered, '#GuptaLeaks: How Bank of Baroda's misadventures dragged it into South Africa's political crisis', *Daily Maverick*, 7 February 2018; amaBhungane and Scorpio, '#GuptaLeaks: Meet the money launderers', *Daily Maverick*, 19 January 2018; Khadija Sharife, 'Guptas, big banks linked to South African–Chinese locomotive deal', Organised Crime and Corruption Reporting Project, 15 November 2017.
5. Hindustan Times, amaBhungane, Scorpio and Finance Uncovered, '#GuptaLeaks: How Bank of Baroda's misadventures dragged it into South Africa's political crisis', *Daily Maverick*, 7 February 2018.
6. David Fine, McKinsey statement to parliamentary inquiry into public enterprises, 11 November 2017.
7. Author's reconstruction of dialogue.

8. Sam Sole, Craig McKune and Stefaans Brümmer, 'How to eat a parastatal like Transnet – chunk by R600m chunk', *Mail & Guardian*, 16 September 2016.

9. Kyle Cowan, 'State capture: Kuben Moodley battles to explain millions paid to Guptas', *TimesLIVE*, 12 September 2017.

10. AmaBhungane and Scorpio, 'A tale of two captures – Alexkor, Gupta Inc and "WMC"', *amaBhungane*, 13 December 2017.

11. Stefaans Brümmer, 'Transnet "kickback" scandal widens', *Mail & Guardian*, 7 August 2015.

12. Stefaans Brümmer, Susan Comrie, Craig McKune and Sam Sole, 'State capture – the Guptas and the R250 million "kickback laundry" unpacked in full', *Daily Maverick*, 29 October 2016.

13. Ibid.

14. Susan Comrie, 'How Transnet cash stuffed Gupta letterboxes', *Daily Maverick*, 23 October 2017.

15. Mosilo Mothepu, Testimony before the parliamentary inquiry into public enterprises, 31 October 2017.

16. Bianca Goodson, Statement released on the Platform for the Protection of Whistleblowers in Africa, 27 September 2017.

17. David Fine, McKinsey statement to parliamentary inquiry into public enterprises, 11 November 2017.

CHAPTER 7: INDECENT PROPOSAL

1. Eskom, *1923–2013 A proud heritage*, May 2013, available at http://www.eskom.co.za/sites/heritage/Documents/90thCoffeeTableBook.pdf.

2. Anton Eberhard, Testimony before the parliamentary inquiry into public enterprises, 17 October 2017.

3. Brian Dames, Testimony before the parliamentary inquiry into public enterprises, 18 October 2017.

4. Dentons report, 2 July 2015.

5. Lynley Donnelly, 'Eskom upheaval: The case against Maroga', *Mail & Guardian*, 6 November 2009.

6. The Economist, 'South Africa's power crisis is having wider repercussions', *The Economist*, 31 January 2008.

7. Carol Paton, 'Too many cooks', *Financial Mail*, 25 June 2010.

8. Christelle Terreblanche, 'Switch on probe leaves Hogan high and dry', *IOL News*, 20 June 2010.

9. Thuli Madonsela, 'State of Capture', Public Protector Report 6 of 2016/17.

10. Lynley Donnelly, 'Gigaba takes over', *Mail & Guardian*, 8 November 2010.

11. Kyle Cowan, 'The Gigupta collusion: Another Gigaba adviser linked to the Guptas', *TimesLIVE*, 26 June 2017.

12. Sabelo Skiti, 'Guptas tried to "buy" SAA boss with R500k', *Sunday Times*, 17 March 2013.
13. Lionel Faull, Stefaans Brümmer, Matuma Letsoalo and Sam Sole, 'State adviser's R5m Gupta house', *Mail & Guardian*, 20 June 2014; amaBhungane reporters, 'Parastatals "bullied" into supporting the "New Age"', *Mail & Guardian*, 17 July 2013.
14. Brian Dames, Testimony before the parliamentary inquiry into public enterprises, 18 October 2017.
15. Aimee Clarke and Chris Yelland, 'A very tender process: Eskom's Koeberg contract ruled unlawful', *EE Publishers*, 13 January 2016.
16. Lynley Donnelly, 'Behind the Eskom purge', *Mail & Guardian*, 10 June 2011.
17. Carol Paton, 'More questions than answers', *Financial Mail*, 1 July 2011.
18. Stephan Hofstatter, 'Acsa board member jumps ship over Gupta scandal', *Business Day*, 8 July 2017.
19. Amy Musgrave, 'Cosatu hunting Eskom's ex-boss', *IOL News*, 6 March 2015; Micah Reddy, 'How Gupta associates "fleeced" Cosatu in HQ deal', *amaBhungane*, 20 July 2017.
20. Tsholofelo Molefe, Testimony before the parliamentary inquiry into public enterprises, 8 November 2017.
21. Brian Dames, Testimony before the parliamentary inquiry into public enterprises, 18 October 2017.
22. Ibid.
23. Lionel Faull, Sam Sole and Stefaans Brümmer, 'French kisses for Eskom's tender team', *Mail & Guardian*, 5 September 2014.
24. Brian Dames, Testimony before the parliamentary inquiry into public enterprises, 18 October 2017.
25. AmaBhungane and Scorpio, 'Another CV, another Eskom chief – then cash for the Guptas', *Daily Maverick*, 14 June 2017.

CHAPTER 8: MAKING HAY
1. Tsholofelo Molefe, Testimony before the parliamentary inquiry into public enterprises, 8 November 2017.
2. Author's reconstruction of dialogue.
3. Tsholofelo Molefe, Memo to Collin Matjila: 'Regiments Service Level Agreement', 9 June 2014.
4. Tsholofelo Molefe, Testimony before the parliamentary inquiry into public enterprises, 8 November 2017.
5. Erica Johnson, Submission to the parliamentary inquiry into public enterprises, 7 November 2017.

6. Erica Johnson, Testimony before the parliamentary inquiry into public enterprises, 7 November 2017.

CHAPTER 9: TURN OFF THE LIGHTS
1. Lionel Faull and Sam Sole, 'Row over Eskom's R43m Gupta breakfast deal', *Mail & Guardian*, 24 October 2014; Tshediso Matona, Testimony before the parliamentary inquiry into public enterprises, 7 November 2017.
2. Loni Prinsloo, Stephan Hofstatter, Mzilikazi wa Afrika and Piet Rampedi, 'Former Eskom boss "bent the rules" to favour Gupta mines', *Sunday Times*, 19 April 2015.
3. Piet Rampedi, Stephan Hofstatter and Mzilikazi wa Afrika, 'Guptas name drop Zuma in effort to get Eskom involved in illegal mine', *Sunday Times*, 7 July 2014.
4. Terence Creamer, 'Eskom sees Majuba output at 1800 MW as it works on full recovery plan', *Mining Weekly*, 7 November 2014.
5. Eugenie du Preez, 'Load shedding hits home on SA economy', *Fin24*, 26 August 2015; BizNews, 'Matt Sharratt: The real cost to GDP of Eskom's load shedding', *Fin24*, 15 January 2015.
6. Dentons report, 2 July 2015.
7. Ted Blom, Testimony before the parliamentary inquiry into public enterprises, 18 October 2017.
8. Ted Blom, 'Unplugging corruption at Eskom', Report submitted to the parliamentary inquiry into public enterprises by the Organisation Undoing Tax Abuse, 18 October 2017.
9. Marisane Thobejane, 'An assessment of the security of coal supply to Eskom in the short and medium term', MBA thesis, Graduate School of Business, University of Cape Town, December 2016.
10. Erica Johnson, Testimony before the parliamentary inquiry into public enterprises, 7 November 2017.
11. Dentons report, 2 July 2015.
12. Ibid.
13. Terence Creamer, 'Nersa grants Eskom 8% yearly increases between 2013 and 2018', *Engineering News*, 28 February 2013.

CHAPTER 10: TSOTSI IN THE BOARDROOM
1. Eskom, 'Statement on the Cabinet meeting of 10 December 2014', Eskom Media Room, 2014.
2. Department of Energy, 'Renewable Energy IPP Procurement Programme (REIPPPP) for South Africa', October 2015.
3. Ray Hartley, Interview on Radio 702, 13 June 2017.

4. Pieter-Louis Myburgh, 'EXPOSED: #GuptaEmails show Ngubane, Guptas linked to CAR "bribe" talks', *News24*, 31 May 2017.
5. Thuli Madonsela, 'State of Capture', Public Protector Report 6 of 2016/17.
6. Zola Tsotsi, Testimony before the parliamentary inquiry into public enterprises, 22 November 2017.
7. Minutes of a meeting with Tegeta-Idwala at Eskom's offices, Megawatt Park, Sunninghill, 30 January 2015.
8. Zola Tsotsi, Submission to the parliamentary inquiry into public enterprises, 22 November 2017.
9. Zola Tsotsi, Testimony before the parliamentary inquiry into public enterprises, 22 November 2017.
10. Ibid.
11. President Jacob Zuma, State of the Nation Address, 12 February 2015.
12. Susan Comrie, 'SAA's R167K a month adviser', *City Press*, 9 August 2015.
13. Zola Tsotsi, Submission to the parliamentary inquiry into public enterprises, 22 November 2017.
14. Memorandum to the Eskom board, 9 March 2015.
15. Viroshini Naidoo, Testimony before the parliamentary inquiry into public enterprises, 21 November 2017.
16. Staff reporter, 'Koko – "I won't resign, my blood is Eskom-blue"', *Business Report*, 24 January 2018.
17. AmaBhungane, 'Tsotsi and Eskom executive at war over tender', *Mail & Guardian*, 27 March 2015.
18. Suzanne Daniels, Testimony before parliament inquiry into public enterprises, 8 November 2017.
19. Abram Masango, Testimony before the parliamentary inquiry into public enterprises, 28 February 2018.
20. AmaBhungane and Scorpio, 'How Eskom was captured', *Daily Maverick*, 9 June 2017.
21. PwC report, 'Coal Quality Management Review', *PwC*, 26 November 2015.
22. Minutes of boardroom meeting, Eskom, 11 March 2015.
23. Dentons report, 2 July 2015; Tshediso Matona, Testimony before the parliamentary inquiry into public enterprises, 7 November 2017.
24. Tshediso Matona, Testimony before the parliamentary inquiry into public enterprises, 7 November 2017.
25. Minutes of boardroom meeting, Eskom, 11 March 2015.
26. Venete Klein, Testimony before the parliamentary inquiry into public enterprises, 21 November 2017.
27. Minutes of boardroom meeting, Eskom, 11 March 2015.

28. Zola Tsotsi, Submission to the parliamentary inquiry into public enterprises, 22 November 2017.
29. Interview with Zola Tsotsi, Johannesburg, February 2018; Zola Tsotsi, Testimony before the parliamentary inquiry into public enterprises, 22 November 2017.
30. Lynne Brown, Testimony before the parliamentary inquiry into public enterprises, 22 November 2017.
31. Eskom, 'Suspension of Executives', Eskom report to minister of public enterprises Lynne Brown, 4 June 2015; Tshediso Matona, Testimony before the parliamentary inquiry into public enterprises, 7 November 2017.
32. Tshediso Matona, Testimony before the parliamentary inquiry into public enterprises, 7 November 2017.
33. Eskom media statement, 12 March 2015.
34. Antoinette Slabbert, 'Eskom CEO, FD, two other top executives suspended', *Moneyweb*, 12 March 2015.
35. Internal Eskom correspondence, 13 March 2015.
36. Zola Tsotsi, Letter to Lynne Brown, 18 March 2018.
37. Zethembe Khoza, Eskom board submission to the parliamentary inquiry into public enterprises, 5 December 2017.
38. Caiphus Kgosana, 'Eskom wants Tsotsi out', *City Press*, 22 March 2015.
39. Email from Nazeem Howa to Salim Essa, 31 March 2015.
40. Tshediso Matona, Testimony before the parliamentary inquiry into public enterprises, 7 November 2017.

CHAPTER 11: STACKING THE DECK
1. Matthew le Cordeur, 'Molefe could be Eskom's saviour – Yelland', *Fin24*, 21 April 2015.
2. eNCA, 'Brian Molefe takes on Eskom with firm hand', *eNCA*, 18 April 2015.
3. H.S. Marshall, P. Coleman, D. Bolton and A. Caldwell, 'GPS Applications at Optimum Colliery', *Journal of the South African Institute of Mining and Metallurgy* 98 (3), May/June 1998, pp. 127–134.
4. Marcia Klein, 'One company. Three deals. So many questions.', *Fin24*, 29 April 2016.
5. Atsuo Sagawa, 'Outlook for International Coal Market', *The Institute of Energy Economics, Japan*, 10 July 2015.
6. Confidential discussion with Eskom negotiator.
7. Thuli Madonsela, 'State of Capture', Public Protector Report 6 of 2016/17.
8. Ibid.
9. Nicola Miltz and Steven Gruzd, 'Mired in Guptagate, Pamensky claims innocence', *SA Jewish Report*, 20 July 2017.

10. Thuli Madonsela, 'State of Capture', Public Protector Report 6 of 2016/17.
11. Ibid.
12. Matshela Koko, Submission to the parliamentary inquiry into public enterprises, 24 January 2018.
13. Bonolo Selebano, 'Molefe vows to clear name', *The New Age*, 5 November 2017.
14. Thuli Madonsela, 'State of Capture', Public Protector Report 6 of 2016/17.
15. Dentons report, 2 July 2015.
16. Eskom board minutes, 14 August 2015.
17. Dentons report, 2 July 2015.
18. Sikonathi Mantshantsha, 'Eskom Investigation: Anatomy of a corporate cover-up', *Financial Mail*, 9 February 2017.
19. Ibid.
20. Dentons report, 2 July 2015.
21. Ibid.
22. Ibid.
23. Sikonathi Mantshantsha, 'Damning Eskom Report Exposed: Awkward details, family dealings and self-inflicted load shedding', *Financial Mail*, 9 February 2017.
24. Eskom board minutes, 14 August 2015.
25. Statement issued by Eskom chairperson Ben Ngubane, 16 July 2015.
26. Abram Masango, Testimony before the parliamentary inquiry into public enterprises, 28 February 2018.
27. David Fine, McKinsey statement to parliamentary inquiry into corporate governance at Eskom, 11 November 2017.
28. AmaBhungane and Scorpio, 'How Anoj Singh sang for his supper', *Daily Maverick*, 6 September 2017.
29. RAK Offshore Company, available at http://www.dubai-offshore.com; Watermill Consultants, 'Doing Business in Dubai', available at http://www.watermillconsultants.com.
30. AmaBhungane and Scorpio, 'How Anoj Singh sang for his supper', *Daily Maverick*, 6 September 2017.
31. Ibid.
32. Ibid.
33. AmaBhungane and Scorpio, 'How Anoj Singh sang for his supper', *Daily Maverick*, 6 September 2017.
34. China South Rail spreadsheet, '359, 100 and 95 Project Workings', March 2015.
35. Business Development Services Agreement, China South Rail (Hong Kong) and Tequesta, signed by Salim Essa and Guo Bingqiang on 18 May 2015.
36. Khadija Sharife, 'Guptas, Big Banks Linked to South African-Chinese Locomotive Deal', Organised Crime and Corruption Reporting Project, 15 November 2017.

37. AmaBhungane and Scorpio, '#GuptaLeaks: Guptas and associates score R5.3bn in locomotives kickbacks', *amaBhungane*, 1 July 2017.

CHAPTER 12: ENGINEERED EMERGENCY

1. Mxolisi Mgojo, Submission to the parliamentary inquiry into public enterprises, Exxaro, 14 February 2018.
2. Lynne Brown, Letter to Eskom chairperson, 17 April 2017.
3. Mxolisi Mgojo, Submission to the parliamentary in quiry into public enterprises, 14 February 2018.
4. Ibid.
5. Ibid.
6. Ibid.
7. Ibid.
8. National Treasury report on the verification of compliance with SCM legal framework – appointment of Tegeta Exploration and Resources (Pty) Ltd, 5 April 2017.
9. Dentons report, 2 July 2015.
10. Matshela Koko, Letter to Tegeta, 31 August 2015.
11. Ravindra Nath, Letter to Matshela Koko, 4 September 2015.
12. National Treasury report on the verification of compliance with SCM legal framework – appointment of Tegeta Exploration and Resources (Pty) Ltd, 5 April 2017; Fundudzi Forensic Services, National Treasury, Second draft report: Forensic investigation into various allegations at Transnet and Eskom, July 2018.
13. Ibid.
14. Ibid.
15. War on Want, 'Extracting Minerals, Extracting Wealth', 2015; UK Parliament, International Development Committee, 'Written evidence submitted by Glencore International Plc', April 2012.
16. Ben Doherty, Oliver Zihlmann and Petra Blum, 'Revealed: Glencore's secret loan to secure DRC mining rights', *The Guardian*, 5 November 2017.
17. Brendan Ryan, 'Guptas' Oakbay sells Optimum Coal export rights for R3.6bn', *miningm*[x], 5 September 2016.
18. Eamonn Ryan, 'Glencore and Optimum: Is the government playing "dare"?', *Mineweb*, 7 August 2015.
19. Lameez Omarjee and Matthew le Cordeur, 'Ramatlhodi: I told the Guptas to back off', *Fin24*, 16 May 2017.
20. Press Council, 'Kuben Moodley vs. *Sunday Times*', 3 April 2017.
21. Asset Forfeiture Unit *ex parte* application, Case 168 2018, Bloemfontein High Court, 18 January 2018.
22. Ibid.
23. Thuli Madonsela, 'State of Capture', Public Protector Report 6 of 2016/17.

24. Ibid.
25. Brian Molefe, Submission to the parliamentary inquiry into public enterprises, 21 November 2017.
26. At the time of writing it was expected that Suzanne Daniels would approach the courts to contest her dismissal.
27. Thuli Madonsela, 'State of Capture', Public Protector Report 6 of 2016/17.
28. Nazeem Howa, Letter to Piers Marsden, 9 November 2015.
29. Jan de Lange, 'Eskom "bought" coal mine for the Guptas', *News24*, 23 July 2017.
30. Thuli Madonsela, 'State of Capture', Public Protector Report 6 of 2016/17.
31. Matshela Koko, Optimum Coal Mine Options letter to Piers Marsden and Peter van den Steen, 5 November 2015.
32. Ibid.
33. When confronted with this evidence in Parliament, Matshela Koko confirmed that the email address used to send the documents was his private account, but he claimed that it had been hacked.
34. Legal memo to Matshela Koko, 4 November 2015.
35. Email from Tony Gupta to Ashu Chawla sent at 8.03 a.m. on 5 November 2015, with a draft of Matshela Koko's Optimum Coal Mine Options letter attached.
36. Franz Wild and Paul Burkhardt, 'Zuma son got stake in Tegeta weeks before it bought Optimum', *Bloomberg*, 7 March 2016.
37. Eskom minutes, Exploratory Discussions on Sustainable Hendrina Coal Supply, 24 November 2015.
38. Piers Marsden, Testimony before the parliamentary inquiry into public enterprises, 1 November 2017.
39. Ibid.
40. Thanduxolo Jika, 'Mounting evidence of Zwane-Gupta collaboration', *Sunday Times*, 16 July 2017.
41. Piers Marsden, Testimony before the parliamentary inquiry into public enterprises, 1 November 2017.
42. Matshela Koko, Submission to the parliamentary inquiry into public enterprises, 24 January 2018; Matshela Koko, Letter to Dr Thibedi Ramontja, director-general of the Department of Mineral Resources, 6 December 2015.
43. Piers Marsden, Testimony before the parliamentary inquiry into public enterprises, 1 November 2017.
44. Thuli Madonsela, 'State of Capture', Public Protector Report 6 of 2016/17; Thanduxolo Jika, 'Mounting evidence of Zwane-Gupta collaboration', *Sunday Times*, 16 July 2017.
45. Franz Wild and Bloomberg, 'Zwane's advisor linked to the Guptas', *Moneyweb*, 19 February 2016.
46. Nazeem Howa, Email to Tony Gupta, 2 February 2016.

47. Ibid.

48. Piers Marsden and Peter van den Steen, Business Rescue Report, 4 December 2015.

49. Matshela Koko, Submission to the parliamentary inquiry into public enterprises, 24 January 2018; Matshela Koko, Letter to Dr Thibedi Ramontja, director-general of the Department of Mineral Resources, 6 December 2012.

50. Thibedi Ramontja, Letter to Matshela Koko, 7 December 2015.

51. Matshela Koko, Submission to the parliamentary inquiry into public enterprises, 24 January 2018.

52. David McKay, 'DMR turmoil deepens as Ramontja quits', *miningm^x*, 15 December 2015.

53. Submission to Eskom board, 'Prepurchase of coal from Optimum Coal Mine', 8 December 2015.

54. Email contained in the Gupta leaks sent by Mark Pamensky to Atul Gupta and others, 10 December 2015.

55. Deloitte report for the Reserve Bank, 24 February 2017.

CHAPTER 13: TRILLIAN'S BILLIONS

1. Mindy Weisberger, 'The Bizarre History of Tetris', *Live Science*, 13 October 2016.

2. Matthew le Cordeur, 'How classic game Tetris saved Eskom', *Fin24*, 24 November 2015.

3. Mosilo Mothepu, Testimony before the parliamentary inquiry into public enterprises, 31 October 2017.

4. Anoj Singh, Testimony before the parliamentary inquiry into public enterprises, 23 January 2017.

5. Mosilo Mothepu, Testimony before the parliamentary inquiry into public enterprises, 31 October 2017.

6. Ibid.

7. AmaBhungane, 'McKinsey caught up in Trillian lies', *Daily Maverick*, 30 June 2017.

8. Bowmans report, 2 August 2017; Strategy Report submitted to Eskom, 18 May 2015.

9. Ibid.; Edwin Mabelane, Board tender committee submission, 22 June 2015.

10. Board tender committee submission, 22 October 2015.

11. Round-robin resolution signed by Viroshini Naidoo on 6 July 2015, Nazia Carrim on 3 July 2015, Chwayita Mabuda on 6 July 2015 and by Zethembe Khoza on 1 July 2017.

12. When asked about these allegations in Parliament, Singh denied them. Mosilo Mothepu, Testimony before the parliamentary inquiry into public enterprises, 31 October 2017.

13. Bowmans report citing emails from Aziz Laher, 2 August 2017.

14. Bowmans report, 2 August 2017. The report cites a submission to the board tender committee that was prepared and signed by Matshela Koko and Anoj Singh.

15. Email correspondence between Salim Essa, Tony Gupta and Pieter van der Merwe, with share subscription agreement attached, 11 June 2014.

16. Stephan Hofstatter, 'How McKinsey and Trillian milked billions from SA Inc', *Financial Mail*, 5 October 2017.

17. Bianca Goodson, Statement released on the Platform for the Protection of Whistleblowers in Africa, 27 September 2017. Author's reconstruction of dialogue.

18. Ibid.

19. Ibid.

20. Ibid.

21. Ibid. Goodson's statement contains a copy of Trillian and McKinsey 'meeting notes' that detail these concerns.

22. Ibid.

23. Werksmans memos, sent to Transnet on 14 October 2016.

24. Bianca Goodson, Statement released on the Platform for the Protection of Whistleblowers in Africa, 27 September 2017.

25. Budlender report, 29 June 2017.

26. Mark Pamensky, Email to Atul Gupta and others, 18 September 2015.

27. Trillian confidential submission to Transnet, April 2016.

28. Mark Pamensky, Letter to Michail Shapiro, forwarded to Mosilo Mothepu and Eric Wood.

29. Bianca Goodson, Statement released on the Platform for the Protection of Whistleblowers in Africa, 27 September 2017.

30. Bianca Goodson, Testimony before the parliamentary inquiry into public enterprises, 3 November 2017.

31. Mosilo Mothepu, Testimony before the parliamentary inquiry into public enterprises, 31 October 2017.

32. Hypec proposal, 10 January 2016.

33. Bowmans report, 2 August 2017.

34. Legal opinion for Eskom by Paul Kennedy SC, 4 December 2015.

35. Presentation to McKinsey leadership meeting, 19 January 2016.

36. Bianca Goodson, Testimony before the parliamentary inquiry into public enterprises, 3 November 2017.

37. Bianca Goodson, Meeting notes, January 2016; Testimony before the parliamentary inquiry into public enterprises, 3 November 2017.

38. Ibid.

39. Letter from Anoj Singh to Alexander Weiss, 19 February 2016.

40. Bianca Goodson, Testimony before the parliamentary inquiry into public enterprises, 3 November 2017.

41. David Fine, McKinsey statement to the parliamentary inquiry into corporate governance at Eskom, 15 November 2017.

42. Bianca Goodson, Statement released on the Platform for the Protection of Whistleblowers in Africa, 27 September 2017.

43. Oliver Wyman and Marsh, Review of supplier agreement between Eskom and McKinsey/BBBEE Partner, 15 December 2015.

44. Mosilo Mothepu, Testimony before parliament's inquiry into public enterprises, 31 October 2017.

45. Jessica Bezuidenhout, 'No winnable criminal case against Trillian whistleblower', *Daily Maverick*, 3 April 2018.

CHAPTER 14: SHOW ME THE MONEY

1. Kyle Cowan, 'The mystery of the great Dubai gathering', *TimesLIVE*, 21 August 2017.

2. Jessica Bezuidenhout, 'Guptas turn R3m into R900m in mystery-shrouded mining deal', *Mail & Guardian*, 9 December 2016.

3. Mxolisi Mgojo, Submission to parliamentary inquiry into public enterprises, 14 February 2018.

4. Deloitte report for the Reserve Bank, 24 February 2017; Thuli Madonsela, 'State of Capture', Public Protector Report 6 of 2016/17.

5. Thuli Madonsela, 'State of Capture', Public Protector Report 6 of 2016/17.

6. Piers Marsden, Section 34 report to the Directorate for Priority Crime Investigation, 1 July 2016.

7. Suzanne Daniels, Testimony before the parliamentary inquiry into public enterprises, 8 November 2017.

8. Dialogue reconstructed from the parliamentary testimony of Suzanne Daniels, 8 November 2017.

9. Ntuthuzelo Vanara, Proceedings of parliamentary inquiry into public enterprises, 8 November 2017.

10. Eskom board tender committee submission, addendum to coal supply agreement for Arnot power station, 11 April 2016.

11. Piers Marsden, Section 34 report to the Directorate for Priority Crime Investigation, 1 July 2016.

12. Antoinette Slabbert, 'Renewables have disappointed us – Molefe', *Moneyweb*, 12 May 2016.

13. Paul Burkhardt, 'How Molefe, govt stalled SA's renewable power programme', *Bloomberg*, 1 February 2018.

14. Cited in Thuli Madonsela, 'State of Capture', Public Protector Report 6 of 2016/17.

15. Correspondence between Tegeta and the Department of Mineral Resources, 4–5 May 2016.
16. Deloitte report for the Reserve Bank, 24 February 2017; Thuli Madonsela, 'State of Capture', Public Protector Report 6 of 2016/17.
17. Letter from Sanjiv Gupta, CEO of Bank of Baroda South Africa, to Koornfontein Mines, 23 August 2016. Accessed by Pieter-Louis Myburgh, 'Guptas' "unlawful" loan backed by mine rehab fund', *News24*, 15 September 2017.
18. Letter from Solly Tshitangano to Brian Molefe, 22 August 2016.
19. Letter from Solly Tshitangano to Brian Molefe, 1 September 2016.
20. AmaBhungane, 'R10bn in 15 days – another massive Eskom boost for the Guptas', *Daily Maverick*, 22 April 2017.
21. Kyle Cowan and Sabelo Skiti, 'Coal crisis mints profit for Tegeta', *Business Times*, 13 May 2018.

CHAPTER 15: THINGS FALL APART
1. Eskom board's response to the Public Protector, 13 October 2016.
2. Mondli Makhanya, 'The tragic fall of Brian Molefe', *City Press*, 13 November 2016.
3. Monica Laganparsad, 'Meme's the word, Mr Molefe – bottoms up!', *Sunday Times*, 6 November 2011.
4. Brian Molefe, Testimony before parliamentary inquiry into public enterprises, 21 November 2017.
5. Testimony of Sibusiso Luthuli, chief executive of the Eskom Pension and Provident Fund, to the parliamentary inquiry into public enterprises, 20 October 2017.
6. Email from Mark Pamensky to Baldwin Ngubane, 15 November 2016; Eskom board resolution, 24 November 2016.

CHAPTER 16: 'A BRAZEN THIEF'
1. Report for Eskom by Cliffe Dekker Hofmeyr Attorneys and Nkonki Incorporated, 13 June 2017.
2. Ibid.
3. Report for Eskom by Cliffe Dekker Hofmeyr Attorneys and Nkonki Incorporated, 23 June 2017.
4. Eskom sole source justification for Impulse International, October 2015; Report for Eskom by Cliffe Dekker Hofmeyr Attorneys and Nkonki Incorporated, 23 June 2017.
5. Ibid.
6. Legal opinion for Eskom on the Cliffe Dekker Hofmeyr and Nkonki report, Advocate Azhar Bham, 22 June 2017.

7. Suzanne Daniels, Supplementary submission to the parliamentary inquiry into public enterprises, 18 April 2018; Venete Klein, Submission to parliamentary inquiry into public enterprises, 21 November 2017.

8. Matshela Koko, Testimony before the parliamentary inquiry into public enterprises, 24 January 2018.

9. 'Whistleblower's report' to Ben Ngubane, 1 March 2017.

10. In his submission to the parliamentary inquiry into public enterprises, Khulani Qoma claimed that Zethembe Khoza had told him of the events during a visit at Khoza's home in Durban. This, he said, took place shortly after Khoza had been appointed acting chairperson of Eskom, following Ben Ngubane's resignation in June 2017.

11. Khulani Qoma, Submission to parliamentary inquiry into public enterprises, 14 November 2017.

12. Lynne Brown, Zethembe Khoza and Ben Ngubane, Testimony before the parliamentary inquiry into public enterprises, 22 November 2017 to 7 March 2018.

13. Abram Masango, Submission to parliamentary inquiry into public enterprises, 27 February 2018.

14. Sikonathi Mantshantsha, 'What Brian Molefe's return to Eskom means for SA', *Financial Mail*, 18 May 2017.

15. Brian Molefe, Testimony before the parliamentary inquiry into public enterprises, 21 November 2017.

16. Mzilikazi wa Afrika, 'Billion rand babe', *Sunday Times*, 26 March 2017.

17. Report for Eskom by Cliffe Dekker Hofmeyr Attorneys and Nkonki Incorporated, 13 June 2017.

18. Ibid.

19. Ibid.

20. Report for Eskom by Cliffe Dekker Hofmeyr Attorneys and Nkonki Incorporated, 13 June 2017.

21. Legal opinion for Eskom on the Cliffe Dekker Hofmeyr and Nkonki report, Advocate Azhar Bham, 22 June 2017.

22. Report for Eskom by Cliffe Dekker Hofmeyr Attorneys and Nkonki Incorporated, 23 June 2017.

23. AmaBhungane, 'The Nkonki Pact Part 2 – Eskom's new billion-rand consulting deal for Essa & Co', *Daily Maverick*, 29 March 2018.

24. Stephan Hofstatter and Sikonathi Mantshantsha, 'Anoj Singh holds meetings on the quiet in a week of Eskom drama', *Business Day*, 21 August 2017.

25. Khulani Qoma, Submission to parliamentary inquiry into public enterprises, 14 November 2017.

26. Sikonathi Mantshantsha, 'Eskom drags its feet acting against Matshela Koko', *Business Day*, 18 August 2017.

27. Suzanne Daniels, Memo to Zethembe Khoza, 31 July 2017.
28. Suzanne Daniels, Letter to Johnny Dladla, 4 August 2017.
29. Sikonathi Mantshantsha, 'Eskom acting CE admits to nepotism warning', *Business Day*, 12 October 2017.
30. Kyle Cowan, 'Queries raised on memo that got Koko off hook', *TimesLIVE*, 17 December 2017.
31. Suzanne Daniels, Testimony before the parliamentary inquiry into public enterprises, 8 November 2017.
32. G9 Forensic, Investigation report for Eskom, August 2017.
33. Bianca Goodson, Testimony before the parliamentary inquiry into public enterprises, 3 November 2017.
34. Matshela Koko, Testimony before the parliamentary inquiry into public enterprises, 24 January 2018.
35. Ibid.
36. Judgment in the Labour Court, Case J200/18, delivered on 21 February 2018; Yolandi Groenewald, 'Koko - I won't resign for the sake of patriotism', *fin24*, 24 January 2018.

CHAPTER 17: SECRETS AND LIES

1. Thanduxolo Jika and Sabelo Skiti, 'The dark heart of state capture', *Sunday Times*, 23 October 2016.
2. Eskom statement, 'Eskom has no contracts with Trillian and associated companies', 27 October 2016.
3. Email from Nwabisa Tyupu to Khulu Phasiwe, contained in an email from Eskom Media Desk to, inter alia, Suzanne Daniels, Matshela Koko and Khulani Qoma, 3 May 2017.
4. Suzanne Daniels, Supplementary submission to the parliamentary inquiry into public enterprises, 18 April 2018.
5. Plea explanation, Suzanne Daniles, 5 June 2018.
6. Ruling by Nazeer Cassim, 20 July 2018.
7. The response was initially provided to the *Daily Maverick*. When contacted by the author, Daniels provided the same response.

CHAPTER 18: TEA MONEY

1. Stephan Hofstatter, 'Eskom offered Dongfang secret R800m sweetener', *Business Day*, 3 July 2017.
2. Abram Masango, Testimony before the parliamentary inquiry into public enterprises, 28 February 2018.
3. Term sheet between Eskom and Huarong Energy Africa, 14 March 2017.
4. Email from Adrian Lawrence to Andre Pillay, 12 March 2017.

5. Internal correspondence among officials from Eskom's legal and treasury divisions, March to August 2017.

6. Ibid.

7. Stuart Theobald, 'Eskom's financials reveal how deep a hole its executives have dug for the government', *Business Day*, 31 July 2017.

CHAPTER 19: ON THE RUN

1. Affidavit of Export Development Canada, South Gauteng High Court, Case number 2018/6151.

2. Reuters, 'Indian tax officials raid properties linked to wealthy Gupta family', 6 March 2018.

3. Karyn Maughan, 'State hunts Gupta assets … in Dubai', *TimesLIVE*, 5 June 2018.

4. Kyle Cowan, 'How the Guptas stripped Optimum of R3bn', *Times Select*, 14 May 2018.

CHAPTER 20: GARDEN OF HOPE

1. Eskom annual results presentation, 23 July 2018.

Index

municipal debt 240
Murray & Roberts 197, 222–224
Murray, Christo 156
Myeni, Dudu 108–109, 118–119
Myeni, Thalente 108

Nahyan, Mohammed bin Zayed Al 14–15
Naidoo, Pat 101
Naidoo, Viroshini 99, 100–101, 124–125, 142, 159, 185–186
Narayan, Ashok 70
Nath, Ravindra 105, 139, 154
National Energy Regulator 86, 98
National Prosecuting Authority *see* NPA
National Treasury 6, 42, 61, 97–98, 138–139, 143, 154–155, 167–168, 170, 190, 206, 232, 238
Nedbank 64, 67, 124
Nene, Nhlanhla 6–7, 42, 153
Neotel 70
New Age, The (now *Afro Voice*) 35, 43–44, 79–81, 89, 106, 126
Ngcaba, Andile 38–39
Ngema-Zuma, Bongi 63
Ngonyama, Smuts 39
Ngqulunga, Bongani 16, 35
Ngubane, Ben 99–100, 116, 118–120, 124, 128, 130, 141, 192, 196, 199–200, 204, 207, 220
Nkandla homestead 19, 20
Nkonki Incorporated 197, 204–206, 211, 213
Nobanda, Namhla 228
NPA 20–21, 230, 235
Nteta, Ayanda 186, 239
Ntsebeza, Dumisa 38
Ntsokolo, Mongezi 117
nuclear energy 42, 153, 182, 188, 195–196
Nyembezi-Heita, Nonkululeko 26–27, 31
Nyhonyha, Litha 64, 69, 71, 158, 161, 167
Nzimande, Blade 18, 23–24

Oakbay group 7, 146–147, 152, 166
Oakbay Investments 32, 119, 133, 185
Oakbay Resources and Energy 68, 101, 119, 124–125, 234
Oakbay Resources and Exploration 196

Obiang Nguema Mbasogo, Teodoro 18, 23, 40
Obiang, Teodorin 23–24
OCCRP 133
O'Flaherty, Paul 84, 85
oil 23, 25, 100, 151
Oliver Wyman (management consultancy) 64, 173, 176–178, 217–218
Olsen, Susan 76
Optimum mine 1–5, 69, 100–101, 123–127, 140–155, 167, 182–191, 203, 213, 227–228, 236, 242–243
Organisation Undoing Tax Abuse *see* OUTA
Organised Crime and Corruption Reporting Project *see* OCCRP
Orizio, Riccardo 8–9
Osmany, Zeenat 56
OUTA 95, 145

Pahad, Essop 40
Pajitnov, Alexey 156
Palacios, Gabriela 226
Pamensky, Mark 68, 101, 116, 119, 124–125, 148, 154, 166–168, 195–196, 243–244
Pan, Wang 62
Parekh, Jagdish 31–32
parliamentary inquiry into public enterprises 51–52, 61, 71–72, 74, 80, 86–87, 102, 108–109, 115–116, 144, 148, 174, 180, 184, 186, 195, 199–200, 202–203, 212–214, 218–219, 228–229, 235
Parsons Brinckerhoff Africa 197
Passenger Rail Agency of South Africa *see* PRASA
Patel, Mitesh 206
Patel, Tarina 57
Pather, Pragasen 197–198, 204–206
Pavadia, Ashok 50
Pembani 146
Phasiwe, Khulu 5, 216–217
PIC 32, 36, 37–39, 41, 240
Pillay, Andre 225
Pillay, Jay 239
Pillay, Niven 64–65, 69, 71, 158, 161, 167
Pita, Garry 66, 173